Introduction to Ethics

A Primer for the Western Tradition

by
Frank Scalambrino

Dubuque, IA: Kendall Hunt Pub. Co.
MMXVI

Cover image: A Pathway in Monet's Garden, Giverny, 1902 (oil on canvas),
Monet, Claude (1840-1926)/Osterreichische Galerie Belvedere, Vienna,
Austria/Bridgeman Images

Kendall Hunt
publishing company

www.kendallhunt.com
Send all inquiries to:
4050 Westmark Drive
Dubuque, IA 52004-1840

Copyright © 2016 by Kendall Hunt Publishing Company
Revised printing 2017

ISBN 978-1-5249-1694-7

All rights reserved. No part of this publication may be reproduced,
stored in a retrieval system, or transmitted, in any form or by any means,
electronic, mechanical, photocopying, recording, or otherwise,
without the prior written permission of the copyright owner.

Printed in the United States of America

Dedication:
To my students
future, present, and past.

"To give a few words of truth,
and what you make of them
will be your test…"
~Ptah-hotep (c. 2350 BC)

"[W]here there is no contract of service, those who give up something for the sake of the other party cannot (as we have said) be complained of (for that is the nature of the friendship of virtue), and the return to them must be made on the basis of their purpose (for it is the purpose that is the characteristic thing in a friend and in virtue). And so too, it seems, should one make a return to those with whom one has studied philosophy; for their worth cannot be measured against money, and they can get no honor which will balance their services, but still it is perhaps enough, as it is with the gods and with one's parents, to give them what one can."

~Aristotle, *Nicomachean Ethics*, Bk IX (1164a33–1164b5)

"The young are not proper hearers of lectures on moral philosophy and how to run a city. For they are inexperienced in life and conduct, and it is these that supply the premises and the subject matter of this branch of philosophy. And moreover they are led by their feelings; so that they will study the subject to no purpose or advantage, since the end of this science is not knowledge but action.

And it makes no difference whether they are young in years or immature in character: the defect is not a question of time, it is because their life and its various aims are guided by feeling; for to such persons their knowledge is of no use, any more than it is to persons of defective self-restraint."

~Aristotle, *Nicomachean Ethics*, Bk I (1095a1–1095a11)

Table of Contents

Preface — xiii

Introduction — 1
    §1 *Chapter Overview* — 1
  Introduction: Categories, Distinctions, and Abstract Notions — 1
    §2 *Historical Periods: Fourfold & Ninefold Models* — 1
    §3 *Division of Ethics: Historical & Analytic* — 2
    §4 *The Terms "Ethics" and "Morality"* — 3
    §5 *Spheres of Justice* — 4
    §6 *Traditional Political Interpretations of Justice* — 5
    §7 *State of Nature: Optimistic & Pessimistic* — 5
    §8 *Contributions from Contemporary Psychology: Development & Characterology* — 5
  Meta-ethics — 7
    §9 *Absolutism, Relativism, Nihilism: Cultural Relativism & Incommensurability* — 7
    §10 *Ownership: Realty & Personalty Property Rights* — 10
    §11 *Divine Command Theory: What to do with Revelation?* — 11
    §12 *Freedom & the Role of Judgment in Action: Self-Mastery* — 12
    §13 *Theodicy: The Future and Freedom* — 13
    §14 *The Structural Model: Species-Specific Organic Conditions of Experience* — 14
    §15 *Happiness: More than a Feeling* — 14
    §16 *Supervenience: Harmonic Manifestation* — 15
  Normative Ethics — 15
    §17 *Virtue, Duty, Utility: The Good & The Right* — 15

Chapter 1 Plato: Amidst Divine Presence — 17
    §1 *Chapter Overview* — 17
  Moral Psychology — 17
    §2 *The Cave Allegory: Turn-ing to the Absolute Good* — 17
    §3 *The Charioteer Allegory: The Tri-Partite Soul* — 19
    §4 *Platonic Love: The Scala Amoris to the Beautiful Itself* — 20
    §5 *The Virtues: Philosophy as Caring for Souls* — 22

TABLE OF CONTENTS

Original Nature — 23
- §6 *The State of Nature: Celestial Be-ing* — 23
- §7 *Anamnēsis & Appropriate Logos: The Target Analogy* — 24
- §8 *Natural Law: The Rational Order-ing of Nature* — 27

Happiness: The Good Life & The Good Death — 31
- §9 *Eudaimonism: Perfection & the Practice of Dying* — 31
- §10 *The Noble Lie vs. The Myth of Er: Initiation Into Mysteries* — 34
- §11 *Persephone's Flower: Fate, the Future, and the Daimon* — 35

Chapter 2 Aristotle: The Master of Those Who Know — 43
- §1 *Chapter Overview* — 43

Original Nature — 43
- §2 *Four Causes* — 43
- §3 *Potentiality & Actuality* — 44
- §4 *Types of Life & Types of Love* — 45
- §5 *State of Nature: Family* — 45
- §6 *Justice: Natural Law & Rule of Law* — 46

Moral Psychology — 48
- §7 *Divisions of the Soul* — 48
- §8 *Two Inclinations toward the Good: Inclination & Interest* — 48
- §9 *Nature, Function & Excellence* — 49
- §10 *Pre-Requisites for Virtuous Action: Habit, Choice, and Knowledge* — 49
- §11 *Choice: Freedom of Will & Intention* — 50
- §12 *Character Types: The Spectrum of Self-Mastery* — 52
- §13 *Moral & Intellectual Virtues: The Doctrine of the Mean* — 53
- §14 *Self-Realization: Panoramic Wisdom* — 55
- §15 *Pleasure: The Supervening Indication of Completion* — 57

Happiness: The Good Life & The Good Death — 58
- §16 *Self-Love: The Great-Souled Person* — 58
- §17 *Friendship: Different Types & the Virtue of Trust* — 60
- §18 *Teleological Eudaimonia: Happiness as Human Destiny* — 62

Chapter 3 Ancient Greek "Socratic" Wisdom Schools: Cynicism, Hedonism, Skepticism, Stoicism — 65
- §1 *Chapter Overview* — 65

Cynicism — 66
- §2 *Nature over Convention: Askēsis & Cosmopolitanism* — 66
- §3 *Freedom: Autarkeia, Eleutheria, Parrhēsia* — 67

Hedonism — 68
- §4 *Types of Hedonism: Cyrenaic & Epicurean* — 68
- §5 *Ataraxia: Positivism, Individualism & Contractarian-Justice* — 68

TABLE OF CONTENTS

§6 *The Dynamics of Pleasure & Types of Desires: Food, Sex & Fame*	69
Skepticism	70
§7 *Types of Skepticism: Academic & Pyrrhonian*	70
§8 *Ataraxia: Swaying in the Clearing of Aporia*	71
§9 *Skeptic Askēsis: Modes for Suspending Judgment and Sustaining Tranquility*	72
Stoicism	73
§10 *Stoicism: Corporealism, Determinism & Spirit*	73
§11 *Natural Law: Pantheism & Katalepsis*	74
§12 *Stoic Askēsis & Relation to Desire: Apatheia & Ataraxia of the Sage*	76
Chapter 4 The Catholic Revolution: Augustine, Aquinas, Bonaventure, and Duns Scotus	79
§1 *Chapter Overview*	79
§2 *Theological Virtues*	83
§3 *From the Transcendentals to the Trinity*	83
§4 *Providence, Predestination, and Grace*	84
§5 *The State of Nature: Introducing Sin & Evil*	85
§6 *Natural Law & Justice: From the Garden of Eden to Just War*	86
§7 *From the Daimon to Agent Intellect to Conscience as Divine Illumination*	87
§8 *From Eudaimonia to the Super-Natural Happiness of Beatitude: Angelic Subsistence*	87
Augustine: Intentionalism	88
§9 *The Fall & Roman Law: From Family Innocence to the Guilty City*	88
§10 *Theodicy: Providence & Predetermination in Harmony with Free Will & Intention*	89
Aquinas: Dominican Intellectualism	91
§11 *Intellectualism: Synderesis*	91
§12 *Theodicy & Providence: On the Relationship between God and Hell as Punishment*	93
Bonaventure & Duns Scotus: Franciscan Voluntarism	94
§13 *Voluntarism: Miracles & the Will of God*	94
§14 *Theodicy & Beatitude: Future Contingents*	95
Chapter 5 The Protestant Reformation of the Catholic Revolution I: Machiavelli & Hobbes	97
§1 *Chapter Overview*	97
Machiavelli: Kingdom Making is the Art of War	99
§2 *The Masculinity of Virtue & The Necessary Relation between Justice and Violence*	99
§3 *Necessity & Virtue: Fate, Providence, Fortune & Autonomy and Prudence*	101
§4 *Dirty Hands & Clean Gloves: Authority & Dissimulation*	102
Hobbes: Leviathan as an Immortal Clockwork Kingdom of Man	103
§5 *Voluntarism Conceives Natural Law as Positive Law*	103
§6 *The State of Nature: Meat Machines at War*	105
§7 *Natural Right & The Social Contract: The Innocence of Existence in the Chaos of Freedom*	106
§8 *The Separation of Church and State: The Distinction between Submission and Subjection*	108

TABLE OF CONTENTS

Chapter 6 The Protestant Reformation of the Catholic Revolution II: Hume & Utilitarianism — 111
- §1 *Chapter Overview* — 111

Hume: Influencing Motives of the Will — 112
- §2 *The Role of Judgment in Action: The Path to Nihilism* — 112
- §3 *Dynamic Tension of the Passions: The Will Unmotivated by Reason* — 112
- §4 *The Relation between Is and Ought: The Tension between Right and Good?* — 113
- §5 *A Naturalistic Account of Virtue: Sympathy & the Virtue of Natural Sentiments* — 114
- §6 *Convention vs. Contract & Public Interest* — 115
- §7 *Relations of Ideas: Conventionalism & Nihilism* — 115

Utilitarianism in General Principles of Happiness — 116
- §8 *Principle of Utilitarianism in General: Justice as Utility* — 116
- §9 *Structural Model: The "Jeffersonian Democratic" Reading* — 117
- §10 *Act vs. Rule Utilitarianism* — 117

Bentham's Utilitarianism — 117
- §11 *Principles Specific to Bentham: Positivism & Egoism* — 117
- §12 *Hedonic Calculus* — 118

J.S. Mill's Utilitarianism — 118
- §13 *Mill's Critique of Bentham: "Better to be Socrates dissatisfied than a pig satisfied."* — 118
- §14 *Principles Specific to Mill's Utilitarianism: Liberty & Harm* — 119

Criticisms of Utilitarianism — 120
- §15 *Non-Casuistical; Yet Navigating Blindly?* — 120
- §16 *Criticisms: Human Sacrifice & The Utility of Promises* — 120

Chapter 7 The Kantian Revolution & The Return to the Greeks of German Idealism — 123
- §1 *Chapter Overview* — 123

Moral Psychology — 124
- §2 *The Kantian Copernican Revolution* — 124
- §3 *Concerning the Original Predisposition to Good in Human Nature* — 125
- §4 *Types of Self-Love: In terms of Animality, Humanity, and Personality* — 125

Original Nature — 126
- §5 *The Propensity to Evil in Human Nature & the Distinction between Propensity and Predisposition* — 126
- §6 *Types of Imperatives: What is Natural Law?* — 127
- §7 *The Natural Human Obligation to be Morally Excellent: Virtues as Duty-Based* — 129
- §8 *The Categorical Imperative: The Supreme Principle of Morality in the Analogy of the City and the Soul* — 131

Happiness: Good Will, Goodness in the Heart, & The Kingdom of Ends — 133
- §9 *Freedom/Autonomy of the Will: What is a Good Will?* — 133
- §10 *Difference Between a Person of Good Morals and a Morally Good Person* — 135
- §11 *The Kingdom of Ends: The Starry Heavens Above & the Moral Law Within* — 136

TABLE OF CONTENTS

Hegel: The Phenomenology of Spirit & The Philosophy of Right	137
§12 *Return to an Optimistic-Trinitarian Reading of Spirit*	137
Schopenhauer: The World as Will & Representation	137
§13 *Return to a Pessimistic-Skeptical Reading of the Stoic Craftsman-like Fire*	137
Appendix I	141
§1 *Ancient Greek "Socratic" Wisdom School Charts*	141
Appendix II: 19th-Century Existentialism: The Solitude of Existence & The Mystery of Life	143
Kierkegaard: Purity of Heart is to Will One Thing	143
§1 *Stages Along Life's Way: Life is not a Problem to be Solved; it is a Mystery to be Lived*	143
§2 *Mysterium Coniunctionis: The Hierosgamos of Piety*	145
Nietzsche: Will-to-Power & Original Nature	146
§3 *On Schopenhauer: From Will to Will-to-Power*	146
§4 *The State of Nature: The Homeric Contest*	147
§5 *On the Genealogy of Morals: Autonomy and the Great-Souled Person*	148
Amor Fati: Nietzsche's Return to the Myth of Er	152
§6 *On Truth & Lies in a Non-moral Sense: From the Ubiquity of Interpretation to Daimonic Self-Love*	152
§7 *Amor Fati: "Then I will be one who makes things beautiful…"*	154
Nietzsche's Cheerful Science: The Secret to Happiness is Overcoming Yourself Again and Again and …	159
§8 *Freedom, Destiny, & Self-Realization: Becoming Who You Are*	159
§9 *Full Throttle Heart: The Craftsman-like Spirit-Fire Dances through Me*	160
Notes	163
Bibliography	165
Index	171

Preface

The purpose of this preface is to explain the choices made for this book regarding content, organization, and style. Each of the numbered sections within each of the chapter divisions is intended to state the key idea under discussion or to concisely explicate the relevant concept from the primary source in question. Thus, this book truly is intended to be a "primer" for understanding the key ethical elements and theories in the Western tradition.

Given the importance and depth of the primary sources which these chapters discuss, for example, Aristotle's *Nicomachean Ethics*, size of the chapters may vary significantly. The suggestion is, of course, to divide the chapters across a semester as instructors see fit, keeping in mind more time may need to be devoted to discussion of the Introduction and the first two (2) chapters than the subsequent chapters.

After using this textbook students should be able to see the arrangement and re-arrangement of the elements of ethical theories across the Western Tradition. It is my belief that this is unique for an Introduction to Ethics textbook. In accordance with the standard way of presenting the Western Tradition, this book contrasts the various ethical theories spanning the history of the Western Tradition. However, at the same time, this book strives to show the similarities across the puzzles with which these Western philosophers were grappling and the sense in which later thinkers by utilizing similar concepts and strategies for solving puzzles in ethics essentially established the Western Tradition.

I have set out to balance breadth of scholarly references with the amount of content and explication needed for an Introduction to Ethics course. I have organized the material across the three major parts of the book, in such a way that students may more easily compare the elements and theories of ethics across multiple thinkers and historical periods of Western philosophy. I remain neutral regarding whether the changes across history reflect some larger form or progress toward some purposeful end.

Hopefully, you will find the material digestible in a semester's time, and hopefully its organization will help facilitate theoretical and historical thinking in regard to ethics in the Western tradition. Organizational and additional editing changes have been made to this Second Edition to increase clarity and usability.

Northeast Ohio 2016

Introduction

> "It makes no small difference, then,
> whether we form habits of one kind or of another from our youth;
> it makes a great difference, or rather *all* the difference."[1]
> ~Aristotle, *NE* Bk II.1

§1 *Chapter Overview*

The following information will be relevant throughout the entire book. It is even possible to think of this chapter as providing a kind of general vocabulary for use in both introducing ethics and facilitating critical thinking and discussion regarding ethics. This book is organized historically in regard to the philosophy of ethics in the Western Tradition. Further, the entire book presupposes the following categories, distinctions, and abstract notions featured in the first part of this introductory chapter. Further, as we will see throughout this book, the various components discussed in the second and third parts of this chapter comprise the very terms and topics needed for an introduction to ethics. Therefore, this introductory chapter should be treated as a reference to return to as needed.

Introduction: Categories, Distinctions, and Abstract Notions

§2 *Historical Periods: Fourfold & Ninefold Models*

The two standard ways to divide up the history of philosophy in the Western Tradition we will examine are the "Fourfold" and the "Ninefold" divisions. The four (4) historical periods of the Fourfold division and their time spans are as follows:

1. **Ancient** (600 BC – 400 AD)
2. **Middle Ages** (401–1600 AD)
3. **Modern** (1601–1900 AD)
4. **Contemporary** (1901 AD – Today)

Before viewing the Ninefold division, consider the following "themes" said to characterize the role of philosophy per historical period:

1. **Ancient** – philosophy in this historical period is standardly characterized as "a way of living," that is, philosophy in this period is concerned with determining how to live the best life possible for humans.
2. **Middle Ages** – philosophy in this historical period is standardly characterized as "the handmaiden of theology," that is, philosophy in this period is concerned with clarifying claims regarding God's existence and attributes, and His various relations to humans.
3. **Modern** – philosophy in this historical period is standardly characterized as "the handmaiden of science," that is, philosophy in this period is concerned with determining the basis for scientific knowledge and the possible characterization of philosophy as a science.
4. **Contemporary** – this is philosophy now, that is, the historical period in which we find ourselves. Standardly we say, on the one hand, that the appropriate characterization of our historical period has yet to be determined. On the other hand, in this historical period, philosophy may be characterized as "critical," that is, the ability to criticize the other disciplines, society, and historical events.

The nine (9) historical periods of the Ninefold division and their time spans are as follows:

1. **Pre-Platonic** (600–300 BC)
2. **Hellenistic** (301–100 BC)
3. **Roman** (101 BC–400 AD)
4. **Medieval** (401–1400 AD)
5. **Renaissance** (1401–1600 AD)
6. **Early Modern** (1601–1800 AD)
7. **19th Century** (1801–1900 AD)
8. **20th Century** (1901–2000 AD)
9. **21st Century** (2001–Today)

§3 *Division of Ethics: Historical & Analytic*

Philosophically speaking, ethics is divided in terms of historical periods and the different branches of investigation regarding ethical ideas, concepts, and their applications. Thus, for mnemonic convenience, here is a list:

Historically—In terms of the historical periods of the philosophers, theories, or events under consideration.

Analytically—This means divided into the different branches or levels of investigation.

1. Meta-ethics deals with the primary ideas, principles, and judgments involved in the study of ethics. For example, what does "Freedom" mean; what does "Goodness" mean; what is "Justice," what is a "Right," what is a "Duty," what is "Virtue," and so on. When we make judgments about moral judgments, we are doing Meta-ethics.
2. Normative Ethics refers to the justifying of why an action should or should not have been performed. Normative ethics is what most people think of when they think of activities they would call "doing

ethics." In other words, when we make judgments regarding the ethics of a situation, action, or person, we are doing Normative Ethics. Thus, Normative Ethics may be divided further regarding the different aspects of such activity. Normative Ethics gets its name because it refers to the examination of different theories of standards or norms. Of course, norms characterize what is normal or what is a proper, acceptable, usual, or expected behavior.

   a. Comparative: This means comparing two different ethical theories to determine which is better or to compare the different outcomes prescribed by each theory.
   b. Prescriptive: This means using some ethical theory to prescribe a certain action or behavior. It also refers to the activity of attempting to justify various actions and behaviors. For our purposes, the term "action" puts the focus on the event and the term "behavior" puts the focus on the agent performing an action.
   c. Descriptive: This means gathering empirical data regarding various norms. For example, how many people in America abide by the promises they make to others?
3. Applied Ethics refers to the application of ethics to specialized issues and disciplines. Thus, bioethics and business ethics, as much as ethical analysis of political issues such as abortion, euthanasia, animal welfare, death penalty, eugenics, and transhumanism, constitute the activities of "Applied Ethics."

§4 *The Terms "Ethics" and "Morality"*

Though the question of the relation between the terms "ethics" and "morality" may be merely linguistic, or perhaps more strictly academic, characterizing the difference may provide clarity in regard to classifying and systematizing the relations between various vocabulary terms learned when introduced to the study of ethics. Therefore, we will approach this distinction briefly in three ways, that is, etymologically, historically, and philosophically. First, note that the term "ethics" originates from the Greeks, and the term "morals" originates from the Romans. "Ethics" stems from the words *ethos* and *ethikos*. *Ethikos* originally meant "arising from use," such as a "habitat" or an "accustomed place" like someone's "usual haunt" (cf. Liddell and Scott 1883, 411). "Morals" comes from the Latin "*moralis*," and the term was coined by Cicero (106–43 BC) to translate *ethikos*, and "morals" relates, of course, to "mores." Thus, "morality" is related to terms like "custom," "manners," and "convention."

The Greek verb *kharassein* means to carve or engrave, and is, thereby, related to the Greek verb *graphein*, insofar as engraving may be seen as a kind of writing. In this way, the Greek *kharakteristikos* was used by the Skeptic Sextus Empiricus (c. 160–210 AD) to mean "designating characteristic" or marking or sign indicating what something is (cf. Liddell and Scott 1883, 1714). Further, *êthos* originally could mean "nature" or "disposition" (cf. Liddell and Scott 1883, 412). Hence, the otherwise originally Latin term "character" refers to a significant indication left by an agent performing an action, as if your character somehow leaves your "signature" on the situations in which you participate.

Historically speaking, we could discuss the different uses of these terms across the Western Tradition, just in case there have been peculiarities, and so on. However, this would take us into discussions beyond the scope of an introduction to ethics. Therefore, we will address this distinction philosophically. As we will see below, we will characterize something we call the "Structural Model" in regard to various features which motivate humans. For our purpose, its use here will be self-evident enough to provide the needed clarification. Basically, "morality" refers to the regulation of human passions and emotions. This regulation may stem from conventions or customs, or it may ultimately refer back to Laws, whether they be Civil or Divine. In contrast, "ethics" refers to actions and life more globally than the location of regulation regarding the passions. That is to say, ethics is concerned with discerning the best courses of action. What exactly that means is the topic of this book.

§5 *Spheres of Justice*

Among the highest of philosophical questions asks: To what does the term "Justice" refer? This is a difficult and complicated question, and in some ways the entire rest of the book is needed to fully introduce you to the appropriate relation for answering the question. However, we may begin by enumerating five (5) different "spheres" of Justice, that is, (1) Commutative, (2) Distributive, (3) Legal, (4) Social, and (5) Divine. The term "sphere" is merely intended to signify the "range" of influence to which the different uses of the term extend. Here are the relevant spheres of Justice for our introduction to ethics:

1. Commutative (or Retributive) Justice: This refers to activities of exchange. Therefore, it would be unjust to trade something of low value for something of high value. For example, pricing an object is supposed to be within the jurisdiction of commutative Justice. Of course, some types of evaluation are subjective; however, this will work for a general characterization of the range of this kind of Justice. This kind of Justice also includes the exchange of punishment for breaking laws. In other words, it is possible to think of just punishment for a crime as if it were aiming for a proper exchange of punishment to fit the crime.
2. Distributive Justice: This refers to the distribution of goods and regulation of distributed goods. For example, how should schools distribute scholarships? What kind of tax incentives are Just, and what kind of taxes are Just? Here are some of the principles on which decisions regarding such questions may be based:
    a. Principle of Need: Some portion of resources should be distributed based on need.
    b. Principle of Merit: Some portion of resources should be distributed based on ability or achievement.
    c. Principle of Effort or Sacrifice: Some portion of resources should be distributed based on effort exerted or sacrifices made.
    d. Principle of Productive Contribution: Some portion of resources should be distributed based on actual productive contribution.
    e. Principle of Equality: Some portion of resources should be distributed equally.
    f. Principle of Common Good: Some portion of resources should be distributed based on the requirements of the common good or public interest.
    g. Principle of Stimulus: Some portion of resources should be distributed to motivate.[2]

3. Legal Justice: This refers to the exercising of rights between individuals and entities in a community. Imposing laws on a community belongs to Legal Justice.
4. Social Justice: Social Justice is supposed to be wider in scope than Legal Justice. The idea is that there may be some actions that are right or wrong regarding the community, whether they are subject to laws or not.
5. Divine Justice: Divine Justice is supposed to be wider even than Social Justice. The idea here is that in relation to the Divine, some actions may be right or wrong, good or bad, good or evil, whether they are considered conventional, customary, legal, or not.

§6 *Traditional Political Interpretations of Justice*

In regard to what may be called "Traditional Political Interpretations of Justice" we may enumerate three (3). The idea here is that when someone refers to Justice, we may generally differentiate between three different interpretations:

1. The Mythico/Religious
2. In terms of Order
3. In terms of Utility

In terms of the Mythico/Religious, the idea is that Justice ultimately refers back to Divine Justice. In terms of Order, the idea is that Justice ultimately refers back to some kind of Order. For our purposes, Order, here, is essentially rationality. In terms of Utility, Justice ultimately refers back to satisfaction at some level, whether it be individual, communal, legal-reciprocal, and so forth.

§7 *State of Nature: Optimistic & Pessimistic*

The "State of Nature" refers to what is supposed to be our original natural state. Standardly different theories regarding the State of Nature are categorized as "optimistic" or "pessimistic." The exemplary optimistic characterization is "The Garden of Eden" as a kind of paradise. The exemplary pessimistic characterization comes from Thomas Hobbes. According to Hobbes, the State of Nature is a state of war, and in it human life is "nasty, brutish, and short."

§8 *Contributions from Contemporary Psychology: Development & Characterology*

For our purposes, there are just three theoretical components we will mention here, all of which are standard for introduction to ethics textbooks. First, we will list the stages of Lawrence Kohlberg's (1927–1987) theory regarding "Stages of Moral Development." The second and third components both fit into what may be the category of psychological theories of motivation. Thus, the second component we will briefly examine involves "Egoism," and the third involves sociopathy and psychopathy.

The Pre-Conventional Level: At this level, value judgments are made in regard to the physical dimension and in terms of pleasure.

1. Stage 1: The Punishment and Obedience Orientation.
   Decisions at this stage are made in response to authority.
2. Stage 2: The Instrumental/Relativist Orientation
   Decisions are conditioned by self-interest.

The Conventional Level: Individuals at this level are unreflective, without much concern or regard for conscience, and are primarily motivated by conforming to standards exhibited by the actions of, and in the expectation of, social groups, that is, family, friends, and social media.

3. Stage 3: The Interpersonal Concordance or "Good Boy–Nice Girl" Orientation:
   Individuals at this level are "people pleasers." They seek to live up to the expectations of others and value good intentions.
4. Stage 4: The "Law and Order" Orientation:
   Individuals at this level work to keep the "*status quo*," that is, trying to keep everything just as it is and for its own sake.

Post-Conventional Level: Individuals at this level are reflective and have successfully completed an introduction to ethics insofar as they can think through various normative claims and justify their ethical decisions.

5. Stage 5: The Social Contract Orientation:
   These individuals comprehend that there may be goals, purposes, and ends beyond those established by custom or even law. They view the conventions and positive laws of their community and social group as amendable and as part of a "Social Contract."
6. Stage 6: The Universal-Ethical-Principle Orientation:
   These individuals define what is right in terms of their conscience which is constituted, at least in part, by ethical principles, which even if inherited, they consciously affirm Kohlberg's examples are "The Golden Rule," "The Categorical Imperative," or "The Ten Commandments" (Kohlberg, 1976).

Psychological Theories of Motivation:
Varieties of Egoisms:

Generally speaking Egoism is contrasted with Altruism. Whereas Egoism is Self-Centered, Altruism is Other-Centered. There are different varieties of Egoism, so we will enumerate them here. As far as Altruism goes, the idea is that I should always make decisions with the best interests of others in mind, even if it is to my own detriment. Not so with Egoism.

1. Descriptive Psychological Egoism is the belief that everyone *always* acts in his or her own self-interest.
2. Prescriptive Psychological Egoism is the belief that everyone *should* act in his or her own self-interest.

3. Ethical Egoism—Objectivism—is a universal normative ethical theory which holds that everyone should act in his or her own best self-interest.
4. Ethical Egoism—Personal Egoism—is a prescriptive normative ethical theory which one holds when someone suggests: "personally" I should act in my own best interest.
5. Characterological Disorder—Narcissism—is a disorder of character or personality in which an individual behaves as if everyone ought to act in the interest of that individual, that is, the Narcissist.
6. Pathology:
    a. Psychopathy: Psychopaths are individuals who can violate norms and harm others with no regrets, feelings of shame, or pangs of conscience. If we look at the etymology of the word, we clearly see that "*pathos*," i.e. emotions, feelings, and passions, override the logical rational capacities. These individuals may be able to recognize that others deem their behaviors unacceptable, since they are good at reading the feelings of others so that they might mask their motivations and manipulate others for their own pathological gratification.
    b. Sociopathy: Sociopaths differ from psychopaths. Whereas psychopaths are concerned with others only to the extent they need to be to gratify their own pathology, sociopaths concern themselves with others so that they can gratify themselves by witnessing others suffer.

One last clarification. Notice, "psychopathy" and "sociopathy" both differ from the term "psychotic." Two points should help clarify the difference. First, psychopathy and sociopathy are more long-standing types of attitudes and tendencies of behavior. When psychosis is long-standing, we tend to think of it as the thought disorder "schizophrenia." Moreover, there are three (3) ways a person can be psychotic: in thought, in mood, or drug-induced. Again, all of these types of psychotic episodes seem more temporary than the more characterological pathologies. Thus, someone with a mood disorder such as major depression or bipolar disorder may experience psychotic episodes or features, and someone who ingests entheogens or psychedelics may experience "psychotomimetic" effects, that is, effects which imitate the symptoms of psychosis. However, the psychoses and the pathologies are essentially on different spectrums in terms of how they manifest and influence behavior.

Meta-ethics

§9 *Absolutism, Relativism, Nihilism: Cultural Relativism & Incommensurability*

There are a number of different ways to take an ethical stance in regard to some normative claim or to justify some normative theory. The following list presents them in relation to the coherency of their internal relations to each other. This organization will become clearer after presenting the list:

1. Absolutism
    a. Divine Command Theory
    b. Functionalism – Objective Naturalism

2. Relativism
    a. Traditionalism – Subjective Naturalism
    b. Moral Conventionalism
    c. Subjectivism
3. Nihilism

After discussing the three major types of evaluation, we will discuss the subtypes, and then provide additional vocabulary terms for further clarification. First, Absolutism holds that the value under consideration is absolute, that is, its value cannot change. For example, if you hold that killing another human is *absolutely* wrong, then under no circumstances is the *value* of killing considered good. Second, Relativism holds that the value under consideration does change, and is therefore dependent upon something. That is, to say in some situations killing another human being is good, then the value of killing is relative. Finally, Nihilism holds that there are no values, either good or bad. In other words, an action occurs, and there may be unanimous agreement that it has some value or great disagreement; however, Nihilism holds that to attribute any value whatsoever, i.e. good or bad, to the action would be a mistake.

In regard to Absolutism, essentially, there are two types. The first type grounds the immutability of value in the Divine. That is, somehow the Divine commands us, for example, to follow some code, and the value of those actions does not change. There is nothing we can do to change those values. The second type grounds the immutability of value in Nature, specifically in the organic functions of a species. In the same way, then, though there is variation across the species, insofar as the individuals in question are members of the species, they will be subject to the species-specific functions which distinguish the species. Therefore, these functions cannot change; were they to change essentially, i.e. beyond mere species-internal alteration and deviation, then the individual in question would no longer be of the species. Were the individual no longer of the species, then the fact that the value may no longer apply to that individual does not change the fact that it still applies to all members of the species to which the individual previously belonged.

There are multiple ways to be a relativist. The most common forms suggest that knowledge and truth are relative to:

1. Culture/Spiritual Practices
2. Society/Convention
3. History
4. Context/Situation

On the one hand, we tend to explore different normative theories in ethics to determine the better/best theory. On the other hand, when we praise or blame someone or some group for their actions or beliefs, it implies, first, that some actions and beliefs are better than others and, second, that the individuals performing those actions or holding those beliefs could have acted or could believe differently.

Essentially, there are three types of Relativism. The first type suggests that the value under consideration is relative to Tradition. This is also known as Subjective Naturalism, since the value is determined by a decision. In this way, the value is relative; however, of all the types of relativism this is the type with the most potential stability regarding value. The second type, Moral Conventionalism, is also known as Normative Relativism or Relativism proper. This will be clarified further in regard to the notion of Incommensurability. For now, notice that, according to this position, values are less stable than in the previous version of Relativism, because the values change along with conventions. For example, this may be thought of in terms of etiquette. Not only does etiquette change over time but also even within the same time period, conventions change depending on location, situation, and so on. Finally, subjectivism holds that the value under consideration is relative to the subject considering it. Of course, of the positions of Relativism, this one is the least stable, since the individual could just simply change their mind. Further, notice how the lack of stability makes this type of Relativism very close to Nihilism.

In regard to Nihilism, the essential feature is that there is no value. This position is often referred to as a kind of noncognitivism. The "cognition" piece of noncognitivism refers to Judgment. In other words, when we make a moral value Judgment, for example, killing is wrong or bad, Judgment is a cognitive activity; if the cognitive activity matches reality, then we say the Judgment is true. If I form the Judgment that the image on the cover of this book depicts a Monet painting, then the Judgment is either true or false, and if the Judgment is true, then we may say *it is a fact* that the cover of this book depicts a Monet painting. Notice, both Absolutism and Relativism hold that there are moral facts. Nihilism, however, holds that *there are no moral facts*. In this way, it is noncognitive, because the content of your cognition cannot match reality. That is, there are no values in reality. Hence, for Nihilism, you may think or judge that there are values, but judging and thinking do not cause or create value in reality, just "in your head."

Two final pieces to discuss. First, where should Cultural Relativism be situated regarding the above list of value position types? Second, how does Incommensurability function to differentiate relativism proper from the other types of relativism? Regarding the first question, Cultural Relativism should be considered a type of Traditionalism. The idea here is that the values of a culture are taken to be more stable than the values of convention. However, a "Multi-Cultural" situation or setting should be considered a type of Conventionalism. For, if the situation is such that it can tolerate many different evaluations simultaneously, the value of the situation itself is, of course, relative. Further, because the relative value of the situation can change with whatever cultures happen to be represented, then the value of the situation is not stabilized by deferring to one Tradition. In other words, the value of the situation must remain "open" to greater variability than what Traditionalism allows. Moreover, any attempt to treat Multi-Culturalism as a Tradition would be equivocating on the term Tradition. That is to say, the very meaning of the term Tradition does not allow it to tolerate the relativity of meaning which a truly Multi-Cultural situation would require.

Lastly, consider the quite important philosophical notion of Incommensurability. Visualize a movement through the subtypes of Relativism one at time, and suppose there is a dispute between two perspectives, neither of which have the same point of view, and both of which are regarding the same action. Now, were we to ask within the context of Traditionalism which perspective's evaluation of the action is right, or at least better, then the answer would be that it depends on, that is, it is relative to, the Tradition to which you belong. Thus, we can decide between the two different perspectives and points of view by siding with the Tradition to which we belong. Notice, this means that insofar as we belong to that Tradition, the value does not change for us. For all intents and purposes, unless we abandon the Tradition, the value that is relative to the Tradition is Absolute for the Tradition's participants. This is why Traditionalism, though a Relativism, is located just below Absolutism.

Were we to go through the same exercise for Moral Conventionalism, notice the outcome would differ. That is, in a truly relative situation regarding values in which the determination of a value depends on convention, different perspectives from different points of view would be truly *incommensurable*. For example, if the situation is such that what is good or bad, or right or wrong, depends on Convention (and if the two perspectives, though regarding the same thing, refer back to different Conventions), then there will be no further all-encompassing context which could determine the value of the thing. Thus, Conventionalism illustrates Incommensurability.

Finally, notice the relation between Subjectivism, Nihilism, and Incommensurability. There is no Incommensurability between conflicting perspectives if you take the position of Subjectivism. This is because, though everyone else may believe differently than you regarding the value in question, still you take the value to be determined however it is that you determine it. So, it is as if the all-encompassing context which determines value is the individual subject, according to the position of Subjectivism; hence, there is no Incommensurability. Moreover, whereas Subjectivism holds there is value based on one individual's perspective, regardless of how anyone else sees it, Nihilism holds that any ascribed value is illusory, regardless of how anyone at all sees it. Thus, again, no Incommensurability, since conflicting value judgments are based in something nonfactual like illusion or wish.

§10 *Ownership: Realty & Personalty Property Rights*

For the purpose of an introduction to ethics, there are just two (2) questions we want to examine regarding ownership. Examining these questions, however, will provide us with a base from which to do a good deal of philosophical thinking. The questions are: First, on what authority does our claim to ownership stand? Second, what are the Rights a person has to use that which they own, that is, their property? These questions are, of course, interrelated.

In regard to property, there are two general kinds, that is, realty and personalty. Realty, of course, refers to real estate and material belongings, including animals but not humans. Personalty refers to persons, that is, one's own person, one's children, possibly one's spouse, and, in some cultural and historical settings, slaves (chattel). There are many Rights about which we could enquire. For example, consider the Right to Privacy. Do we have the Right to Privacy regarding whatever we do with, or to, our property? In some ways, this question is tied to the question of what are we allowed to do with, or to, our property? And, the answer to both of these questions stems from the authority on which our ownership stands.

If, for example, Divinity is the authority on which our ownership stands, then there may be rules, i.e. Divine Commands, regarding how we may or may not treat our property. If Civil Law is the authority, that is, the positive law put forth by lawmakers for a community, then our Rights regarding our property depend on those laws. Lastly, if our own power is the authority, for example, our power to acquire and secure property, then our Rights depend on our power to do as we desire and defend ourselves against the powers of others who would have us do otherwise, or who desire to take our property.

To further understand Personalty, it is helpful to understand the concept of Personhood. Consider the following analogy. Just as when you join a gym or some club, you are assigned a membership number, and that number designates your relation to the rest of the members of the organization; well, in the same way, by participating in a society governed by laws and conventions or by being "a Child of God" or basing one's identity on a relation to the Divine, you become a "Person." Thus, there is such a thing as the legal concept of a Person, and there is such a thing as the Theological or Religious concept of a Person.

To be a Person in any of these ways means to have Rights and Duties assigned to one as an individual member of the whole (community), whether that whole be defined by promises, laws, customs, or Divine Revelations or Commands. In fact, the legal concept of a Person may be further divided into Natural Persons and Juridical Persons. The latter type refers to entities with a legal status as Persons because they have Rights and Duties in regard to the communities in which they participate; however, these entities are not human, for example, corporations are considered Juridical Persons. Just as the term "Person" comes from the word persona meaning "mask," such as the masks worn by actors on ancient Greek stages, Natural Persons animate the authoritative covering which protects them, granting them Rights and Duties.

As a quick clarification regarding terminology, philosophers tend to use the term "individual" when talking about the individual in relation to a group, "agent" when talking about the performance of an action, "self" when talking about the individual's differentiation from an "other" or others of a group, or in regard to the internal development of the individual which individuates it from others in terms of actualized potentials and capacities, "person" when referring to an individual receiving an identity from the group to which it relates, "human" to emphasize the species aspect of the individual, and "being" to speak of the individual at the highest level of metaphysical abstraction.

§11 *Divine Command Theory: What to do with Revelation?*

In his popular and influential introduction to ethics textbook *The Elements of Moral Philosophy*, James Rachels defines Divine Command Theory in the following way:

> In the major theistic traditions, including Judaism, Christianity, and Islam, God is conceived as a lawgiver who has laid down rules that we are to obey. He does not compel us to obey them. We were created as free agents, so we may choose to accept or to reject his commandments. But if we are to live as we should live, we must follow God's laws. (2003, 50).

Thus, Divine Command Theory holds that what is Good and what is Right do not depend upon anything other than Divine Commands. Rachels offers three (3) closely related criticisms of Divine Command, and we will examine each in turn.

The three criticisms may be stated in question form, that is, the "how to apply Divine Commands," "how to interpret Divine Commands," and "what to do when the Shepherds become corrupt" criticisms. First, he claims that given Relativism, it is not always clear how to apply Divine Commands. Second, he suggests that whatever Scriptures contain the Divine Commands, a person may question how these Scriptures are to be interpreted and who is supposed to be able to interpret them appropriately. Third, he points out that some religious organizations support political agendas, and if the agendas they support do not seem to coincide appropriately with the Divine Commands, then are we supposed to accept their authority in regard to political commitments as well?

It has been suggested, however, that if these three criticisms of Divine Command Theory were branches on a tree, then the following insight might cut them off at the trunk. The idea is that though Divine Commands are commands, ultimately these commands are an expression of love. That is, it is as if were we trapped in a dark Fallen place, the light of the Divine Commands represents an act of Love for us from God to help us see the place in which we are trapped and to help us navigate its darkness. In other words, if there is a Natural logic or system of rules, that is, Laws, regarding how to operate best in this place, then living a life in harmony with such rules would lead to the best possible life. However, as we will see, not everyone finds this argument persuasive, and usually those not persuaded by this argument also reject the faith-based argument that living appropriately here will ensure the best afterlife. Thus, even if there are Divine Commands, not everyone seems motivated to abide by them.

§12 *Freedom & the Role of Judgment in Action: Self-Mastery*

Throughout the different historical periods of the Western Tradition, we will see different understandings of Freedom. Hence, because there are multiple ways to understand its essential components, namely, the Will and responsibility, Freedom will be one of the more difficult ideas to understand. In order to introduce the complexity, note that when we think of Freedom, freedom from duress or external compulsion seems to pertain to the Will, and there seems to be some sense in which an agent who performs an action is in *control* of the performance. Thus, an examination of noncompulsion and control may guide us toward comprehending the complexity of Freedom as a central concern in ethics.

We can address Freedom in regard to noncompulsion simply. That is, if no one forced you to perform an action or if you were not unconscious, then you most likely meet the nonexternal constraint condition for Freedom. Though we should briefly characterize four (4) positions regarding Freedom in terms of external causation and compulsion, that is, Fatalism, Hard Determinism, Soft Determinism, and Indeterminism. For our purposes, the term "Fatalism" refers to events that cannot be changed. Thus, if they are in the future, then they are on the way here, and nothing can be done to stop them from arriving. This theme will recur throughout this book, so for now just one more comment for clarification. It is possible to take the position of Fatalism without thinking that all events are fated.

The idea is that if you are a Determinist, then you believe that all events are caused by prior events in a chain, and as a result, "Freedom of the Will" has no real place in the causal system. Therefore, such would be the position of Hard Determinism. If you are a Soft Determinist, then you believe that humans can evoke change in the causal chains of events. Thus, "Freedom of the Will" could have a real place in the causal system. Lastly, the position of Indeterminism suggests "Chance" and "Freedom" have real places in the causal system. That is to say, Indeterminism holds that not everything is causally determined.

In regard to the responsibility component, we encounter the question of the role of judgment in action. There seem to be four (4) standard positions here. First, you may suggest, as David Hume will later in the book, that judgment cannot control passions and emotions. In contrast, there are three different understandings of how judgment can exert control over passions and emotions. Thus, second, the agent may have "rational control" in performing the action if the requisite skill capacity and knowledge is present and the action accords with these aspects. In other words, a plumber may be thought to be responsible for fixing the plumbing in virtue of the fact that the plumber had specialized knowledge and the application of that knowledge was required to complete the action.

Third, because the characterization of rational control seems to leave out the desires which may account for the individual's self-willingness to perform the action, philosophers speak of "volitional control" or "conative control." In this way, the self seems free in that we may point to the desires and intentions of the agent itself, not merely those requisite for performing the action, to suggest the individual freely performed the action and is responsible. Fourth, because none of these characterizations include an individual's concern for its determination of itself in relation to Justice, philosophers speak of "discursive control." The term "discursive" here invokes the idea of being in a "discourse" with conventions, customs, and the law. Thus, the free person, beyond the free agent and free self, is one who understands how its actions relate to the various relevant rule structures. The free agent is not compelled and has the knowledge and capacity to be responsible for performing an action. The free self has, in addition to being a free agent, the desires requisite to perform the action and be held responsible for it. The free person, in addition to being a free agent and a free self, understands the performance of the action in such a way as to be held personally responsible.[3]

Interestingly, then, notice how coinciding with the extent to which one can free one's self is the extent to which one can master one's self, and because this requires directionality, self-mastery coincides with a kind of self-realization and self-perfection in regard to self-understanding (cf. Scalambrino 2015b). We will also explore this theme throughout the book. For now, just notice that in regard to all of these pieces in constellation with one another, perfection may be understood as a kind of harmony.

§13 *Theodicy: The Future and Freedom*

The ancient Greek roots of the term "Theodicy" are "Theos," meaning God, and "Dikē," meaning Justice. Therefore Theodicy is the study of God's Justice. This is also known as "The Problem of Evil," since the central question in Theodicy may be characterized as: If God is Good, then why is there evil in the world? Theodicy is a primary component of the philosophy of religion. However, it is inevitable that we encounter issues related to Theodicy when discussing ethics. The two primary concerns of Theodicy in this book emerge regarding Divine Justice and Providence. Just as we saw in the previous section, in this section we examine human Freedom in relation to the Divine. This examination is different regarding Freedom because it raises the question that even if we are Free, doesn't God know what we are going to do in the future?

A number of questions unfold from the question of God's foreknowledge regarding the future. Since this will be a central issue of chapters discussing Fate, Freedom, and Divine Justice, we will briefly sketch a general depiction of the positions. On the one hand, if God knows we are going to perpetrate evil, then why doesn't God stop us? And, since God does not stop us, is it right to characterize our punishment in terms of Justice? On the other hand, if God knows the future and, thereby, our future actions, then to what extent can we really consider ourselves Free? Further, if God knows the future, is there a way we may be able to access this knowledge in any way? Hence, notice this is a different approach to the question of human freedom than the approach in regard to the role of judgment in performing actions. Yet, at the same time, it is possible to combine these approaches into a more complicated description of the predicament of human existence.

§14 *The Structural Model: Species-Specific Organic Conditions of Experience*

To begin, we want to be sure to keep in mind that this *is not* the "Structuralist Model," it *is* the "Structural Model." The Structural Model explains the Natural human conditions for a human experience. Thus, these conditions are "species-specific," which means they pertain to the conditions which belong to humans, and therefore no attempt is made within this model to account for the experiences of non-human beings.

If we move from the "level" of concrete contact with the physical world and move "upward" toward levels understood more abstractly, then we begin with sensation. After sensation we move to perception, and after perception we move to conception. Because we use concepts to think, we understand thinking to be the highest level. Each of these levels can then be understood as organized conditions for having a human experience. Hence, we call the total structure of these conditions from bottom to top, the Structural Model.

We will refer to the Structural Model throughout this book. However, we want to notice here that the Structural Model naturally divides in a number of ways. First, sensation and perception pertain to the body, and conception and thinking belong to the intellect. Second, emotion, affection, feelings, and passions belong to the lower division coinciding with the body. Third, though we can locate a specific kind of memory at each level of the Structural Model (cf. Scalambrino 2011), for our purposes, habit refers to the tendency of the overall organization. Thus, we can assign three very important ancient Greek terms—to the lower division, we assign *pathos*; to the upper division, we assign *logos*; to the habit, we assign *ethos*.

§15 *Happiness: More than a Feeling*

So much can be said about Happiness, and yet without exposure to philosophy, it seems many individuals may understand Happiness as some kind of feeling. By the end of this book, we will have a much more intricate understanding of Happiness. This is not to say that there are no elusive aspects to achieving Happiness. Rather, through ideas such as the Structural Model, Justice, and Natural Law, we should gain a better understanding of the target at which we are aiming when we wish to be Happy. Borrowing from Plato's *Republic*, to speak of an "analogy between souls and cities is helpful in a number of ways. First, keeping this analogy in mind throughout the book will help us recognize the relation between ethics and politics. Second, the analogy helps illuminate the sense in which theories of societal Good are inseparable from theories on Goodness for the individuals who people societies. Third, the elements in play in the construction of ethical theories regarding individuals may also be in play in the determination of what makes a city excellent. Thus, Happiness may be understood as referring to individuals and to cities."

Across the history of the Western Tradition, Happiness is characterized differently. What we may say at a general level to get started is that there are soteriological (Divine), teleological (Order), and psychological (Utility) aspects which receive varying degrees of emphasis across the history of philosophy. In brief, the teleological aspect of Happiness suggests that Happiness seems to relate to our Natural capacities, i.e. it is Natural to be, and to want to be, Happy. The Soteriological aspect suggests that Happiness has some quality about it which is "saving" or "redeeming" for human existence. In other words, the possibility of Happiness motivates us. Finally, the psychological aspect of Happiness suggests that we will relate internally to ourselves and externally to others differently when we are Happy. Focusing on the internal changes, to be Happy means something like achieving a kind of harmony which allows one to relate to existence with less resistance.

§16 *Supervenience: Harmonic Manifestation*

Supervenience receives its own brief section here because it is an important concept for us that may seem awkward at first. It will be important for us during our later conversations regarding Happiness and Virtue, especially Justice as a Virtue. As a perennial citation has it: "We have supervenience when there could be no difference of one sort without differences of another sort." (Lewis 1986, 14). Thus, if we have two qualities, A and B, and B supervenes onto A, then there can be no changes to B without changes to A. However, more importantly, for our purposes, is the insight that in some contexts, we may only be able to directly causally effect A qualities. Supposing this is the case, then in order to acquire the B qualities, we would need to aim at and achieve the A qualities. As we will see, this is what philosophers mean when they say Happiness supervenes on being Virtuous. It may also be the case that Virtues supervene on perfecting certain qualities which may be located in regard to the Structural Model.

One last metaphor for the sake of priming further thinking in this book regarding supervenience. We may think of musical harmonics. The idea being that we need to perform certain operations at the concrete physical level, that is, in contact with a musical instrument, to be able to produce sounds, which ultimately harmonize with one another. Thus, from the perspective of the ear, it may be as if the harmony manifests out of nowhere, though, of course, the sounding of the appropriate notes at the right time is prerequisite and, therefore, the only way to causally effect the harmony is by causally effecting the sounding of the notes. Hence, we may think of a supervenient quality as a kind of harmonic manifestation.

Normative Ethics

§17 *Virtue, Duty, Utility: The Good & The Right*

Recall from §3 above that Normative Ethics deals with the justifying of why an action should or should not have been performed. Now, what philosophy shows us is that there are three concepts from which the various normative justifications stem. These are Virtue, Duty, and Utility. Further, these categories ultimately relate to two different ideas in ethics, that is, the Good and the Right. Lastly, a distinction may be made between normative theories which emphasize character and those which emphasize conduct, that is, Character versus Conduct ethics.

If we cross-reference these distinctions, we can gain even further clarification regarding the various ways to categorize normative justifications. That is to say, Virtue pertains to the Good in regard to character emphases, and Duty and Utility contrast with each other in terms of the distinction between Obligation and Value, respectively. In philosophy, the formal study of obligation is called "deontology," and the formal study of value is called "axiology." The idea of Right is associated with the notion of Obligation, and the idea of Good is associated with the notion of Value. Thus, if we are obliged to someone due to a verbal promise, a contract, and so on, then we have a duty to fulfill our obligation, and if we value some activity, then we deem the activity to have utility. Further, it is possible to differentiate between Duty in terms of obligation stemming from Natural Function or from concern regarding Consequences. Lastly, not that Utility is often considered synonymous with "satisfaction."

1

Plato: Amidst Divine Presence

> "The safest general characterization of the European philosophical tradition
> is that it consists of a series of footnotes to Plato."[4]
> ~Alfred North Whitehead

§1 *Chapter Overview*

Given the style of Plato's writing, that is, dialog form, we charitably tend to say we cannot be certain of Plato's views. However, traditional and standard readings of Plato's writings have come down to us through history. The following presentation of Plato's ideas, then, corresponds to the themes we will pursue throughout this book. As we will see, it is clearly the case that the Western philosophical tradition stands on the work of Plato and its subsequent systematization by his most famous student Aristotle. The following introduction to key themes in ethics found in Plato's writings revolve around the famous mythical and allegorical passages in his dialogs.

Moral Psychology

§2 *The Cave Allegory: Turn-ing to the Absolute Good*

Plato's "Cave Allegory" comes from *Republic* Book VII (514a2) and is usually said to extend to (Stephanus number) 519c5. It is supposed to "compare the effect of education and the lack of it on our nature" (514a1). It describes "prisoners" chained inside a cave, forced to watch shadows play on a screen-like wall in front of them. The description refers analogously to the experience of having a human sensorium, that is, the five senses of embodiment. The experience of being freed from one's chains and climbing out of the cave to see the reality of that to which the shadows were supposed to indirectly refer is understood as a description of the effect of education on the soul (*psychē*/ψυχή).

Now, "Plato notoriously never explicitly states two points regarding the Cave Allegory which are of great importance for both memorizing the narrative and the journey it describes."[5] First, he does not tell us how or why a "prisoner" is freed from the chains binding them to the shadowy dimension of the Cave. Second, Plato never tells us why a liberated prisoner who had seen outside the Cave would ever return. Plato's *Republic* consists of ten (10) "books," and if we recall the famous opening lines of the *Republic*—Plato has Socrates begin by saying, "I went down" (327a1)—, then we may be able to envision the entire ten books of the *Republic* itself as following the schematic presented in the Cave Allegory. Read in this way, Socrates represents a freed prisoner who has returned to the Cave.

There is much on which we could meditate regarding Plato's Cave Allegory; however, for the purpose of an introduction to ethics, there are three (3) elements we want to note for further examination. First, there are two ways to relate to what appears to us due to our embodied condition, i.e. our five senses. In fact, we may relate to each experience as an isolated *particular*, or we may relate to the content of experience by understanding the *universal* in which it *participates*. We say "participates" to refer to the one universal to which multiple particulars may be referred. The classic example invokes chairs. There are many chairs; however, to be a chair and to be recognizable as a chair each of the particular things in question must actually meet certain criteria to be a chair. Those criteria refer to the universal *form* of "chair."

Notice, the form of chair is not material, yet since every particular chair must be material, it is possible to standardize a number of phrases here. (a) Each chair is a "material instance" or "material instantiation" of the form of chair. (b) Each chair "participates in the form" of chair. (c) Forms are the "conditions for the possibility of" instantiated material things. (d) Finally, the dimension[6] of the material aspect of things refers to a continuous changing, often referred to by philosophers as "the dimension of Becoming," since what is always changing is always becoming something else. Further, this dimension is contrasted with the dimension of the form(al) aspect of things, that is, the universals in which the particulars participate. Philosophers often refer to this dimension as "the dimension of Being," since forms are immutable, that is, they do not change.

Second, if it is the case that the forms of things do not change, then what is happening when we are learning? It cannot be that we are learning something new, because the forms are not new. Moreover, insofar as the forms are the conditions for the possibility of our recognizing things, then we must already "know" or "have" the forms if we are able to recognize things at all.

Learning, then, according to Plato, is a kind of "remembering." The Greek term is *anamnēsis*, and it is usually translated as "recollection" to help us keep it distinct from everyday remembering. However, it is a kind of remembering. In other words, when the body comes into contact with some particular thing, in order for us to know what that thing is, we refer it to the dimension of universals, i.e. we must identify its form. This can be really deep water; so, we'll move through this slowly.

Because the forms do not change, the question of how they occupy time may be quite perplexing. For our purpose here, we can simply note that if forms cannot change, then they cannot be destroyed. If they cannot be destroyed, then they last forever. If they last forever, then they already were before we were born into this embodiment. Therefore, when we refer something to them, we are "remembering" or "recollecting" them. This leads us directly to the third point.

Third, *know thyself*. In light of the above description of learning and above understanding of the process of having knowledge, does this help us understand ourselves any better? Firstly, we may say that there is a form of human being. That is, in order for something to *be a human*, consistent with what we've been saying, that something needs to participate in a form. Therefore, there must be a form of human being. We refer to that form when we use the word "soul." Thus, because forms cannot be destroyed, we believe—following Plato—that the soul is immortal. Now, there will be much further discussion of this in the chapter on Aristotle; however, suffice to say here that as the principle of our animation, that is, as the form of our very being, the soul refers to the power to commune (or, if you prefer, "communicate") with other forms.

Secondly, in what will be a theme at the end of this chapter, because the soul is immortal, Plato is concerned to understand what happens after the body dies. In other words, if the soul won't die, then what will the "experience" of a disembodied human soul be like? As we will see, this is an important question for ethics, since if how we live while embodied has an influence on our soul, then it may, thereby, influence our future, however embodied, for example, materially instantiated, or not.

Lastly, because we are concerned about the future, we will need to examine the question of time as it relates to the soul as a form. In other words, if the soul as a form survives the death of the material body, then how does the soul occupy time? This is a deeply metaphysical question; however, for the purpose of ethics, we may simply note the two options which will be discussed further in this book. On the one hand, if the soul is immortal, then—even just strictly logically speaking—there is a possibility it may become materially instantiated again. This refers, of course, to a doctrine of reincarnation. Further, if we think of this reincarnation as cyclical, and as we shall see this idea is present in Plato's writings, then we may refer to the cycle of reincarnation as the Wheel of birth and rebirth or the Wheel of (re)incarnation. On the other hand, if it is possible to be liberated from the Wheel, then the idea of this liberation's occurrence may be understood (in Western terminology) as "ascending to Heaven." Because these ideas involve a number of perplexities, we will reserve discussion of them until the final section of this chapter.

§3 *The Charioteer Allegory: The Tri-Partite Soul*

Another famous myth, or allegorical figure, is that of "the Charioteer" from Plato's *Phaedrus*. Though there may be clear reference to the poem "The Way of Truth" written by the Pre-Platonic philosopher Parmenides of Elea (515–460 BC), who has been characterized as a poet and a "shaman-like figure for whom spiritual journeys are a regular experience" (Guthrie 1979, 7), Plato's image invokes the famous "tripartite soul," which he discusses further in *Republic* Bk IV. As the Italian Renaissance Neo-Platonic philosopher and Catholic priest Marsilio Ficino (1433–1499 AD) noted regarding the Charioteer, "before Socrates can affirm that love restores us to heaven, he has to examine a number of things concerning the condition of the soul, both divine and human." (Ficino 1981, 86). Thus, this section will provide us opportunity to discuss Plato's tripartite soul and prime us to discuss the Platonic notion of love.

In the Charioteer Allegory from *Phaedrus*, Plato speaks of "a pair of winged horses and a charioteer" (2416a). The chariot may be understood as referring to the body, the charioteer as the intellect, and the horses as the forces of impulsion. The horse "on the right" Plato calls "noble" and a "lover of honor." The horse "on the left" Plato calls "ignoble" and a "lover of pleasure" (253a–254e). In the *Republic* Plato's characterization of the impulsion to which the ignoble horse refers speaks of "avarice," the love of gain, and the love of money. In regard, then, to the combination of all of the elements, "the Charioteer" may be thought to allegorize individual human beings. Though much may be said, for our purposes there are only a few aspects of the allegory we will examine. First, Plato discusses an encounter with love through the allegory. Second,

Plato discusses the manner in which the charioteer gains mastery over the horses. Third, we should be sure to notice how these two aspects together relate to what today we may call "virtue theory."

First, Plato discusses the encounter with love. It is as if the body relates to love through the impulsions of the horses, and the intellect relates to love more form(al)ly. Thus, on the one hand, the noble horse controls itself in relation to the beloved in the spirit of closeness and mutuality. On the other hand, the ignoble horse desires to pounce on the beloved in the hope of limitless pleasures. As the allegory goes, *erôs* originates the motion of the horses. In this way, it is as if *erôs*, that is, erotic desire or love, refers to a kind of soul-base and the nobility of the noble horse a kind of soul-center. The peak of the Charioteer figure refers, then, to a higher kind of desire or love. Finally, "as if by a bolt of lightning," according to Plato, "When the charioteer sees that face [of the beloved], his memory is carried back to the real nature of Beauty." (Plato 1997h, 254b4). Notice the reference to *anamnēsis*, that is, the awareness of the presence of the Beautiful as the condition for the possibility of the experience of the embodied beauty of the beloved awakens the intellect to the dimension of true Being.

Second, Book IV of Plato's *Republic* discusses the tripartite soul as logical (*logistikon*), spirited (*thumos*), and appetitive (*epithumētikon*). The Greek terms make it clear, that is, the "*epi*" in "*epithumia*" for appetites and "*thumos*" for spirited or passion part, that the appetites derive from spirited embodiment. The reference to "logical" is not entirely to be understood as "calculative" or in terms of "calculation." Rather, this higher part of the soul refers to the dimension capable of grasping *logos*. For our purposes, *logos* means "to give an account of." For example, "psychology" would etymologically refer to the discipline that provides accounts of *psychē*, that is, "soul."

Thus, combining the descriptions from *Republic* with the Charioteer Allegory, we see the suggestion that the charioteer may be able to control the horses by providing accounts to them of their activity. There is a lot here, especially if we think about the quality of the *logos* to include rhetorical aspects like the sound of the charioteer's voice, as if he were a "horse whisperer." For our purposes, it will suffice to say that the charioteer is motivated to control the horses in such a way so that he can continue to commune as much as possible with the forms in general, and specifically the form of Beauty in Itself. Therefore, the charioteer is motivated to discover the best *logos* for controlling the horses. Notice, because the best *logos* will be the most beautiful *logos*, it is as if the charioteer—out of its encounter with love—has the "purity of heart" to will one thing, that is, communion with the form of Beauty in Itself. As this entails bringing forth excellence in regard to all the aspects involved in the Charioteer Allegory, it entails virtue and the quality of the desire or love motivating the charioteer and horses.

§4 *Platonic Love: The Scala Amoris to the Beautiful Itself*

Recalling that the horses are motivated by *erôs*, that is, embodied erotic desire or love, and the charioteer is motivated by a "higher" love, it becomes possible to think of the control of the horses along a spectrum referring to desire for and ability of the charioteer to commune with the higher forms. This type of love, according to Plato, is called *philia*, and it is the word for love in the etymological definition of philosophy as the love of wisdom (*sophia*). Thus, *philia* is thought of as Platonic, or platonic, love in that it is the kind of love one has for family and friends. Recall, just as *delphos* is Greek for brother, Philadelphia is the "city of brotherly love."

The dialog which speaks directly to this spectrum is Plato's *Symposium*. Specifically, this refers to a speech given by Plato's character "Socrates" who recalls his discussion with the goddess Diotima in which he learned of the *scala amoris*, (Plato 1997m, 210a–211b). The "*scala*" is often taken to mean "ladder," and thus *scala amoris* is taken to refer to the "ladder of love." However, *scala* may also refer to a stairway or a scale, as in a musical scale (cf. Kennedy 2011).[7] It is helpful to think of the *scala*, then, as both a musical scale and a ladder, since the former points to harmony and the latter points to ascension.

In this way, the intellect's ability to recollect (*anamnēsis*) the forms corresponds to (a) its ability to have true knowledge about the dimensions of Becoming and Being, (b) its ability to harmonize its soul with absolute Being, and (c) its ability to control its embodied soul, that is, the charioteer controlling the horses. This latter aspect of *anamnēsis* and having the appropriate *logos* (*logoi*, plural) can be understood as a kind of virtue ethics. Thus, as the intellect is able to better control the passions and appetites of the embodied soul, it increasingly gains access, i.e. recollects, to more beautiful *logoi* and understands itself and its soul more deeply. Further, as it understands itself and its soul more deeply it communes not just with the condition for the possibility of all Beauty but also with the condition for the possibility of all that is Good.

In sum, the embodied soul of a human being comes into contact with love, and the process in which it—to the extent it masters this process—harmonizes its desires with the higher forms, refers to its ascending, that is, re-turning, to the dimension of true Being from its contact with the dimension of embodied Becoming. Keeping in mind *anamnēsis* is movement in an "inward" direction, so too *scala amoris* moves from the material dimension inward through the spiritual dimension toward the forms. In this way, the soul's love leads it simultaneously to ascend and to a higher self-love—ultimately, a (re)turning to its origin and "true home." Thus the steps of the *scala amoris* are characterized in Plato's *Symposium* as moving from love (*erôs*) directed toward "a beautiful body" to desire directed toward "all beautiful bodies," upward with *philia* toward "beautiful souls," then beautiful laws and beautiful knowledge (*logoi*) toward the Beautiful Itself.

Lastly, then, notice how the *scala amoris* indicates a kind of liberation (cf. Scalambrino 2016). As Ficino brilliantly articulated it:

> To the extent that the soul turns toward itself and toward divine things and shows that it has its own motions, which may surmount the corporeal condition, it testifies too that it does not depend on the body and that it agrees with divine things and that therefore, separated from the body, it can live united with divinity. (Ficino 1981, 88).

In this way, the intellect is "self-moved" and exists as the principle of its own motion. This becomes fully apparent when the soul makes progress in its life and studies together, and exercises its free will to improve itself." (Ficino 1981, 88). The question, then, which emerges here is: What are the best and most beautiful *logoi* with which to control the passions and appetites of the body, harmonize oneself with true Being, and live as best one can while "imprisoned" by the dimension of Becoming? As the next section will show, this question—in asking to account for *excellences* of the soul—is asking for *an account of* virtue.

§5 *The Virtues: Philosophy as Caring for Souls*

Though technically anachronistic to speak of the "Cardinal Virtues" regarding Plato's dialogs, it will have tremendous heuristic value for our introduction to ethics. According to the Western Tradition, the four (4) cardinal virtues are: Temperance (*sōphrosynē*), Fortitude or Courage (*andreia*), Practical Wisdom or Prudence (*phronēsis*), and Justice (*dikaiosynē*). Cicero's famous remark regarding the "Cardinal Virtues," may be helpful here: "Virtue may be defined as a habit of mind in harmony with reason and the order of nature." (Cicero 1976, 159). Thus, Temperance, as Plato points out in *Charmides* (190c8–d5) functions as a kind of base for the health of the soul and the body. In addition, Piety (*hosios*) is discussed as if it were a theological virtue, that is, reverence in regard to the divine. The Platonic dialogs most often associated with the above listed virtues are Temperance (*Charmides* & *Symposium*), Fortitude (*Laches* & *Crito*), Justice (*Republic* & *Laws*), Prudence (*Gorgias* & *Meno*), and Piety (*Euthyphro* & *Phaedo*).

In regard to the "Structural Model" discussed in the Introduction chapter of this book, we can say that Temperance is the virtue of the pursuit of pleasure. Fortitude or Courage is the virtue of the avoidance of pain. Prudence or Practical Wisdom is the virtue of rational judgment regarding practical matters and situations. Technically, Wisdom, then, is the highest virtue, and, recall in regard to the Cave Allegory and Charioteer Allegory Wisdom refers to knowing the truth of the dimension of Becoming and Being and the appropriate *logoi* with which to control the passions of the embodied soul, respectively. Thus, in thinking about how the *scala amoris* leads to harmony in the soul, we arrive at the fourth virtue, Justice.

Though Wisdom may be the most important virtue for Plato, Justice is quite interesting indeed. On the one hand, Justice in regard to the individual indicates the accomplishment of the Good Life. In Plato's final dialog *Laws*, he explicitly states that the most pleasant life is one lived in accordance with Justice. From the perspective of an individual's moral psychology, the soul's harmony, and the Structural Model, this seems pretty straightforward. In other words, if you compare the life lived solely in pursuit of pleasure, it turns out to be less pleasant than the life lived in accordance with Justice. On the other hand, Justice is interestingly complicated. The beauty of the complexity comes out when we begin to compare two ideas: first, the idea that Justice results from *logoi* and, second, that Justice indicates not only an excellent individual but also the excellent society. This latter idea, of course, reminds us of Plato's centerpiece to the *Republic*, that is, the Analogy of the City and the Soul.[8]

From Book II in the *Republic*, Plato has Socrates suggest that showing how a just city is always happier than an unjust city will provide insight into how it is the case that the just person is always happier than the unjust. Recall, this is in response to various items in the *Republic* such as Thrasymachus' suggestion that Justice is the advantage of the stronger or whatever benefits whoever has the most power (338c) and the infamous "Ring of Gyges" story (359c), that is, the story which influenced Tolkien's *Lord of the Rings*, and asks us to decide whether we would act in accordance with Justice if we possessed a ring with which we could become invisible and perpetrate evil without being noticed.

There are two aspects to the Analogy of the City and Soul which we will examine as it relates to Justice. The first is the idea that if the *logoi* may function as laws (*nomon*) for the city, that is, *logos* as *nomos*, then the *logoi* may be understood as "coming from above," as it were, for the betterment of humankind. The second is the idea, then, that from the perspective of chance and fate, we can see that if an individual were born into a city where the *logoi* were present for helping the individual to achieve happiness, it may be understood as a kind of boon. Plato acknowledges this, suggesting the laws may be brought "from one of the gods or some human expert" (Plato 1997e, 645b). In this way, the stage is set for later theories of Grace, as we will see in the Augustine chapter.

Original Nature

§6 *The State of Nature: Celestial Be-ing*

As we noted in the Cave Allegory above and in regard to the highest form, that is, the Good and the Beautiful, in Itself, if we ask Plato in regard to our original nature, we discover that our true home is not to be found in the dimension of Becoming. That is, we are not terrestrial beings of the material Underworld originally; rather, we are celestial beings. We belong to the dimension of forms and that dimension's be-ing.

Plato's "creation myth" derives primarily from his dialog *Timaeus*. So, we will briefly examine the following passage.

> The god wanted everything to be good and nothing to be bad so far as that was possible, and so he took over all that was visible—not at rest but in discordant and disorderly motion—and brought it from a state of disorder to one of order, because he believed that order was in every way better than disorder. (Plato 1997o, 30a).

Notice, (1) there is disorderly material, (2) there is the force of "the god's" will or desire, (3) there is the form of orderliness, and (4) the god wanted to put the material into an orderly form, so that it could be "all good."

In regard to the Charioteer Allegory, the charioteer is located on the side of "the god's" will. The soul, through its contact with the material dimension of disorderly Becoming, manifests through the will of "the god." Further, the original motivation of the horses is the desire of "the god" to work on the material dimension of Becoming for the sake of making it better; that is, raising it to the level of harmony with the good order of "the god." Therefore, it is as if our natural state is not the disorderly material dimension of Becoming; rather, the State of Nature which we are able to recollect is a place in the divine will of "the god." It is as if, according to Plato, what we most are was originally part of the celestial be-ing of "the god" who created human reality, and human reality, in turn, was created in the process through which "the god" brings the dimension of Becoming into Being.

The following comes from a philosopher whose philosophy we will not examine until later; however, the following is helpful for envisioning what we call Celestial Be-ing. According to Immanuel Kant in his *Lectures on Metaphysics*,

> Since the soul has through the body a sensuous view of the corporeal world, when freed from the sensuous view of the body it will have a spiritual view, and this is the other world. In going to the other world one does not enter a community of other things, as it were on another planet, one stays in this world but has a spiritual view of everything. (2001, 177).

As we will come to see, the process through which we obtain this spiritual view is the same in both Plato and Kant. That is, by turning away from the Pleasure of animality and the Honor of humanity, it is as if we see through the provision of the higher spiritual be-ing which, through its order-ing Nature, conditions all human be-ings.

§7 *Anamnēsis & Appropriate Logos: The Target Analogy*

There are four (4) goals for this section: (1) Introduce the Target Analogy; (2) Grasp the idea in Plato that ignorance is to blame for evil; (3) Introduce—in the context of the first two goals—Plato's account of moral responsibility; (4) Provide a brief example of the logic of decision making, in the context of the first three goals. The Plato-inspired phrase "It's all Good!" captures the first two goals, and the second two goals resolve the apparent tension in regard to how one may be *accountable* for their actions in a context understood as being "all Good."

The Target Analogy comes from Plato's dialog the *Laws*, where we hear the following:

> And if the ruler of a state were obviously ignorant of the target at which a statesman should aim, would he really deserve his title 'ruler'? Would he be capable of ensuring the safety of an institution whose purpose he entirely failed to appreciate? …if our settlement of this territory is to be finished off properly, it looks as if we shall have to provide it with some constituent that understands (a) this target we have mentioned—the target, whatever we find it is, of the statesman, (b) how to hit it, and (c) which laws (above all) and which persons have helpful advice to give and which not. (Plato 1997e, 962a–b).

Thus, there is the straightforward aspect to the Target Analogy and a more subtle aspect. Straightforwardly, we must determine (1) at which target to aim, and next (2) we must determine how best to hit it. More subtly, notice how the identity of the ruler (e.g., the sovereign) depends on the very ability to pick the correct target and determine how to hit it.

The idea that ignorance is to blame for evil, though present in a number of places in Plato's writings (cf. Plato 1997j, 358d), is often referred back to his dialog *Meno*. In the context of a conversation in which Plato's character Socrates laments the fact that (the character) Meno will not be able to stay long enough to experience the "mysteries," (e.g., a reference to the Eleusinian Mysteries) and "be initiated" (cf. Plato 1997f, 76b–77a). The passage which follows suggests the perhaps peculiar idea that no one willing performs evil acts.

> **Meno:** I think, Socrates, that virtue is, as the poet says, 'to find joy in beautiful things and have power.' So I say that virtue is to desire beautiful things and have the power to acquire them.
> **Socrates:** Do you mean that the man who desires beautiful things desires good things? – **Meno:** Most certainly.
> **Socrates:** Do you assume that there are people who desire bad things, and others who desire good things? Do you not think, my good man, that all men desire good things?

Meno: I do not know.

Socrates: But some desire bad things? – **Meno:** Yes.

Socrates: Do you mean that they believe the bad things to be good or that they know they are bad and nevertheless desire them? – **Meno:** I think there are both kinds.

Socrates: Do you think, Meno, that anyone, knowing that bad things are bad, nevertheless desires them? – **Meno:** I certainly do.

Socrates: What do you mean by desiring? Is it to secure for oneself?

Meno: What else?

Socrates: Does he think that the bad things benefit him who possesses them, or does he know they harm him?

Meno: There are some who believe that bad things benefit them, others who know that the bad things harm them.

Socrates: And do you think that those who believe that bad things benefit them know that they are bad?

Meno: No, that I cannot altogether believe.

Socrates: It is clear then that those who do not know things to be bad do not desire what is bad, but they desire those things that they believe to be good but that are in fact bad. It follows that those who have no knowledge of these things and believe them to be good clearly desire good things. Is that not so? – **Meno:** It is likely.

Socrates: Well then, those who you say desire bad things, believing that bad things harm their possessor, know that they will be harmed by them? – **Meno:** Necessarily.

Socrates: And do they not think that those who are harmed are miserable to the extent that they are harmed?

Meno: That too is inevitable.

Socrates: And that those who are miserable are unhappy?

Meno: I think so.

Socrates: Does anyone wish to be miserable and unhappy?

Meno: I do not think so, Socrates.

Socrates: No one then wants what is bad, Meno, unless he wants to be such. For what else is being miserable but to desire bad things and secure them?

Meno: You are probably right, Socrates, no one wants what is bad. (Plato 1997f, 77b4–78b1).

Notice, then, from this exchange between Socrates and Meno regarding virtue that "every arrow aims at some target." That is to say, whenever a person is about to perform an action, they believe the action to be good. In this way, it is as if "It's all Good!" refers to the sense in which all that is good participates in the form of the Good in Itself. If the Good in Itself is the condition for the possibility of all that is good, then it seems as though ignorance of the appropriate good at the appropriate time is the factor that makes an agent both susceptible to performing an evil action and the condition for the action which makes the agent ultimately responsible. Just as impatience is its own punishment, ignorance is its own judgment. In other words, a person must be responsible for their level of knowledge and, thereby, responsible for their action.

Recalling our discussions from the Moral Psychology section of this chapter, we briefly examined the Platonic notion that learning, and thereby the state or level of a person's knowledge, is a kind of remembering or recollection, that is, *anamnēsis*. Further, recall that we discussed a person's spiritual perfection or accomplishment of self-realization—becoming who one truly is—as intimately and inextricably linked with *anamnēsis*. For example, here is a reminder from Plato in the *Theaetetus*.

> Now when a man gets a true judgment about something without an account (*logos*), his soul is in a state of truth as regards that thing, but he does not know it; for someone who cannot give and take an account of a thing is ignorant about it. But when he has also got an account of it, he is capable of all this and *is made perfect* [emphasis added] in knowledge. (Plato 1997n, 202c).

Thus, it is in this way that a person is culpable for the role knowledge plays in the determination and subsequent performance of an action. We will return to the relation between *anamnēsis* and self-realization again at the end of this chapter. For now we will look more closely at the logic of the action-situation to clarify the role of knowledge and the knower's culpability.

First we will look at the logic of decision-making in regard to time, and then we will look at the logic of decision-making in regard to its purely logical form. In regard to time, there are four (4) parts to this logic. First, there is the chain of events materially taking place in which a decision is also to take place. Second, there is the psychological force, so to speak, of the past. This force is, of course, different from the material force of the past, that is, the chain of events, and it should be understood as twofold. On the one hand, it is characterized by desire, that is, our desires related to the situation and the possible decisions which can be made in the situation. On the other hand, it is characterized by habit, that is, the decisions we tend to make and have made in the past have a kind of psychological momentum influencing our presence in situations. Finally, there is the moment of our decision making. This moment is always "a Now."

Notice, then, whatever account (*logos*) we have of the Good, it is in the moment of the Now in which it functions in the "making" (or "taking," if you're British) of a decision. In this way, out of all of the other features of the decision-making, this is the feature over which we exercise the most control. For example, it may very well be the case that the material dimension is causally determined. Moreover, the question of our desires may also be determined, for example, in terms of biology or fate. Further, though it is true that we influence our habits by the manner in which we choose in each Now, we exercise less control over this aspect of our situatedness in the Now than we do over the self-realization and knowledge or understanding-base with which we *anamnēsis* a *logos*. Hence, our character (êthos) is based in habit (*ethos*), and we are culpable for each decision made resulting from our understanding of the situation, despite any causally determined aspects of the situation.

The purely logical form regarding decision-making should further clarify the ground we've gained so far. If a person has the *desire* to be healthy, and he or she believes the *account* that to be healthy a person should go for a walk at dusk, then when the person perceives it is dusk, he or she *will* go for a walk. If thought of in terms of a syllogism (i.e., a three-line argument in which the third line logically follows from the combination of the first two), then we have:

A: If a person is to be healthy, then they should walk at dusk.
B: I desire to be healthy, and it is dusk.
C: Therefore, I will go for a walk.

In this way, "A" refers to the Universal aspect, "B" refers to the Particular aspect, and "C" refers to the subsequent action in the decision-making situation. Further, consistent with our discussion of the forms above, "A" refers to the *logos* a person applies in the decision-making situation. This may also be thought of as one's "Maxim" or their "Code of Conduct." Hopefully, now you can see how, insofar as "B" and "C" are determined by "A," the appropriate *logos* makes all the difference for Plato in determining the good of the situation and the good course of action, and as we emphasized above, the appropriate *logos* is gained through the process of *anamnēsis*.

A deeper distinction should be made here for the sake of greater clarification. This distinction is found in a number of Plato's dialogs, for example, *Gorgias*, *Meno*, *Theaetetus*, and *Laws*, and it helps us recognize the unity and depth of *anamnēsis* and self-realization. In a word, it is knowing "why." That is, we can recognize a difference between two people who both have the appropriate *logos* in a decision-making situation. Knowing why the appropriate *logos* is the appropriate *logos* will strengthen an individual's tendency to sustain the appropriate *logos*, thereby making them less likely to waver or make incorrect choices. Insofar as an account of the "why" is like the *logos* regarding *logoi*, or a *logos* become *mythos*, then perhaps it is appropriate—as we shall see—to consider its origin divine.

To sum, consider two thoughts. On the one hand, notice regarding all that has been said in this section of the chapter, we have explained how one may be *accountable* for their actions in a context understood as being "all Good." On the other hand, notice how it may be possible to "give" to another person the most appropriate *logos* for a situation they may encounter. First, at the human level and in regard to society, this is the question of which *logoi* should function as laws. Also at the human level and in regard to the individual, this is the question of how to raise and train children. At the level of the divine and in regard to society this invokes questions related to providence, and at the level of the divine and in regard to the individual this invokes questions regarding predestination. Unsurprisingly, we will discuss such questions in the final section of this chapter and in subsequent chapters through a discussion of Theodicy, which is, of course, the study of the relation between the divine (*theos*) and justice (*dikē*). Insofar as our happiness—as emphasized by Socrates in his discussion above with Meno—depends on having the appropriate *logos*, then these questions are not unimportant.

§8 *Natural Law: The Rational Order-ing of Nature*

Recall the distinctions noted in the Introduction regarding Traditional Political Interpretations of Justice. Though Plato's dialogs depict all three positions, we associate the mythico/religious and order positions with his philosophy, and not the position of utility. Pulling from the previous sections, we can articulate criteria regarding how to identify an appropriate law (*nomos*), understood analogous to the appropriate *logos* in the previous section. Ultimately, we need to grasp the analogy between law at the social level and universal accounts at the individual level to more deeply appreciate the second of the two ideas with which we concluded the above section; put in the form of a question: How should we characterize the individual's relation to divinity? In order to more deeply appreciate this aspect of the Analogy of the City and Soul, we must grasp two distinctions, that is, between nature and convention and between a command and a law. Whereas the first distinction will help us understand Natural Law as Plato's use of divine law to validate civil law, the second distinction will help us understand the complexity of the human relation to happiness and divine justice. This last distinction is complicated because it points to different origins of command (e.g., divine, civil-legal, and social-conventional) and the relation between jurisdiction and obligation.

To begin, consider a question central to Plato's dialog *Gorgias*. *Is it better to suffer an injustice than to commit an injustice?* According to Socrates in the dialog, it is better to suffer an injustice than to commit one because committing one corrupts the soul; this is consistent with Socrates' discussion in the *Apology* (30a–b) when he describes the activity of doing philosophy as "caring for souls," since "Injustice, then, lack of discipline and all other forms of corruption of soul are the worst thing there is" (*Gorgias*: 477e; cf. *Crito* 47d–48, *Republic*, BK I: 353d–354a).

Further, notice this question links clearly with the Ring of Gyges, noted above, and the "advantage of the stronger" theme which suggests Justice is whatever those with power say it is. For the idea put forward against Socrates in the *Gorgias* is that if you had enough power you would never have to suffer injustice because everyone would be too afraid to punish you, even when you obviously deserve to be punished. To gain such a status is often referred to as being a "Tyrant," and to be a Tyrant one has to have a tyrannical state of soul. This is the state of the soul which Socrates seems to suggest is *the worst possible state* in which to be. The idea in the background here is that there is a natural order to human life, and it is against this natural order to be a Tyrant. The question against which Socrates is often working, for example, in *Republic*, Protagoras, and Gorgias to name just a few dialogs, is whether it is possible to become a Tyrant without violating the natural order?

On the one hand, certainly some humans are born with more strength and intelligence than others. Doesn't this mean that they are *naturally* fit to rule? Not necessarily. Though Plato's discussion of "Philosopher-Kings" in his *Republic* suggests these individuals do need strength and intelligence, it is the condition or state of their souls that makes them fit to rule. Here, in fact, is where we find Plato advocating for Moderation: "excessive emphasis on athletics [(strength)] produces a pretty uncivilized type, while a purely literary and academic training leaves a man with less backbone than is decent." (410d). In regard to Moderation, then, for example, as noted above, the laws of a city are supposed to help its citizens conform to the natural order, and by conforming to the natural order the citizens will become excellent.

Notice, however, there is a distinction to be made here. Wouldn't we say there is a difference between two types of people in regard to following orders, both of which we would call good? First, envision someone who has been given good rules to follow, and this person is also good at following rules. Second, envision someone who is given good rules to follow, *knows why* those rules are good, and follows the rules also. The second person seems to have a better state of soul than the first because the second person's soul also has a better grasp on the *logoi* involved in performing the good action.

Interestingly, though, notice a problem that we can see more clearly now. If it is true that there is a difference between merely following rules and following rules of which we know why they are good, then it seems as though it is possible to be good at following rules that are not good, and also to not know that they are not good rules when you are following them. Perhaps the most straightforward example here would be the *command* of a Tyrant. If you believe you should follow the *orders* of the King, then you may end up following orders which are not good, especially if you do not understand, that is, have the *logoi* needed, to tell the difference between good and bad orders.

Thus, the question asked in the *Gorgias*, i.e. "Is it better to suffer an injustice than to commit an injustice?" points directly at the problem of following unjust commands or orders. On the one hand, even if you don't know that the order you are following is bad, it will still have an effect on your soul. Hence, it is important to know *why* orders are good, so you can know if what you have been commanded to do is good. On the other hand, if you do not perform the action you have been commanded or ordered to perform, then you will be punished. However, notice that if it is truly the case that not performing the action was just, then, generally speaking, that would make your punishment for not performing it unjust. Yet, as we have already heard, Socrates thinks it would be better to suffer the unjust punishment than to perform an unjust action.

There are two straightforward contexts to which this ethical insight is relevant. First, as we just discussed, this insight is important in regard to civil law and political life, for example, even the commands ordered by your employer or perhaps even your parents. This means "civil disobedience" seems to rightly refer to disobeying orders when those orders are against, at least, civil order.[9] Second, in regard to everyday life and the following of "conventions," following the conventions of the society or group you happen to have fallen in with will provide you with certain rewards; however, according to Socrates, though what you are doing may be good in the eyes of your social group, you may ultimately be committing injustices. So, what is the ultimate determining factor? For Plato we may say it is the divine order as it manifests in nature. Thus, the ultimate determining factor is the Natural Law, that is, performing actions "according to nature." (Plato, *Laws*: 686d).

Civil law makers, and even those "trend setters" who establish convention, should be wise enough to establish rules which are "agreeable to nature." (Plato, *Republic*: 456c; cf. *Laws* 890d). Thus, if those setting trends are doing so for the love of money, then participating in those trends may be committing an injustice. In the *Protagoras* Plato notes, "For like is akin to like by nature, but convention, which tyrannizes the human race, often constrains us contrary to nature." (337d). In fact, the *knowing why* factor is linked with excellence in regard to "excellence of soul" and actually accomplishing what is potentially within our nature to accomplish. This is called Happiness or being a "Master," rather than a "Slave." The Master is directed in regard to the appropriate *logos*, and, thereby, habitually motivated by the appropriate pleasures and pains. Nature, in this way, is understood as moral, rational, and purposeful in accordance with its divine order. Thus the State of Nature associated with divine justice and "celestial be-ing" is not the State of Nature in which becoming a Tyrant seems like the greatest good.

This is important, since it seems as though the Tyrant is one who is motivated by what amounts to injustice. This is best characterized, then, in terms of the Cardinal Virtues; for the Tyrant is not temperate, the Tyrant pursues excessive pleasure; the Tyrant is not courageous in that the Tyrant attempts to set itself up against feeling the pains of natural living; the Tyrant is not Prudent in that the Tyrant operates with the wrong *logos* regarding what is natural; and, lastly, the Tyrant is not Just. The Tyrant is neither Just in its treatment of others nor is it in harmony with the natural order, i.e. its soul is not in a state of Justice.

Since the Tyrant neither has the appropriate *logos* nor the appropriate relation to pleasures and pains, that is, Moderation, the Tyrant has not achieved excellence in regard to the art of living, that is, a person thought virtuous and *happy*. For, Happiness involves possessing the excellence characterized in terms of habitual and harmonious excellence; whereas habitual excellence involves habits established through appropriate *logoi*, harmonious excellence involves the knowing why established through appropriate *logoi* as *logoi* which reveal divine order-ing.

We have now seen the different origins of command (e.g., divine, civil-legal, and social-conventional). The relation between jurisdiction and obligation was laid out above in regard to command, so we can complete our account of it here. That is, "*knowing why*" shows us the distinction between jurisdiction and obligation. By *knowing why* we are able to see that though we are within the jurisdiction of social-convention and civil-law, we are also within the jurisdiction of divine justice. Thus, we may have conflicting obligations in regard to the "laws" of society, civil law, and the divine. Interestingly, this emphasizes the Analogy between the City and the Soul again. Just as in the soul *knowing why* makes us a Master over conflicting desires, so too knowing why we should civilly disobey a command safeguards our soul from corruption. For, Happiness "isn't a matter of getting rid of something bad; it's rather a matter of not even contracting it to begin with." (Plato 1997c, 478c). Here is an excellent example from Plato's *Apology* regarding this distinction between jurisdiction and obligation:

> Listen to what happened to me, that you may know that I will not yield to any man contrary to what is right, for fear of death, even if I should die at once for not yielding. … This happened when the city was still a democracy. When the oligarchy was established, the Thirty Tyrants summoned me to the Hall, along with four others, and ordered us to bring Leon from Salamis that he might be executed. They gave many such orders to many people, in order to implicate as many as possible in their guilt. Then I showed again, not in words, but in action, that if it were not rather vulgar to say so, death is something I couldn't care less about, but that my whole concern is not to do anything unjust or impious. That government, powerful as it was, did not frighten me into any wrongdoing. … Throughout my life, in any public activity I may have engaged in, I am the same man as I am in private life. I have never come to an agreement with anyone to act unjustly… I am equally ready to question the rich and the poor if anyone is willing to answer my questions and listen to what I say. (Plato 1997a, 32a–33b).

As was the case with Socrates, in concrete terms this may amount to being virtuous enough to suffer injustice rather than commit injustice. And, this of course needs to be considered because no matter how virtuous a person may be, the person must still live and dwell among other people who may not be as virtuous.

Notice, then, in a move that may seem difficult to understand at first, it is by submitting to, and as best as one can harmonizing one's self with, Divine Justice that one becomes a Master and Free. Rather than understand oneself as the slavish subject of the Divine Law, Plato suggests that one is the slavish subject of passions and feelings and conventions and Tyrants, until one masters oneself enough to subject oneself to Divine Law. That Plato understood Divine Law as natural, that is, expressed as Natural Law, despite originating from the

Celestial Be-ing which is our true home, shows that the capacity to harmonize one's self with Divine Justice belongs to our very (divine) nature. Thus, we must try to account for the extent to which we are responsible for actualizing that capacity, that is, our self-realization. Structurally at the level of the soul and the city, this is understood in terms of arriving at the *logos* that enables us to *know why*. Thus, Plato speaks in the *Gorgias* (452a) and in the *Laws* (720a–e) about slaves who play the role of doctor to other slaves and the non-slave doctor who tells the slave doctors what to do. It is, of course, only the free doctor who *knows why* that is the right treatment. The same goes for making laws in a city.

It is a bit more difficult to approach the issue of self-actualization and self-realization from the perspective of Divine Justice. Like reentering a Cave, it takes more time than one might like for vision to adjust. However, taking the above discussion as a point of departure, the word "state" works quite well for us as a polyphonic term. We can hear it as state of the soul, as state in terms of the city, and as state in terms of statement. The first meaning points to the habitual excellence of the soul; the second meaning points to the *logos* to which the soul is relating, as if it were a law in the city; the third meaning points to the harmonious excellence of the soul, as if the soul were expressing its excellence by displaying itself in action and leaving the signature of its virtuosity. Of course, the harmony here is action in accordance with Natural Law understood first and foremost as itself the expression of Divine Justice manifested as natural order.

Now, though we needed to move from the soul through the city to gain a better understanding of the divine, if we reverse this trajectory—taking Divine Justice as the original point of departure—we gain an interesting perspective on the first meaning, that is, on the state of one's soul. On the one hand, just as it was possible to think of different accounts (*logoi*) of Justice in a city as competing to become law (*nomos*), it is possible to think of *logoi* in the soul competing to be the guiding *logos*. With such an image, it would be as if you are the Charioteer determining the best *logos* in accordance with your own excellence, since the Charioteer's relation to the Good in Itself is displayed as your excellence. On the other hand, just as it was possible to think of arriving at the right laws to establish a city as receiving divine permission to establish the city, that is, the state's excellence as divinely granted, we can envision our excellence and happiness as divinely permitted and granted. This is complicated and will take us into the final section of the chapter.

Happiness: The Good Life & The Good Death

§9 *Eudaimonism: Perfection & the Practice of Dying*

We are now ready to pull together a number of the ideas from above. The suggestion here is that the following in some way constitutes Plato's *logos* with which we are to characterize our relation to divinity. Recall, we asked the question regarding this relation in §7. The following account, then, not only emphasizes a kind of constellation amidst myths but also provides the "why" for the idea of Divine jurisdiction and Justice.

In Plato's dialog *Phaedo*, which ancient commentators referred to as "On the Soul," we find the memorable definition of philosophy as "the practice of dying." Further, there are two myths to which we find multiple references throughout Plato's dialogs and mysteriously associated with the highest human good, that is, the myth of Persephone and the myth of Orpheus. The former is associated with the sacred ancient Eleusinian Mysteries and the latter is associated with the, deeply related, Orphic Mysteries. Specifically, regarding

INTRODUCTION

Persephone, there is a peculiar passage mentioned in Plato's *Meno* which is associated with liberation from the Wheel of (re)incarnation, that is, the cycle of birth and re-birth. Regarding Orpheus, Diogenes Laertius (fl. c. 3rd Century AD) memorably refers to Orpheus as "the first philosopher" (1925, Prologue), and Ficino famously provided us with the following genealogy:

> In things pertaining to theology there were in former times six great teachers expounding similar doctrines. The first was Zoroaster, the chief of the Magi; the second Hermes Trismegistus, the head of the Egyptian priesthood; Orpheus succeeded Hermes; Aglaophamus was initiated into the sacred mysteries of Orpheus; Pythagoras was initiated into theology by Aglaophamus; and Plato by Pythagoras. Plato summed up the whole of their wisdom… (Ficino 1559, 698; quoted in Mead 1896, 18; cf. Kingsley 1995).

There is a famous ancient Greek maxim, originating from Solon and so known at the time of Plato and Aristotle, that "No one should be considered happy until he is dead." (Herodotus, *Histories*, Bk 1.32). Plato and Aristotle have interesting philosophical readings of this maxim, and we will explicate Plato's reading by way of his relation to the above two myths. Thus, we will return to the myths of Persephone and Orpheus to conclude this section regarding Happiness. To begin, however, we will examine the etymology of the word: *Eudaimonia*.

The ancient Greek prefix "*eu*" means "good" or "well," and "*daimon*" refers to a be-ing who is "in between" humans and the gods. Further, because Greeks seemed to believe these be-ings may be good or bad, *daimons* are often compared to guardian angels *or* tempting *demons*, perhaps even simultaneously as in "*Psychomachia*" or "Soul War." In Modern times, attempts have been made—mainly by psychologists—to reductively define this experience in terms of "conscience." However, as one commentator has pointed out, the concerns of the *daimon* seem to be "confined to future contingencies (as opposed to pangs of conscience after the act) and does not always have to do with judgments of moral value." (Beckman 1979, 76).

Two Platonic dialogs seem to suggest everyone potentially has access to a *daimon*. In the *Timaeus* Plato refers to the *daimon* as "the most sovereign part of our soul as god's gift to us, given to be our guiding spirit." (90a), and in the *Republic* Myth of Er, to be discussed in a moment, we are told that before (re)incarnation we each select which *daimon* will accompany us through our subsequent embodiment. Hence, *Eudaimonia* is supposed to refer to having a good *daimon*, or having a good relationship (friendship) with your *daimon*. If we stick with the theme of "hearing voices in the head," then the idea is that the state of *Eudaimonia* is one in which you are no longer at war with yourself or no longer fighting with the voices in your head. Thus, it sounds right that Happiness or Human Thriving or Human Flourishing would coincide with such a state.

Now, in a dialog—which importantly is on the theme of friendship—*Lysis*, Plato has Socrates introduce the distinction between primary and secondary objects of love, or something loved for itself and something loved for the sake of something other than itself (219c1–d5). This is also the distinction between ends and means, i.e. something loved as an end in itself and something loved as a means to some other end. Whereas in the *Lysis* Socrates speaks of multiple primary objects of love, in the *Euthydemus* (279a–281e) he speaks as if there is one true primary object of love to which all other objects of love ultimately refer;

that primary object of love is *Eudaimonia* or Happiness. Further, when Socrates talks of living in accordance with Justice, he equates that life with Happiness, that is, *Eudaimonia* (cf. *Crito* 48b), and when he suggests suffering an injustice cannot harm a good person, it is because in regard to the good person—who lives in accordance with Justice and has achieved *Eudaimonia*—it is their Happiness (i.e., *Eudaimonia*) that cannot be harmed.

It is as if the relation Socrates had with the *daimon* was one of friendship and love. In fact, taking the indication and end of the Good Life to be Happiness (*Eudaimonia*), it is as if Socrates loves and trusts the *daimon*, and the *daimon* loves him in return. For example, recall how much he trusts the *daimon* when at *Apology* 40b Socrates says he believes going to his death is good because the *daimon* never interrupted him to get him to save himself. Also in the *Euthydemus* Socrates trusts the *daimon* and so waits with apparently no immediate indication of for what it is he is to wait, then suddenly—because he waited—Socrates was present when two students arrived to speak with him (272e–273a). Finally, as further evidence of trustworthiness, at *Apology* 21b, we hear that the *daimon* never lies.

One way to indicate how we may think about the presence of the *daimon* is in terms of "supervenience." Recall, as discussed above and noted in the *Crito* 48b8–9 and the *Apology* 30c6–d5 and 41c8–d2, virtue is sufficient to achieve Happiness. This may be thought of as a series in terms of supervenience. Just as we discussed, the Four Cardinal Virtues above and the sense in which the *logoi* may be thought of as competing with the Charioteer functioning as a judge to determine which ones will rule the soul, it seems as though when the virtues of Temperance, Fortitude, and Prudence are actualized, then Justice supervenes onto them and the individual acting virtuously. Further, then, *Eudaimonia* is supposed to supervene onto the person living in harmony with Justice. In fact, we can think about this musically and suggest that Justice is the sound of the other virtues as they harmonize. In this way, recollecting the idea we mentioned above using the language of "reversing the trajectory" from soul to city to divinity, that is, taking Divine Justice as the original point of departure, we gain an interesting perspective on the state of one's soul; specifically regarding the state of the soul to which "Eudaimonia" refers. So, if as we discussed above, we may envision our moral virtuosity and Happiness as divinely permitted and granted, then we arrive at a twofold conclusion. On the one hand, it is as if we have achieved a conjunction, i.e. a *mysterium coniunctionis*, with the Divine, characterized in terms of love—like a *scala amoris*. On the other hand, it is as if the personified divine offering of friendship is, precisely, the presence of the *daimon*. For further study, look up the term "Theurgy."

Each of these, then, i.e. the Cardinal Virtues bridging with Divine Justice, supervene in regard to the soul, and are therefore as if in a higher dimension. This opening onto, or channeling of, the *daimon* is neither imaginary nor symbolic; rather, it is an awareness of a higher presence, usually said to be indicated by its "voice" or by "hearing" its voice. However, these terms are, of course, not meant literally. Think of how we say we "see" what someone means when the idea they hope to convey comes to us. Awareness of the presence of the *daimon* is not the same, thus we do not say we see the *daimon*. Yet, just as the awareness of the idea we "see" refers to an awareness of something present to us which is not in the physical dimension, so too we may have an awareness of something present to us that is both not in the physical dimension and not as isolatable as the arrival of a coherent idea. Thus, it is as though we hear it from a distance without the localization of on our right or left or only present five minutes ago, and so on. Self-realization, then, individuates us, allowing for the excellence of harmony and friendship with the *daimon*.

This love for the divine is properly self-love. However, it is not narcissism, because it is love for oneself while also a love for Divine Justice, thus we love ourselves as we are in the light of Divine Justice. Hence, we arrive at the theological virtue of Piety.[10] This also resonates well with the translation of *daimon* by some as the "you that is not you." Our discussion of the Myth of Er, momentarily, should help us appreciate the relationship between the individual, the future, the *daimon* and Fate. Suffice to say here that the self-love is directed at the self that is actualized or realized through Divine Justice. This is not chthonic pride, this is celestial love. We strive for excellence and are *happy* with our habitual and harmonious excellence because our original nature is such that our excellence is in accordance with the divine ordering of nature. As the poet Hölderlin articulated it: "Each of us goes toward and reaches the place that he can" (quoted in Heidegger 2001, 93).

In the State of Nature imbued with Divine Justice, laws are determined to be valid if they are in accord with universal Justice. In the State of Nature of the Tyrant, laws operate like "savage commands." There is a spectrum along which to understand the possible human relation to such commands: gifted, imposed, contracted with for security, tyrannically commanded. The *daimon* is gifted to us. Thus, according to Plato from Socrates' death dialog, *Phaedo*, if we do not practice the love of wisdom (which is the general life direction that leads to virtue and self-realization of our natural divine potential), then we will only have "illusory virtue" (69b) or "civic and political virtue" (82a). We will now turn toward the *Republic* and the *Phaedo*, respectively, to examine Plato's articulation of the relations amidst Happiness, Providence, and the practice of philosophy as "the practice of dying."

§10 *The Noble Lie vs. The Myth of Er: Initiation Into Mysteries*

We have now seen—at some depth—Plato's thoughts regarding virtue and happiness. We now hope to appreciate his thoughts at a greater depth by considering three different myths which figure centrally in his dialogs. The first is the infamous "Noble Lie" appearing at Book III in his *Republic* (414e–15c). Basically it is the "lie" Socrates suggests should be told to the citizens of the hypothetical city they are discussing. On the one hand, the Myth is supposed to encourage citizens to treat each other as "brothers and sisters," while at the same time suggesting the legitimacy of the social stratification by assigning a kind of "metal" to different bloodlines in the city, and suggesting that "breeding" should only occur between members of the same class of metals. Here is an excerpt from the Myth:

> the earth, as being their mother, delivered them, and now, as if their land were their mother and their nurse, they ought to take thought for her and defend her against any attack, and regard the other citizens as their brothers and children of the self-same earth. … While all of you, in the city, are brothers, we will say in our tale, yet god, in fashioning those of you who are fitted to hold rule, mingled gold in their generation, for which reason they are the most precious—but in the helpers, silver, and iron and brass in the farmers and other craftsmen. And, as you are all akin, though for the most part you will breed after your kinds, it may sometimes happen that a golden father would beget a silver son, and that a golden offspring would come from a silver sire, and that the rest would, in like manner, be born of one another. (Plato, 1997k, 414e–15).

In this way, the Myth of the Metals functions to explain differences across citizens in terms of *natural* talents, aptitudes, and job placement by associating bloodlines with metals. Notice, this Myth is supposed to provide an understanding which is not too complicated for the citizens to understand. Yet, it is ultimately characterized as a "lie." A "Noble Lie" because it is supposed to direct the citizens appropriately, in regard to Divine Justice, just without providing depth which they would not be able to comprehend. On the other hand, in regard to the Myth of Metals we may ask: Is there another myth in the *Republic* which would provide depth which philosophers could understand? The answer is: Yes. It is called the Myth of Er, and it appears at the end of Plato's *Republic*.

Whereas the Myth of Metals sought a, we might say, material origin for human existence, the Myth of Er describes a celestial origin. "Er" is the name of a poet-warrior killed in battle. He had what we would call an extreme "near death" experience in that he was supposed to be dead for ten (10) days before he was discovered on the battlefield. Placed on the funeral pyre for cremation, he came back to life and told a story about his experience. According to the story, he died and was allowed to witness the process through which souls shed their embodiment and are prepared for (re)incarnation. For our purposes we want to focus on two aspects of the Myth. First, we are told that the various desires which we are to have in the next embodiment, we actually choose for ourselves. There are two aspects to the choosing. We choose the type of life we would like to live based on the types of desires associated with that life, and then this becomes our "character" (êthos) and our soul is then given an "internal ordering" which corresponds to that type of character (618b). Second, we are given the choice between several guiding or guardian spirits. This is how we choose our *daimon*. Thus, we choose our *daimon*, the *daimon* does not choose us (617e).

After making these choices the Fates weave them into the metaphysical fabric of our next embodiment. That is to say, that which is fated to us in this embodiment is governed by necessity, and it cannot be escaped. The idea, then, is that during our embodied existence we are supposed to live in such a way as to be liberated from the Wheel of (re)incarnation, i.e. to not need to receive another embodiment. However, notice that there are a number of fated factors, and even the issue of the role the *daimon* plays in our efforts to live in accordance with Divine Justice for the sake of liberation from the Wheel of (re)incarnation. What this suggests is that Plato believed liberation, that is, return to our true celestial home, requires multiple incarnations to achieve. It also introduces the problem of the relationship between what is fated to us and to what extent "progress" toward liberation is available to us. In later historical periods this will be seen as the tension between Providence, Predestination, and Free Will. Consistent with Plato's theme of Harmony, the Western Tradition tends to articulate the appropriate response to the tension in terms of attitude, that is, attitude toward Fate. For example, notice how the following famous passage from Plato's *Apology* sounds in light of the Myth of Er: "Wherever a man posts himself, thinking it is the best place for him to be, or wherever he is posted by a commander, there he must, as it seems to me, stay and face the risks taking no account either of death or of anything else as against what is disgraceful." (28d). We will turn toward the mythic characterization of the attitude appropriate for liberation, according to Plato, now.

§11 *Persephone's Flower: Fate, the Future, and the Daimon*

For a more complete discussion of the Persephone Myth, see my book *Meditations on Orpheus*. For our purposes, we should note that not only is the Persephone Myth central to the ancient Eleusinian Mysteries, both the Myth and the Mysteries are central to Platonic philosophy (cf. Ruck 1981, 2006; cf. Ruck and Staples 1994). Here is a brief overview of the Persephone Myth: One day as Persephone, gazing into the narcissus flower, reached out to make it her own, Hades emerged from the Underworld and abducted her. Distraught at her daughter's absence, Demeter set about looking for her. Reenacted by initiates to the Eleusinian Mysteries and depicted by Aristophanes in *Frogs*, Demeter initially searched for Persephone until she learned from Helios of her entrance into the Deathlands. At that point Demeter journeyed to Eleusis to grieve the loss of her daughter (Aristophanes 1908, 36–37; cf. Ruck 2006).

Thus, Persephone was tricked by an earthy shadowy realm, and subsequently Demeter, scorching the *earth*, tricked Hades into releasing her daughter for two-thirds of the year. She did this by enthroning herself in the temple at Eleusis. By refusing to return to her Olympian family, "The seed planted in the earth refused to sprout: humankind was faced with extinction, and [were humans to become extinct there would be] no mediation between the realms of spirit and earthy matter" (Ruck and Staples 1994, 320). Therefore, "Zeus sent *Hermes* down *into the House of Hades to summon Persephone back* [emphasis added]" (Ruck and Staples 1994, 320). Yet, by a trick of his own, to ensure Persephone would return, Hades impregnated her with a son "Brimos," meaning "terrible" or "dreadful" one. Who, according to Joseph Campbell (1979, 103) is a continuation of Hades by being a liminal manifestation, that is, Pluto/Brimos.

In fact, this is reflected in the dual meaning of the name "Pluto" which suggests either "rich father" or "giver of wealth" (cf. Hansen 2005, 182). All this is supposed to *account*, then, for the cyclical reunion of Persephone with Hades, reigning as Queen of the Underworld and with her Mother Demeter, thereby, producing "seasons in the abyss" for mortals, conditioning life-sustaining grain and the Sacred Mysteries. Regarding these "seasons," we should note the shift effected by the influence of Orpheus between the time of Hesiod (c. 750–650 BC) and Plato. That is, according to Werner Jaeger, with Anaximander (c. 610–546 BC) we see the

> transfer [of] the concept of diké [, i.e. justice,] from the social life of the city state to the realm of nature, explain[ing] the causal connection between coming-to-be and passing-away as equivalent to a lawsuit, in which things are compelled by the decision of Time to compensate each other for their unrighteousness (Jaeger 1945, 110).

The actual Anaximander fragment, referred to by Martin Heidegger notes: "But that from which things arise also gives rise to their passing away, according to what is necessary; for things render justice and pay penalty to one another for their injustice, according to the ordinance of time" (1984, 20). Hence, we may draw a twofold conclusion here.

First, notice the shift to Natural Law and the emphasis on Divine Justice as having jurisdiction over all be-ings. In this way, our life—right now—is a manifestation in relation to Divine Justice. In a very direct way, the passing of time refers to the passing of Divine Judgment on mortals; this life is our be-ing judged by the divine (cf. de Romilly 1968, 59–85). Second, here is where the Orpheus Myth links with the Persephone Myth and the Myth of Er. Briefly, Orpheus was a poet-musician whose wife died, and because he missed her so much, he made beautifully sad music—to remember her by—lamenting the loss. He descended into the Underworld, a.k.a. the Deathlands, in the attempt to retrieve his *lost love*. His journey through the Underworld may be seen as a series of trials, and his mourning songs help him overcome every trial. When he arrives at the heart of the Underworld he must persuade the King Hades and the Queen Persephone to release his lost love.

As we will see in a moment, a key passage from Plato's *Meno* is directed at exactly this moment which overlaps all of the myths in our discussion. Orpheus persuades Persephone by communicating to her the truth and genuineness of his mourning. This is—as noted by Plato—*how to ascend from the Underworld*. Thus, when we truly mourn our celestial home to a sufficient and genuine degree, it will transform our material imprisonment, and as if granted by Persephone we will be released from the Wheel of (re)incarnation. In a word, we must not attempt to pick the narcissus flower.

In order to conclude this chapter, then, let's consider a number of questions relevant for introduction to ethics which may be analyzed out of the above overlap of myths, prior to further examining Plato's *Meno*. Insofar as the soul is the form of the human body, a number of questions naturally follow for Plato. Recall, Socrates explains "the Beautiful and the Good and all *that kind* [emphasis added] of reality ... just as they exist, so our soul must exist before we are born." (Plato 1997g, 76e). Further, "All would agree ... that the god, and the Form of life itself and anything that is deathless, are never destroyed." (Plato 1997g, 106d). Hence, Socrates concludes in Plato's dialog *Phaedo*, "the soul ... is most certainly deathless and indestructible and our souls ... really dwell in the underworld." (Plato 1997g, 107a).

Thus, first, because forms cannot be destroyed, the soul is immortal. Therefore, what happens to the soul after the body dies? We have already seen a sketch of what happens regarding the Wheel of (re)incarnation, and so forth, from the Myth of Er. Second, because the material aspect of human embodiment substantially changes, that is, generates and perishes, and the formal condition for the possibility of the material body's being in the world does not change, how are we to understand human embodiment and, thereby, worldly concerns? Third, because the human soul evidently requires conjunction with another type of being to exist, for example, material embodiment, what fulfills this requirement after the death of the physical body? Fourth, because there is only one form regarding whatever type of being we examine, for example, the human form. What type of identity can the soul have after it has shed its embodiment? Insofar as the differentiating factor may also count as fulfilling the requirement of celestial embodiment, questions two and three may be answered simultaneously.

There are a number of standard answers to these questions, which are quite important in regard to soteriology and the philosophy of religion. All of these answers appear in Plato in one place or another. One, the soul "re-grows" its wings, if it lives in accordance with Divine Justice while materially embodied. Two, the soul is granted a celestial body by some divine entity. Three, the soul's "personhood" in regard to its participation in Divine Justice constitutes its celestial embodiment. Four, its degree of perfection or habitual and harmonious excellence leaves "inscriptions" on the soul which substantially differentiate it. Five, the mysterious conjunction with the *daimon* accounts for the soul's celestial embodiment.

Returning now to Plato's discussion of the Myth of Persephone and the Myth of Orpheus. These Myths are repeatedly referenced throughout Plato's dialogs, sometimes explicitly and sometimes implicitly. Moreover, they especially appear in Plato's dialog *Meno*, in which he discusses *anamnēsis*, and the dialog *Phaedo* in which he discusses *anamnēsis* in relation to self-realization, that is, the Good Death. Though to begin, consider Plato's *Cratylus*. Much of the following comes from a more in-depth discussion of these themes in my *Meditations on Orpheus*.

In Plato's dialog *Cratylus*, we listen in as Socrates provides an etymological explanation of the terms for "body" and "soul." The following statements are all made by Socrates:

> When you consider the nature of every body, what, besides the soul, do you think sustains and supports it, so that it lives and moves about? ... So, a fine name to give this power, which supports and sustains the whole of nature (*physis*/φύσις), would be 'nature-sustainer' (*phusechē*). This may be pronounced more elegantly, '*psuchē*' [i.e. *psychē*/ψυχή]. (Plato 1997c, 400a-c).

Next, in regard to the body Socrates explains,

> some people say that the body (*sōma*) is the tomb (*sēma*) of the soul, on the grounds that it is entombed in its present life while others say that it is correctly called 'a sign' ('*sēma*') because the soul signifies whatever it wants to signify by means of the body. *I think it is the followers of Orpheus who gave the body its name* [emphasis added], with the idea that the soul is being punished for something, and that the body is an enclosure or prison in which the soul is securely kept—as the name '*sōma*' itself suggests—until the penalty is paid... (Plato 1997c, 400c-d).

Here Plato explicitly connects the understanding of body as prison or tomb with Orpheus. Of course, this is the same understanding upon which the *Phaedo* determines that the proper practice of philosophy is "the practice of dying."

Further, notice in regard to the question of the soul's descent into the body, in the *Meno* Plato explicitly references the Persephone myth. Moreover, Plato at the key point of the dialog—just before the famous "Pythagorean Theorem" passage—introduces *anamnēsis* in the very context of the soul's immortality, noting:

> I know what you want to say, Meno. Do you realize what a debater's argument you are bringing up, that a man cannot search either for what he knows or for what he does not know? He cannot search for what he knows—since he knows it, there is no need to search—nor for what he does not know, for he does not know what to look for. (Plato 1997f, 80e-81).

The idea here is that we are presented with a perplexity the resolution of which reveals the notion of *anamnēsis*. That is to say, learning is recollecting [*anamnēsis*] through the psychic dimension, as if "out" of the body.

Quoting a poem from Pindar (fr. 133), Socrates goes on—after making reference to both the Eleusinian Mysteries and Orpheus—to explain,

> They say that the human soul is immortal; at times it comes to an end, which they call dying; at times it is reborn, but it is never destroyed, and one must therefore live one's life as piously as possible [the following, then, is the Pindar quote]:
>
> > Persephone will return to the sun above in the ninth year
> > the souls of those from whom
> > she will exact punishment for old miseries,

> and from these come noble kings,
> mighty in strength and greatest in wisdom,
> and for the rest of time men will call them sacred heroes.

> As the soul is immortal, has been born often, and has seen all things here and in the underworld, there is nothing which it has not learned; so it is in no way surprising that it can recollect [*anamnēsis*] the things it knew before… (Plato 1997f, 81b–d; cf. Plato 1997g, 72c5–6).

There is much here to discuss; however, for our introductory purposes, let's consider just the following. In the above passages, Plato links the immortality of the soul with descent into the Underworld; *anamnēsis* with liberation and in connection with the Queen of the Deathlands Persephone. Thus, it is as if the above indicates the Platonic accounting (*logos*) for salvation, that is, soteriology.

Thus, keeping in mind that Socrates in the *Cratylus* brought the focus of the question to our "present life," we may ask regarding our own ethics, our own *logos* regarding what is Good, "Where" are we in the hierarchy of liberation? As one commentator aptly put it, with such an understanding of embodiment,

> The question shifted from that of one's status among the dead, in an afterlife that was real in the same way as successive cycles of Eternal Return, to that of whether one had awakened, in *this* life, to a transcending spiritual and interior life that knows its own eternity already and in death is released from the cycle of birth and death and from worldly existence altogether (Manchester 1986, 392).

Recalling the Analogy between the Soul and the City, just as the city may receive its laws through divine dispensation, so too our exposure to *logoi*, such as the Myths discussed in this chapter, and the indication of a Platonic *logos* constellating the myths, may be understood as fated to us, that is, as a "gift from the gods to men" (Plato 1997i, 16c; cf. Plato 1997g, 66b). Further, recalling the two pieces of the Cave Allegory which Plato did not explain, suddenly this Platonic *logos* through the figure of the Wheel of (re)incarnation would explain, at least, the possibility of the prisoners "leaving" and "re-turning" to the Cave.

Finally, then, if we examine this Platonic *logos* by "looking back," as it were, from the ascended point of view (a thought exercise we discussed in §7 above), then we may gain a deeper appreciation for Plato's sense of self-realization and the true meaning of philosophy as "the practice of dying." In language, then, that is clearly reminiscent of the *Meno* and *Phaedo* discussions of *anamnēsis*, Plato has Socrates explain in the *Republic*,

> the power to learn is present in everyone's soul and that the instrument with which each learns *is like an eye* [emphasis added] that cannot be turned around from darkness to light without turning the whole body. This instrument cannot be turned around from that which is coming into being [i.e. Becoming] without turning the whole soul (Plato 1997k, 518c–d).

He concludes *anamnēsis* is precisely the process of turn-ing that which "is like an eye" in psychē "upward." Thus we hear Socrates ask, "Do we say that there is such a thing as the Just itself, or not? … And the

Beautiful, and the Good?" (Plato 1997g, 65d). The philosophers answer, "Of course." Socrates then asks, "have you ever seen any of these things with your eyes? … Or have you ever grasped them with any of your *bodily* [emphasis added] senses?" (Plato 1997g, 65d). Of course, we have not. What we are after here, then, would be an awareness of looking back from the point of view gained by looking upward, that is, from the point of view of Justice and Goodness and the Beautiful in Itself as much as possible.

Plato provides the explicit connection for which we are looking in the following passages from *Gorgias* and *Timaeus*. To begin, we hear "I shouldn't be surprised that Euripides' lines are true when he says:

> But who knows whether being alive is being dead
> And being dead is being alive?" (Plato 1997c, 492d).

And, this statement reminds us of a fragment attributed to the Pre-Platonic philosopher Heraclitus (535–475 BC) "Immortal Mortal, Mortal Immortal: Life of These Death of Those, Death of Those Life of These" (quoted in Heidegger and Fink 1979, 191). Thus, after the following brief remarks from Plato which speak to the sense in which his philosophy is in harmony with the Myths we have discussed:

> Perhaps in reality we're dead. Once I even heard one of the wise men say that we are now dead and that our bodies are our tombs, and that the part of our souls in which our appetites reside is actually the sort of thing to be open to persuasion and to shift back and forth. And hence some clever man, a teller of stories, a Sicilian, perhaps, or an Italian, named this part a jar [*pithos*], on account of its being a persuadable [*pithanon*] and suggestible thing, thus slightly changing the name. And fools [*anoētoi*] he named uninitiated [*amuētoi*], suggesting that that part of the souls of fools where their appetites are located is their undisciplined part, one not tightly closed, a leaking jar, as it were. He based the image on its insatiability. (Plato 1997c, 493a1–b4).

Socrates goes on to explain that this Italian or Sicilian man

> shows that of the people in Hades—meaning the unseen [*aïdes*]—these, the uninitiated ones, would be the most miserable. They would carry water into the leaking jar using another leaky thing, a sieve. That's why by the sieve he means the soul… And because they leak, he likened the souls of fools to sieves; for their untrustworthiness and forgetfulness makes them unable to retain anything. (Plato 1997c, 493b4–c3; cf. Plato 1997k, 364e; cf. Plato 1997e, 9.870d–e).

Notice the manner in which Plato's discussion of the uninitiated follows from the lines which he quoted, above, from Euripides. That the sieve leaks in two ways will refer to the intellectual and moral virtues in the Western Tradition. Virtue, that is, excellence, refers to keeping the soul from leaking, and thereby being released from "the mud" and brought to the experience of Happiness.

In Plato's death dialog the *Phaedo*, he has Socrates refer back to these same ideas in discussing liberation from the Wheel of (re)incarnation.

> It is likely that those who established the mystic rites for us were no fools, but were speaking in riddles long ago when they taught that whoever arrives uninitiated in Hades will lie in mud, but the purified and initiated will dwell with the gods. (1997g, 69c–d).

Further, just as Euripides emphasizes the ambiguity of life and death in light of the ability to shift between the embodied and the celestial point of view, so too the embodied fate of the uninitiated transposes onto their fate in Hades. Perhaps, then, the difference is not to be understood in terms of "location," but rather in terms of the extent of each individual's ethical destiny in terms of self-realization.

In conclusion, then, we may speak of virtue regarding social trends; we may speak of civic virtue; and, we may speak of virtue in regard to the divine. Further, for Plato, since all of these types of excellence ultimately fall within the jurisdiction of Divine Justice, each excellence has an accompanying *logos*. Interestingly, self-realization correlating with our liberation from the Wheel of (re)incarnation would refer to self-ownership, as if to say this life is the property bestowed upon us by Divine Justice through Fate. Thus, Plato's account of our present life in relation to divinity—borrowing the phrase above from Heraclitus to quickly characterize the "celestial point of view" regarding our existence—seems to suggest we should live virtuously so as to "wake up" to the reality that we are immortal beings serving a "life sentence" in the material dimension in accordance with Divine Justice (which is why suicide cannot liberate you from the Wheel, it just gets you a different cell and perhaps a longer sentence). That is, we are to live with an eye toward living through the death of this mortal existence, constituted by our imprisonment in the mud. As we climb the *scala amoris*, we self-realize body and soul as "Mortal Immortal … Death of Those Life of These," and in "dwelling with the gods" through *Eudaimonia*, we are released from the Wheel of (re)incarnation, in accordance with Divine Justice.

2

Aristotle: The Master of Those Who Know

"the virtues we get by exercising them, as also happens in the case of the arts… by doing the acts that we do in our transactions with others we become just or unjust, and by doing the acts that we do in the presence of danger … we become brave or cowardly… In a word, acts of any kind produce habits or characters of the same kind. Hence, we ought to make sure that our acts are of a certain kind; for the resulting character varies as they vary. It makes no small difference, then, whether we form habits of one kind or of another from our youth; it makes a great difference, or rather *all* the difference."[11]
~Aristotle, *NE* Bk II.1

§1 *Chapter Overview*

Aristotle's was truly one of the greatest minds in the Western philosophical tradition. As we will see by the end of this book, essentially all of the remaining chapters can be referred back in some way to the Plato and Aristotle chapters. In fact, with Plato's emphasis on the Divine and Aristotle's emphasis on Natural Function, the rest of the chapters of this book may be seen as emerging from a kind of oscillation between the Plato and Aristotle chapters. It is not surprising, then, that the teacher-student lineage extending from Socrates (c. 469–399 BC) through Plato (424–348 BC) through Aristotle (384–322 BC) to Alexander the Great (356–323 BC) is known as the greatest in the history of the Western philosophical tradition. The following key ideas from Aristotle's ethics, primarily from his *Nicomachean Ethics*, will help facilitate our understanding and discussion.

Original Nature

§2 *Four Causes*

Insofar as Aristotle's "Four Causes" answer the "how and why" of some *being*, then, it might be mnemonically helpful to think of them as the four *be* (-) causes. The "Four Causes" are commonly referred to as: Material; Efficient; Formal; and, Final. Knowing the Four Causes, according to Aristotle, tells us the "why," and provides us with an "explanation" of whatever it is we are investigating. (cf. Aristotle, *Posterior Analytics*: 71 b9–11).

The Four Causes are found at *Physics* Bk II §3 (194b16–195a1), and *Metaphysics*, V §2.

1. **Material Cause**: "that out of which a thing comes to be and which persists," for example, "the bronze of the statue, the silver of the bowl, and the genera of which the bronze and silver are species." (194b23)
2. **Formal Cause**: "the form or the archetype, that is, the statement of the essence and its genera, are called 'causes' ... and the parts of the definition." (194b26)
3. **Efficient Cause**: "the primary source of the change or coming to rest ... and generally what makes of what is made and what causes change of what is changed." (194b30)
4. **Final Cause**: "the sense of end (*telos*) or 'that for the sake of which' a thing is done, for example, health is the [final] cause of walking about." (194b34)

As an example, consider the (**1**) bronze statue, which—because (**2**) its figure is in the "thinker pose"—we call it the "the thinker." It was constructed in 1904 by (**3**) the French sculptor Auguste Rodin, and the statue was originally titled "the poet" in reference to Dante. Rodin sculpted various depictions of scenes from Dante's *Divine Comedy*, and (**4**) intended the statue to depict Dante pondering downward from upon the Gates of Hell.

§3 *Potentiality & Actuality*

There are two points we want to take away regarding Aristotle on Potentiality and Actuality for Introduction to Ethics. First, because actuality refers, among other things, to an action performed by an agent, we may use this schematic to discuss virtuous action. The idea is that our natural functions put us in First Potentiality, and our habits put us in Second Potentiality. This will help us better contextualize Aristotle's discussion of practical decision-making in terms of practical syllogisms. It makes sense for him, that is, with this schematic, that potency has us primed to perform certain actions, then when the circumstances call for actions regarding which we are primed we perform the appropriate action. This will also help us contextualize the discussion below regarding freedom of choice and free will, insofar as it pertains to Aristotle's ethics. The following example may be helpful as a mnemonic:

1st Potentiality	Born with the capacity to speak French.
2nd Potentiality	Have learned but not currently speaking French.
Actuality	*Voilà*—the activity of speaking French.

Second, notice how Potentiality and Actuality in Aristotle may help us think through the meta-ethical question regarding universal equality. According to Aristotle's schematic, though we may be equal in terms of First Potentiality (though this too is questionable nowadays given genetic engineering through selective in vitro fertilization, and so on), we are not equal in terms of Second Potentiality, and therefore we are not Actually all equal.

§4 *Types of Life & Types of Love*

We will return to these ideas again in the section on Happiness below. For now, suffice to say that Aristotle characterizes three (3) specific types of life which correspond with three (3) specific types or styles and habits of desiring.

Type of Life	Type of Love
Contemplative Life	Wisdom
Political Life	Honor/Power
Life of Enjoyment	Pleasure

Thus, we will see Aristotle thinks the Good Life, that is, the best human life, will be a contemplative life. Ultimately, however, it seems for Aristotle that philosophy is a necessary but not sufficient condition for Happiness.

§5 *State of Nature: Family*

Though technically it may be anachronistic to talk about a "State of Nature" theory in Aristotle, it will be helpful to facilitate "dialog" between Aristotle and later thinkers, and it will also add some depth to an understanding of Natural Law as it appears in Aristotle's writings. So, if we were to press Aristotle for his version of the State of Nature, it seems as though he would speak of Families. In his *Politics*, Aristotle speaks of two different types of partnerships from which cities are naturally developed. Moreover, these partnerships are made of "persons who cannot exist without one another" (1252a27). The first are men and women. The idea is that men and women naturally need each other to procreate. The second are masters and slaves. Though it may sound strange to our ears, Aristotle thought of the relationship between a slave and its master as a partnership. It is as if the slave could not survive on its own, or at least not in the way it would like to, and so it therefore naturally enters into a relation of slavery with a being who is naturally a master. This is, according to Aristotle, for the sake of "preservation" (1252a30).

When these two pairs of people band together, they form a kind of commune or household established for the sake of their survival and the meeting of their daily needs. As these "families" get larger, then, they will come into contact and partner with other families, and once enough of these families constellate, then there will be a village. Finally, "The partnership arising from several villages that is complete is the city." (1252b27). Thus, Aristotle sees the city as the natural conclusion of the family. Recall the famous quote from Aristotle which concludes the following passage: "Every city, therefore, exists by nature, if such also are the first partnerships. For the city is their end ... [Therefore,] the city belongs among the things that exist by nature, and ... man is by nature a political animal." (1252b30–1253a3). Man is a political animal, that is, naturally a member of the *polis* (city), in that the natural perfection of the family is the *polis*.

Aristotle goes so far as to say, "one ought not even consider that a citizen belongs to himself, but rather that all belong to the city; for each individual is a part of the city." (1337a26). For Aristotle, this makes sense if we think of how the city is a necessary condition for the citizen's perfection. Similar to what we saw in Plato, the Natural Law is required for an individual to find its completion as a person and develop its self-love in terms of morality. Yet, for Aristotle, the Natural Law is not separable from its material instantiation—this is often characterized as "the tension between the Ideal and the Actual" and Plato and Aristotle, respectively. That is to say, the Law is present in the presence of the city. Therefore, each individual's self-realization requires the city in which and through which it realizes itself. Thus, "One who is incapable of participating or who is in need of nothing through being self-sufficient is no part of a city, and so is either a beast or a god." (1253a27).

§6 *Justice: Natural Law & Rule of Law*

In his *Politics*, Book III §16, Aristotle makes two important points for our introductory purpose. First, he notes "absolute monarchy, or the arbitrary rule of a sovereign over all the citizens, in a city which consists of equals, is thought by some to be quite contrary to nature; it is argued that those who are by nature equals must have the same natural right and worth" (1287a10–14). Thus, Aristotle has a concept of "natural right" which, as we will see, factors into his notion of Natural Law. Second, in order to accomplish equality of natural rights among "those who are by nature equals," Aristotle ultimately advocates for the "Rule of Law," noting: "We thus arrive at law; for an order of succession implies law. And the rule of the law … is preferable to that of any individual." (1287a20). In this same passage he famously announced, "The law is reason unaffected by desire" (1287a30), and "Hence, it is evident that in seeking for justice men seek for the mean, for the law is the mean." (1287b3).

From the *Nicomachean Ethics* Book V §7, we find the following passage which will help us comprehend Aristotle's vision of Justice.

> Of *political justice* part is *natural*, part *legal* – natural, that which everywhere has the same force and does not exist by people's thinking this or that; legal, that which is originally indifferent, but when it has been laid down is not indifferent, e.g. what a prisoner's ransom shall be… Now some think that all justice is of this sort, because that which is by nature is unchangeable and has everywhere the same force … This, however is … true in a sense … with us there is something that is just even by nature, yet all of it is changeable; but still some is by nature, some not by nature. It is evident which sort of thing, among things capable of being otherwise, is by nature, and which is not but is legal and conventional, assuming that both are equally changeable. And in all other things the same distinction will apply; by nature the right hand is stronger, yet it is possible that all men should come to be ambidextrous. The things which are just by virtue of convention and expediency are like measures; for wine and corn measures are not everywhere equal, but larger in wholesale and smaller in retail markets. (1134b18–1135a).

INTRODUCTION TO ETHICS

There are a number of ideas, important on their own and important for later chapters, emphasized in this passage. In general, we may say these ideas represent the shift of perspective found from Plato to Aristotle, that is, a shift often characterized as from Absolute to Relative and from Ideal to Actual. Besides the following discussion of Justice, at this point, the most important of these ideas is the notion of the rules of convention as relative types of measures. Such a notion is the foundation of Traditionalism, Conventionalism, and Nationalism.

In regard to Justice, then, notice Aristotle immediately limits the conversation to "political justice." That is to say, he does not intend to address Divine Justice. However, we should note that in his *Rhetoric* Book I (375a25-b1-8) he accepts that, as in the case of Socrates, reference to the "higher law" may be legitimately used in court. He lists two meanings of Justice, and these receive different labels from different commentators, so we will see a list of possible terms, then we will choose the most appropriate for our purposes. First, there is Natural Justice, also known as "Moral Justice" and "Justice broadly construed." Second, there is Conventional Justice, also known as "Justice in regard to the Principle of Equality" and "Justice narrowly construed." Whereas in the first sense of Justice, appeals are made to Nature or the Natural Order to *justify* decision, in the second sense of Justice, justification may rest solely on decisions. Thus, Conventional Justice exists because a community determines it. It can be changed, and it varies across different communities. Aristotle gives the example of whether it is legal to sacrifice two goats instead of one, and concludes that it depends on, that is, it is relative to, the rules of the community from which you come.

In the first sense of Justice "Law" means more than mere legality in terms of the city's laws. In the second sense, Justice divides into three types: (1) Distributive, (2) Commutative (or "Rectificatory"), and (3) Reciprocal (or "Justice regarding Exchange"). In regard to the distribution of goods, Justice is determined in regard to proportional Equality for Aristotle; however, there are multiple principles which may be used to determine the proportionality:

1) Principle of Need: Some portion of resources should be distributed based on need.
2) Principle of Merit: Some portion of resources should be distributed based on merit.
3) Principle of Stimulus: Some portion of resources should be distributed to motivate.

Commutative Justice involves proportionate equality between two goods. For example, the following types of situations involving Commutative Justice come from John Finnis' excellent book *Natural Law and Natural Rights*:

1) Breeches of trust between two individuals, for example, to fulfill a contract, defamation, perjury, and so on.
2) Duties toward specific others, for example, deliberately or carelessly causing harm to a person or their property.
3) Duties toward the community, for example, to not defraud the public.
4) Duties toward government, for example, to pay taxes and not be in contempt of court.
5) Duties to public office, for example, fair distribution of tax incentives or honest inspections of the lottery or gas station pumps. (1980, 184).

Moral Psychology

§7 *Divisions of the Soul*

The following comes primarily from Book II of Aristotle's *De Anima* or "On the Soul." It is the first work of "scientific psychology" in the Western Tradition. Thus, it treats as a topic ψυχή (*psychē*). We hear from Aristotle that psychē is the "force that animates" the human body. Notice how the Latin *Anima* is the beginning of the word "animation." Aristotle associates the soul with the form in the matter form compound of the body and soul. Thus, his famous analogy: "Suppose that the eye were an animal—sight would have been its soul, for sight is the substance of the eye which corresponds to its *logos*." (412b20).

Aristotle goes on to divide different types of soul based on the different powers with which they are associated. There are two points we want to be sure to remember in addition to being able to reproduce the following chart:

Distinct Part of ψυχή	Distinct Power	Motivating Force
Human or Sapience	Rationality	Use of Reason
Animal or Sentience	Sense Perception & Appetite	Spirit or Will & Desire
Vegetal or Organic Survival	Nutrition & Reproduction	Impulse/Inclination

First, we want to recognize there is a "natural hierarchy" among the distinct parts or types of soul. Second, we want to remember the justification for our belief that such a hierarchy exists. Notice that with each movement "upward" the next level up retains the powers of the "lower" level. Therefore, the human soul has the power of nutrition, reproduction, sense perception, appetite, and rationality.

§8 *Two Inclinations toward the Good: Inclination & Interest*

Because the human soul is materially embodied, we can associate the powers of the animal soul with the body and the power of rationality with the mind. In this way, the human is "inclined toward the Good" in two different ways. First, in terms of its bodily appetites; second, in terms of its intellect's rationality, which technically we will call an "interest" to indicate its rational nature. Though this distinction seems so simple and obvious that it may also seem hardly worth mentioning, it actually deserves its own section to emphasize its central importance. Of all the distinctions we will discuss in Introduction to Ethics, my suggestion has been that the entire course may be understood as crystalizing around this distinction. Lastly, the Target Analogy discussed in our Plato chapter should be mentioned here. The idea—and this will be a point of controversy in later chapters— is that rationality may somehow control and guide the appetites of the body. Thus, we say that rationality can help us determine toward what to direct our appetites and what to avoid, while also determining how best to "hit" our Target.

The perhaps most difficult aspect regarding the notion of the Two Inclinations toward the Good is that they are two inclinations psychologically speaking; however they are two perspectives on the same *thing*, i.e. to say they both regard some thing in the world is to show how the external aspect of the action unifies them. In other words, the bodily desire to drink the beverage and the rational knowledge regarding its caloric content are unified by actually drinking or not drinking the beverage. We will return to this example again with later thinkers.

§9 *Nature, Function & Excellence*

In this section, we want to comprehend Aristotle's understanding of virtue by recognizing its connection with three different ideas. First, just like Natural Justice was said to trace back to the "nature of things," here too virtue will trace back to human nature. Second, we may see how virtue traces back to human nature by recognizing that there are natural functions which may be associated with the Division of the Soul and the Two Inclinations toward the Good noted in §§6–7. Third, when these natural functions are excellently actualized, then virtue is achieved. Thus, virtue may be understood as a state of excellence. Aristotle notes,

> Now each function is completed well by being completed properly in accordance with its virtue. And so the human good proves to be activity of the soul in accord with virtue, and indeed with the best and most complete virtue, if there are more virtues than one. (NE: 1098a17)

Finally, according to Aristotle, "It should be said, then, that every virtue causes its possessors to be in a good state and to perform their functions well." (NE: 1106b17). What remains, then, is for us to understand the various conditions involved in the excellent actualization and completion of the natural functions.

§10 *Pre-Requisites for Virtuous Action: Habit, Choice, and Knowledge*

According to Aristotle's *Nicomachean Ethics* Book II §4 discussion, there are three prerequisites for virtuous action. The prerequisites are important to illustrate the fact that *we cannot be excellent by accident*. For example, just as it is possible for someone to perform some athletic feat such as making a "jump shot" from half court during a basketball halftime show, it does not necessarily mean that the person is an excellent basketball player. In the same way, just because someone performs the same action that a moral virtuoso, or a morally virtuous person would perform, it does not mean that the person is a morally virtuous person. Thus, Aristotle tells us there are three "necessary conditions of a virtuous agent." (1105a30–35).

1) The agent "must have knowledge";
2) The agent "must choose the acts, and choose them for their own sakes";
3) The agent's "action must proceed from a firm and unchangeable character," that is, Habit/Tendency.

Of course, as we discussed at length in the Plato chapter, the first prerequisite involves having a *logos* appropriate to the situation. The second refers to the fact that we must aim for the virtuous action for its own sake, that is, not for the sake of some instrumental gain or other end. This ensures that people who pretend to be virtuous for the sake of obtaining some non-virtuous end are excluded from being deemed virtuous. Finally, the last prerequisite ensures we don't consider accidentally excellent agents to be excellent. That is, in order for an agent who performs an action excellently to be considered excellent, the agent needs to be in the habit of performing the action excellently. As we will see, habit plays quite a significant role for Aristotle. Though the following quote is technically not from Aristotle, it captures the Aristotelian notion excellently (pun intended), so we invoke it:

> We are what we repeatedly do.
> Excellence, therefore, is not an act;
> it is a habit.

§11 *Choice: Freedom of Will & Intention*

As we will see throughout this book, the question of Freedom, which includes the question of Choice and Freedom of the Will, is complicated. There are still disagreements regarding how exactly to understand Aristotle's notion of Choice. However, by the end of this section we should have, at least, a good introductory-level grasp on it. To begin, then, we will examine the differences between: Choice, Wish, Belief, and Intention.

In Book III §2 of the *Nicomachean Ethics*, Aristotle explains that Choice pertains to actions the agent believes they can perform, and Wish pertains to things known to be outside of our control, and this may even include wishes for the impossible. Thus we wish for ultimate ends like Happiness, and we choose actions which may bring about the relevant wished for ultimate end. For the sake of facilitating discussion and for the sake of aiding memory, we will enumerate the following list from *Nicomachean Ethics* 1111b30–1112a13:

1) Whereas Choice is evaluated as either Good or Bad, Belief is evaluated as True or False.
2) As we noted above, Choice is restricted to those actions we believe we can perform; however, Belief is unrestricted in that we may believe anything we like, including impossibilities.
3) This distinction between Choice and Belief is important for Aristotle because Character, as we will see, is determined by the Choices we make and not by our Beliefs. This is quite similar to the familiar saying: "Actions speak louder than words."
4) We choose to pursue or avoid something, but we have beliefs about what we should or should not avoid.
5) We praise Choice for being right, and we praise Belief for being true.
6) Choice supposes what is chosen is known to be good; however, we may believe even what we do not know to be true.
7) We can choose to perform actions which we do not believe to be the best action.

Therefore, Aristotle identifies a chosen action as a voluntary action resulting from deliberation. The word "deliberation" here means having an account (*logos*) regarding that which is chosen. Returning to §6 of the above Plato chapter should suffice for an explanation of how action in accordance with the appropriate *logos* refers to voluntary action from deliberation. In order for us to understand voluntariness better in Aristotle, we will now examine "Intention."

If we recall §6 of the Plato chapter, we will see that having the appropriate *logos* refers to the universal premise, or Maxim, involved in the Practical Syllogism. Further, the second line of the syllogism was the particular premise, in that it included particular aspects of the agent's present situation. This is important to keep in mind, because it is in regard to "ignorance of particulars" that we will come to identify a notion of intention in Aristotle. According to Aristotle, ignorance of particulars means ignorance of

> who is doing it, what he is doing, what or whom he is acting on, and sometimes also what (e.g. what instrument) he is doing it with, and to what end (e.g. he may think his act will conduce to someone's safety), and how he is doing it, for example, whether gently or violently. (1111a4-6).

The extent to which one is ignorant of particulars feeds into a theory of culpability and blameworthiness. In fact, it will be in regard to involuntary actions by carefully distinguishing between the blameworthiness of the actions that we may comprehend a theory of Intention in Aristotle.

Suppose the following scenario. A friend stops by to visit you, and you serve your friend coffee. Further, suppose your friend is lactose intolerant and after drinking the coffee—because they were unaware that you had milk added—your friend becomes ill. Now, Aristotle is quite subtle and brilliant here. When your friend asks if there was milk in the coffee, you answer "Yes," and they tell you, believing you already knew about their condition, that they are now ill due to your action of serving them milk, despite their lactose intolerance, how do you react? There are two different reactions we need to consider. Basically, do you feel regret for your action or not? First, if you truly regret your action, then you are not to blame for making your friend ill. Second, if you do not regret your action, then it suggests you would be willing to make your friend ill—perhaps for "kicks and grins," as they say. In both instances the action is considered involuntary; however, there is a degree of culpability associated with the no regret reaction that is not associated with the regret reaction.

Notice, then, Aristotle's technical language here:

> Now every wicked man is ignorant of what he ought to do and what he ought to abstain from, and error of this kind makes men unjust and in general bad; but the term 'involuntary' tends to be used not if a man is ignorant of what is to his advantage—for it is not mistaken purpose that makes an action involuntary (for it makes men wicked), nor ignorance of the universal ... but ignorance of particulars, i.e. of the circumstances of the action and the objects with which it is concerned. (1110b27-1111a4).

Notice the last word of the passage. Some translations put this last phrase differently, for example, H. Rackman has it: "ignorance of the circumstances of the act and of the things affected by it." In either case, Intention is neither "concern" nor "affect." It is the directedness of the agent toward "the things affected" or "objects with which it is concerned." In other words, regarding the above scenario, in both instances the agent gave the milk involuntarily. However, we may say that what was missing was a directedness toward the possibility of giving milk to someone who may be lactose intolerant.

The distinction regarding regret still stands, and it is a good distinction. However, we want to focus on the fact that Aristotle seems to be aware—though he does not develop it—of the fact that an agent has

Intentions (good or bad), if the agent is related to the particular aspects of a situation in such a way as to bring out relevant circumstances. In other words, the situation is such that a lactose-intolerant person may be on the receiving end of some milk; however, without a kind of *directedness determining various relations to the situation*, then those particular aspects of the situation remain out of awareness for the agent. Or, put more concisely, the agent remains ignorant of those particulars.

Finally, in this way, voluntariness may be understood as the performance of an action without compulsion. However, involuntary may be understood as either being out of the agent's control (i.e. no Choice regarding it) or performed without Intention. Regarding ignorance, some have made the distinction that actions performed with ignorance of particulars are "non-voluntary," and of those actions, the ones performed with regret are "involuntary." This is also a helpful distinction; however, it does not focus on Intention. Therefore, in addition to non-voluntary acts distinguished regarding ignorance of particulars, we may also identify a specific aspect of ignorance of particulars, that is, the Intention to perform an action *directed toward* particular ends.

§12 *Character Types: The Spectrum of Self-Mastery*

We are now in a position to pull together the above distinctions and notions to determine the perhaps most essential element of Aristotle's ethics, that is, Character. The Greek translated as "Character" is actually the term *ethikē*, relating of course to an individual's ethics and "way of living." However, the term "Character" works well, since it refers to an impression left behind, for example, from a signet ring.[12] Thus, the impression you leave on a situation, the way you "stamp it" with your presence, refers to your ethics and your character.

Aristotle works out six (6) different types of Character; however, only four (4) describe "human" types. Notice, they involve various constellations of *logos*, *pathos*, and *ethos*, that is, an intelligible account/reason, passion/desire, and habit. Let's first look at the list, then we will analyze the differences across the Characters.

1) Superhuman virtue
2) Virtuous (*aretē*)—deliberates to the virtuous *logos* and acts virtuously without resistance from *pathos*, experiencing the pleasure of a non-narcissistic self-love at being morally excellent.
3) Continent (*enkrateia*, literally means "mastery")—deliberates to the appropriate *logos* and acts virtuously most of the time, but experiences resistance, that is, desire (*pathos*) to do otherwise.
4) Incontinent (*akrasia*, literally means "lack of mastery")—deliberates to the appropriate *logos*; however, goes against this *logos* as a result of the appetitive part of the soul, that is, performs an action the Intention of which is influenced by some *pathos*, therefore, most often acting viciously.
5) Vicious (*kakia*)—deliberates to the vicious *logos* or cannot hear the *logos*; in either case, there is no conflict between *logos* and *pathos*, since ultimately this type goes along with *pathos*, that is, passions and desires, directed toward vicious ends.
6) Superhuman vice

Notice, given the above descriptions, it makes sense that Aristotle says of the Incontinent Character Type that its appetitive part resists the appropriate *logos*, the Continent Character Type "obeys the *logos*" (1147b3), and regarding the Virtuous Character, "everything agrees with the *logos*" (1102b26–28).

Interestingly, what the Virtuous and the Vicious Characters have in common is a kind of harmony within their souls; in that neither of them experiences the moral conflicts that the Continent and Incontinent Characters experience. However, we will discuss this with more depth in the Happiness part of this chapter; the Virtuous and Vicious Character contrast starkly regarding self-realization and self-love. The vicious person "is in conflict [regarding self-realization], and on account of being vicious, when he is restrained part of him is in pain, part is pleased; one side pulls this way, the other that, as if he is being torn apart" (1166b20). We will discuss this in terms of "Congruence" just below in the section of this chapter on Self-realization. Ultimately, because the Vicious Character is too preoccupied with gratifying appetites and desires they are unable to actualize their Personhood through the virtuous activity of the rational power of their soul. They are not in harmony with Natural Justice.

In regard to what may be called the "phenomenological reading" of the Character Types, Aristotle informed us, "Someone may say that all people aim at the apparent good, but have no control over the appearance, but *the end appears to each person in a form answering to that person's character* [emphasis added]." (1114b1). In other words, "The ends we set up for ourselves are determined by the kind of persons we are" (1114b25). In this way, it is as if the particulars of the situation which "light up," or of which we become aware, are intimately related to the passions and desires which drive us. Further, the manner in which the identity of the situation is determined by the various Maxims or Codes of Conduct (i.e., *logoi*) which we habitually carry with us into new situations, emphasizes the importance of Good Character. The Virtuous Character is supposed to live a better life than the other Character Types, and this is because the kind of life that manifests is relative to the quality of the *logos*, *pathos*, and *ethos* constellating an individual's experience of a situation.

§13 *Moral & Intellectual Virtues: The Doctrine of the Mean*

Regarding the Two Inclinations to the Good, Aristotle informed "Excellence too is distinguished into kinds in accordance with this difference; for we say that some excellences are intellectual and others moral." (1103a4). There are two key differences for us to remember. Whereas Intellectual Virtues are developed through learning, Moral Virtues are established through training. Further, the Moral Virtues can be destroyed by either excess or defect. In contemporary psychological terms, excess may be associated with trauma and defect may be associated with learned helplessness. As we have seen with the list of Character Types, it is not a matter—for Aristotle—of merely having the appropriate *logos*, we must also have trained our appetites and desires to respond to the appropriate *logos* and to tend toward the excellences which the appropriate *logoi* refer. Though it will be a point of controversy when we discuss some Modern perspectives on the relation between the Intellect and the Appetites, it seems clear for Aristotle that the appetites respond to, that is, may be controlled by, *logoi*, since non-physical reward and punishment regulate our passions. That is, it is possible to get a person to act contrary to their desires by providing them with an account in the form of communicating a reward or punishment (cf. 1102b25).

Before looking at the lists of Moral and Intellectual Virtues we may characterize these Virtues in general. Starting with the more straightforward of the two types, the Intellectual Virtues pertain to Prudence or Practical Wisdom. In regard to our previous discussion this means being able to hear the appropriate *logos* for which each situation calls. The Moral Virtues pertain to Temperance and Fortitude in that they are excellences regarding what to pursue and what to avoid. Though all of these Virtues, as Moral, pertain to the appetitive and desiring—bodily—aspect of soul, there are multiple feelings or ways these excellences may manifest. Before considering the example of anger, note the twofold conclusion toward which we are moving. First, we are about to arrive at an understanding of Aristotle's famous "Doctrine of the Mean." Second, because the Virtues are required for Happiness, it is by "Caring for the Soul" that through the Virtues of the soul we arrive at an overall state of excellence, that is, *Eudaimonia*.

Now, despite the use of the word "care" we must not slide into thinking that Aristotle's moral theory is soft. Virtuous kindness is not weakness, it is power in repose. For example, consider anger. Just like Moderation leads to acquiring and sustaining a state of physical health, Moderation in regard to anger means that at times we should be angry. That is to say, we want to have the appropriate amount of anger toward the appropriate individuals at the appropriate time. Therefore, an excess amount of anger is Vicious and a deficient amount of anger is Vicious. Again notice how the excess may be associated with trauma and the deficiency associated with learned helplessness. The point is that there are such phenomena as "righteous indignation" and "nemesis." This idea that Virtue is the mean between two extremes is called the "Doctrine of the Mean."

Here, then, is a list of the Moral and Intellectual Virtues. As per the Doctrine of the Mean, the Moral Virtues are listed in regard to the "Feelings and Actions" which when present in a situation may be enacted excellently or not.[13]

Practicable Feelings and Actions	Excess (Vice)	Mean (Virtue)	Defect (Vice)
Fear of important damages, *esp.* death	Cowardice	Courage	Reckless/foolhardy
Pleasure (bodily) and **Pain**	Self-Indulgence	Temperance	Insensibility
Proneness to **anger**—attitude to slights and damages	Irascibility—Easily irritated	Good Temper/Patience	Apathy—Lack of spirit
Indignation (anger caused by something unjust)	Jealousy/Envy	Nemesis/ Righteous indignation	Spite
Giving money away— management of personal property regarding others	Extravagance	Generosity	Stinginess
Honor—attitudes and actions with respect to one's own worth	Empty Vanity	Pride in regard to greatness of soul	Undue Humility
Self-presentation/expression	Boastfulness	Truthfulness	Self-deprecation
Conversation/Desire to Amuse	Buffoonery	Wittiness	Boorishness
Social Conduct/Desire to Please others	Obsequiousness	Friendliness	Unpleasantness
Susceptibility to **Shame**	Bashfulness	Modesty	Shamelessness

The following represents the Intellectual Virtues:

Productive	Concerned with that which is **contingent**.
technê	Technical knowledge of the process of producing some artifact.
Practical	Concerned with that which is **particular**.
phronêsis	Deliberation concerning the object(s) of perception. (Practical Wisdom)
Theoretical	Concerned with that which is **universal**.
epistêmê	*Demonstrative* knowledge *from* (first) principles.
nous	*Intuitive* non-demonstrative knowledge *of* (first) principles.
sophia	The combination of *nous* and *epistêmê*. (Philosophical Wisdom)

For our introductory purposes, we will not engage in an extended conversation of the Intellectual Virtues. Such a conversation would include recognizing the different relations between *logos* and the Productive, Practical, and Theoretical Virtues. Suffice to say, we would notice an analogous structure across the relations. Moreover, for our purposes, we need to notice Practical Wisdom refers to the Virtue of Prudence. In light of the Doctrine of the Mean, the term Prudence may make more sense now. That is, when the Intellect is Functioning excellently, it will be able to hear the appropriate *logos*, that is, the account of the situation which calls for a non-excessive action. The non-excessive action, in turn, should ensure we act in harmony with Justice and sustain the "healthiness" of our souls by not exposing the soul's appetitive aspects to self-destructive extremes.

§14 *Self-Realization: Panoramic Wisdom*

This section discusses the result of excellence, that is, Virtue, on the soul overall. This coincides with the idea of moral virtuosity, that is, being a moral virtuoso, in Aristotle and the idea of perfection and completion in Plato. Thus, it is as if we must control our passions to be able to arrive at an account of self-knowledge, and when one arrives at an appropriate account of self-knowledge, then one is able to appropriately relate to others and act in accordance with an appropriate understanding of relations to others, that is, to act in accordance with Justice. The notion of "Panoramic Wisdom" comes into play here, then, because it is as if the moral virtuoso, that is, the Sage or the Wise Person, is able to hear—what Plato would call—the *logos* derived from Divine Justice. Therefore, being able to hear the *logos* of Justice allows for the continual activity of virtuously appraising, that is, "seeing" situations and acting in the way which best sustains one's harmony with Justice and its consequent well-being, allowing one to be Happy and life to thrive.

Returning then to the Character Types, we may now articulate a few more differences across the Types. Remember, becoming virtuous is tantamount to "Self-Mastery," and to be Master of one's self is—philosophically—the most important sense of Freedom. That is, to truly be free, we must free ourselves from animalistic tendencies toward Vice. Thus, we perfect the powers of our soul by allowing the Natural

Harmony involved in the "higher" powers ruling the "lower" ones. There are two aspects of Self-Mastery, then, that we will examine here. First, the further clarifications Aristotle provides regarding Incontinence, that is, the individual who lacks Self-Mastery. Second, the idea of "Congruence." Though this idea seems to be present in Aristotle, he does not thematize or emphasize it. Therefore, we will derive a significant amount of the clarification regarding this idea in Aristotle from the contemporary psychologist Carl Rogers.

According to Aristotle, there are two different kinds of Incontinence. Recall, the Incontinent Character Type is one who may hear the appropriate *logos*, however, the force of *pathos* results in the performance of a Vicious action. The different kinds of Incontinence, then, constitute two different ways in which a person may not be able to resist the force of *pathos*. They are "impetuosity" and "weakness." In regard to the hierarchy of Character Types, impetuosity is located just below weakness and just above Viciousness. Thus, weakness refers to proper Incontinence. That is to say, the weak person hears the appropriate *logos*; however, the weak person also experiences a conflict between *logos* and *pathos*, and ultimately is too weak to resist the influence of *pathos*. Whereas the Vicious person neither experiences conflict between *pathos* and *logos* nor experiences regret after performing the Vicious action, the impetuous Incontinent does not experience conflict between *pathos* and *logos*; however, this type of individual does experience regret after performing the Vicious action.

In Aristotle's discussion of these two kinds of Incontinence, he focuses on two types of *pathos*: Pleasure and anger. Because both can influence Incontinence, a matrix may be developed, and this further develops the hierarchy internal to the Incontinent Type and within the overall hierarchy of Character Types. Thus, we ask: What is the essential difference between Pleasure and anger? According to Aristotle, whereas Pleasure can influence the soul without a *logos*, anger seems only able to influence the soul through a *logos* (1149a33). The internal hierarchy then would be: "at the top" of Incontinence, (1) weakness caused by anger; followed by (2) weakness caused by pleasure; followed by (3) impetuosity caused by anger; and, lastly, (4) impetuosity caused by pleasure.

We now turn to the idea of Congruence. Congruence refers to the Virtuous and Continent Character Types, and Incongruence refers to the Incontinent and Vicious Character Types. Recall above, we noted that the psychological experience of the Vicious Type is as if they are being "torn apart." Similarly, Rogers tells us that a general anxiety and feeling of vulnerability accompanies Incongruence. Explicitly, Incongruence refers to "a discrepancy between the actual experience of the organism and the self picture of the individual insofar as it represents that experience." (Rogers 1957, 96).

Rogers's discussion of Incongruence helps us understand what may be the role of Conscience and the silent *logos* of the Daimon's protest to performing the Vicious action. According to Rogers,

> If the individual dimly perceives such an incongruence in himself, then a *tension state* [emphasis added] occurs which is known as anxiety. The incongruence need not be sharply perceived. It is enough that it is subceived—that is, discriminated as threatening to the self without any awareness of the content of that threat. (Rogers 1957, 97).

Before discussing this quote, consider the following clarification, "Such anxiety is often seen ... as the individual approaches awareness of some element of his experience which is in sharp contradiction to his self concept." (Rogers 1957, 97). Now, what Rogers means by "self concept" here is what Plato and Aristotle meant by self-understanding. Of course, insofar as self-understanding involves *logos*, then this takes us directly back to the idea of Justice as the Virtue of the capacity to appropriately "see" the self's relations. Remember, "Know Thyself" requires the actualization of capacities with which to Know Thyself. Therefore, the excellent actualization of these capacities refers us back to the sense in which we may ascend the *scala amoris* by becoming a virtuoso regarding our self's relations to Pleasure and pain, and then excelling at our capacity to hear the appropriate *logos* for which a particular situation calls. Finally, the culmination of these Virtues, recall, is the excellence of Justice, which *provides* us the capacity to understand our self's relations in accordance with Justice. Thus, by appropriately understanding our self's relations we arrive at a self-understanding, that is, what Rogers calls a "self concept," which is Congruent with our *actual* self that has now self-actualized.

This is the connection between the panoramic view acquired through Wisdom in Harmony with Justice and self-realization. Moreover, the Incongruent and Vicious Character Types, due to their lack of excellence regarding their Natural Functions, are unable to self-actualize (and thereby self-realize) in regard to the Virtues of Wisdom and Justice. Referring to the rest of the above Rogers quote beyond his notion of "self concept," notice how the question of an individual's Congruence becomes operable. When an individual is about to perform an action, it is possible for the individual to "subceive" that the actions they are about to perform in accordance with *pathos* are in "contradiction" with their *logos* associated with self-realization.

§15 *Pleasure: The Supervening Indication of Completion*

Aristotle's primary discussions of Pleasure occur in the *Nicomachean Ethics* in two places, that is, Book VII §§11–14 and Book X §§1–5. For our purposes, we will focus on the discussion from Book X. Aristotle's analysis of Pleasure will yield the result that though the Highest Good is a Pleasure, it is not Pleasure. The reason the analysis is important is because if every Good is pleasant, and the Good is that toward which all actions aim, then why is the Good not Pleasure? The reason is that it is the Nature of Pleasure to accompany something else. The idea of supervenience is helpful here. We say that both eating food and finishing writing a paper are pleasant; however, they are not pleasant in the same way. Yet, notice, Pleasure in each case may be seen as accompanying the completion of an activity. In the poetic translation of W.D. Ross, Pleasure "supervenes as the bloom of youth does on those in the flower of their age" (1174b33).

In this way, "Since activities differ with respect to goodness and badness, some being worth choosing, others worth avoiding, and others neither, the same is true of pleasure as well" (1175b24–5). Of course, Pleasure may be associated with activities which are ultimately harmful to us. Thus, Aristotle thinks of the Virtuous person as the standard in determining which Pleasure should be pursued (cf. 1176a15–19). We must keep in mind two ideas, then, regarding Pleasure. First, extremes can destroy the capacity of the appetites to respond to *logoi*; though heroin and crack cocaine are pleasurable, we should not consume them. In fact, doing so may harm us to the point of becoming more animal-like than human, and the same may be said regarding various sexual activities. Second, since Pleasure is the supervening indication of completion of the various Natural Functions, we should not pursue Pleasure in itself. Rather, we should pursue the excellent, that is, Virtuous, completion of the Natural Functions, and we will thereby experience the appropriate Pleasure.

Therefore, we are now in a position to solve what may seem puzzling regarding Aristotle's characterization of the best human life, that is, the Good life. Aristotle, following Plato, says that the best life will be one filled with "Contemplation." This is like the idea that the best life available to a human is a life lived "doing" philosophy. We may now comprehend this claim in two ways. First, recall the highest power of the human soul is Intellectual activity. Corresponding to the Two Inclinations toward the Good, the human is the "rational animal." Thus, when we "Contemplate" we are in a continuous state of completing the activity associated with the Function of the Intellect, that is, actualizing the capacity of the human soul's highest power. Second, the continual actualization of the Intellect corresponds with both the Virtue of Wisdom and of Justice. Hence, recalling the above section discussion of self-realization and panoramic Wisdom, it is as if with each moment the Wise person pulses forth the actualization of an awareness of the *logos* corresponding to *Eudaimonia*. This is contemplation. The self-realization not only regarding self-understanding but also regarding the fact that one has gained this "vision" is a Pleasure. Insofar as the Sage or the Wise Person may sustain such a relation, then it is as if that person "dwells with divinity," in that God, for Aristotle, is a be-ing that continually enjoys its be-ing as a "single and simple pleasure" (1154b26).

Happiness: The Good Life & The Good Death

§16 *Self-Love: The Great-Souled Person*

To begin, notice the Greek terms around which Aristotle's discussion revolves. The term Aristotle is using for love, which will also be the term he uses for friendship, is *philia*, and the term for "Great-Souled" is a combination of "mega" and *psychē*. Some translate this as "Pride," "Dignity," or "Magnanimity," however, we will stay as close to Aristotle's term as possible by simply saying "Great-Souled." For instance, this is also consistent with Rackman's Loeb translation of the *Nicomachean Ethics*, where Book IV §3 initiates the discussion of Greatness of Soul. For our purposes the two questions to emphasize inquire how the Self-Realization of the Virtuous person influences its own self-relation and relation to others. If we recall how Incontinence was distinguished into weakness and impetuosity, it is as if Virtue is being distinguished into Virtue proper and being Great-Souled as "a crowning ornament of the virtues" (1124a2). Thus, there is a spectrum here too spanning from Vicious individuals to Virtuous individuals and up to the Great-Souled Person. Aristotle's "scientific" way of stating Plato's concern for celestial be-ing and relation to divinity appears here with the Great-Souled, since this individual "aims at Superhuman Virtue." It is as if the glow of Superhuman Virtue adorns the Great-Souled with a crown—like a halo.

The challenge for contemporary readers of Aristotle regarding self-love is distinguishing it from "narcissism." We need to understand that there are two pieces to narcissism, and it is really the second piece which makes narcissism bad. It is also the second piece that differentiates narcissism from self-love. Just like the Myth of Narcissus, narcissism refers to an individual's preoccupation with self. This may or may not be bad. However, the second piece, and you must have them both to be truly narcissistic, is that the narcissist does not allow external relations to influence their internal relation to self. Notice, then, self-love is similar to the first piece of narcissism, at least insofar as it requires attention and awareness to self, though "preoccupation" may be too strong of a term to characterize that relation. In contrast, self-love does not resonate with the second piece of narcissism. That is to say, as we will see with the Great-Souled Person, virtuous self-love is consonant with Justice. The Great-Souled Person has self-love because the Great-Souled Person recognizes his or her own greatness. The external relation ensures that Greatness of Soul is neither narcissism nor empty vanity.

Because the Great-Souled Person truly is great-souled, Aristotle thinks of all those who deserve Honor, the Great-Souled deserves it most. Interestingly, in order for the Great-Souled Person to remain great-souled, they must relate appropriately to the rewards and honors bestowed upon them. This is the key to understanding why the Great-Souled Person seems to care little for external goods and worldly rewards, that is, the Great-Souled Person seems to be a Wisdom lover and not an Honor lover, despite being the most deserving of Honor. According to Aristotle, "a person is thought to be great-souled if he claims much and deserves much; he who claims much without deserving it is foolish, but no one of moral excellence is foolish" (1123b2–4). Yet, in one respect, the Great-Souled Person does seem like a child. In Aristotle's *Rhetoric* he notes "the young and the great-souled" are among those who "deem themselves worthy of goods they do not possess" (1388a38). The difference being that the Great-Souled Person actually is worthy of great things and Honor.

At the same time, the Great-Souled Person will not be excessively joyed at receiving Honor for being Great-Souled, because—keeping in mind Panoramic Wisdom and a discernment of relations in accordance with Justice—Great-Souled Persons accept what to their minds should belong to them already and "because others are not able to give them anything greater in tribute" (1124a5–9). However, because they do not believe the rewards are worthy of pursuit, that is, they are Good for the sake of Goodness not the instrumental gains which *should* be associated with it, they will not "lower themselves" to pursue such ends (notice how this thought coincides with translations of Greatness of Soul as pride and dignity). Famously Aristotle held, "The life of money-making is one undertaken under compulsion, and wealth is evidently not the good we are seeking; for it is merely useful and for the sake of something else." (1096a5). Thus, in regard to the Doctrine of the Mean, we may say, the Great-Souled Person believes itself to be worthy of Honor at the right times, for the right reasons, and so on. Whereas persons with the Vice of excess, that is, vanity, think they deserve Honor at the wrong times, for the wrong reasons, persons with the deficient Vice, that is, "Smallness of Soul, will fail to think themselves worthy when they may, in fact, be." (1123b25). In this way, Aristotle criticizes undue humility.

Consider the distinction between praise and Honor. Whereas praise is supposed to be relative, Honor is supposed to be absolute in regard to Justice. "Thus we praise the just man and the courageous man and generally the good man and virtue, on account of their actions and achievements." (1101b14–15). However, that which is choice worthy as an end in itself, for example, Happiness, deserves "something greater and better" than praise, and that is, according to Aristotle, Honor. This is why Aristotle says we should not "praise" the gods, rather we should Honor them. For we should think of the Goodness of the gods beyond merely how they contribute to the accomplishment of human ends. The difference is similar to the one between the Great-Souled and those who attempt to imitate them. Aristotle holds,

> in reality only the good man ought to be honored ... without virtue it is not easy to bear good fortune becomingly, and such men, being unable to carry their prosperity, and thinking themselves

superior to the rest of mankind, despise other people, although their own conduct is no better than another's. The fact is that they try to imitate the great-souled man without being really like him, and only copy him in what they can, reproducing his contempt for others but not his virtuous conduct. For *the great-souled man is justified in despising other people—his estimates are correct*; but most proud men have no good ground for their pride [emphasis added]. (1124a25–1124b7).

We may praise cleverness and wittiness; we may recognize a savvy transaction that leaves one rich or in possession of another's goods; however, such transactions are not worthy of Honor.

Perhaps the difficulty with understanding such a Virtuous Character Type is that the Great-Souled Person is, for the most part, indifferent to external goods, including honor, and yet by aiming at Superhuman Virtue is concerned with deserving the highest Honor, that is, recognition of one's value by the gods. Aristotle examines a good example of a situation in which the distinction is clear. That is, Aristotle points out that by bearing misfortunes, the Great-Souled Person wins Honor (1100b30). Moreover,

> The great-souled person, because he does not value anything highly, does not enjoy danger. He will avoid trivial dangers, but will face great ones, and, again because of his attitude to goods, will be unsparing even of his own life. (1124b6–9)

This kind of "self-possession" is reminiscent, as Aristotle points out, of Socrates or the philosopher in contemplation. Recall the story of the death of the Sicilian philosopher Archimedes (287–212 BC) who, according to Plutarch, when accosted by a Roman soldier during the siege of Syracuse in the Second Punic War famously refused to stop working on his diagram, and so was killed while contemplating some theorem.

Finally, the above discussion allows us to draw a conclusion regarding self-realization, self-love, and being Great-Souled. Recall, self-realization manifests with the supervenience of the Virtues. Thus, Prudence and Justice allow us to correctly appraise relations, and thereby a person arrives at a correct self-evaluation. Though love may be characterized in many ways, it may be characterized as a kind of "evaluative attitude." This will be the centerpiece of the next section; for now, notice through the self-realization and consonant self-evaluation; it is as if one sees oneself in the vision of Panoramic Wisdom, and, as a result, there is a genuine psychological response to perceiving one's own Goodness and Virtue. Hence, one truly manifests self-love.

§17 *Friendship: Different Types & the Virtue of Trust*

The kind of self-love the Great-Souled Person has may be characterized in terms of Friendship. This characterization will be helpful for differentiating the different kinds of Friendship found in Aristotle. The basic idea is that just as the Great-Souled Person's self-evaluation manifests self-love, what we love expresses the state of our soul. Therefore, Aristotle is critical of the general notion of Good Will, because it seems as though we need to experience another person's presence to be able to discern if our being with them is like "one soul in two different bodies."

There are four (4) characteristics of friendship found in *Nicomachean Ethics* Book IX §4: (1) wishing and doing good, or things that appear to be good, for another's sake (cf. 1122b31); (2) wishing that another exist and live, for his sake (cf. 1159a31–32); (3) spending time with another and choosing the same things (cf. 1157b18–22); (4) sharing in another's joys and sorrows (cf. 1156b14–17). With important implications for Care Ethics: Aristotle cites the relation between mother and child as a model regarding characteristics 2 and 4 (cf. 1159a31), 1 refers to completeness, and 3 refers to closeness and mutuality. Further, in §§2–3 of Book VIII, Aristotle provides a list of what he takes to be the possible characterizations of objects of love, that is, the Pleasant, the Useful, and the Good. The Pleasant is, of course, loved because of the Pleasure received from it; the Useful from the Utility we gain by it. Finally, the Good differs from the others in that the others treat the object of love as a means to those ends, and the Good treats the object of love as an end in itself; moreover, recalling our discussion of Pleasure in §15, there is Pleasure associated with the Good, which should be differentiated from the Pleasure associated with the object of love as a means to Pleasure.

Aristotle thinks the best friendships are ones in which both individuals are Good. This results in a harmony of self-love between the two individuals. Think of how the great-souled man in friendship with others displays the frankness which both characterizes his honesty with himself and characterizes the honesty of a genuine friend. Further, notice how wishing and doing good things for the other's sake and wishing that the friend exist and live for their own sake (1166a4–5) naturally follows when one is wishing the same for oneself for the same reason, that is, just as a person may be a friend to himself and, thereby, perform actions wishing good for himself, so too it may follow in regard to someone of the same Character Type.

Thus, it seems so long as both individuals have the same primary object of love, then they may expect to have an excellent Friendship; however, Aristotle provides greater insight here. The best Friendships are those "between equals" and those which last longer. Ultimately, this is because the best Friendships are capable of Trust. Aristotle seems to list them as follows:

1) *Good-Good* (Strongest bond: lasts longest and is best)
2) *Pleasure-Pleasure* (Typical of youth)
3) *Utility-Utility* (Weakest bond)

Notice, how in terms of Congruence and capacity for Trust Aristotle's hierarchy of Friendships seems Natural and based in psychological Function. In this way we can understand how Trust may be a Virtue or excellence of the Friendship. For example, if a Good person pursues a friendship for the sake of Pleasure, the Good person may eventually experience Incongruence if faced with compromising Justice and acting in contradistinction from self-understanding.

Lastly, consider the relation between Congruence and Trust. Just as self-love is not possible for the Incontinent and Vicious Character Types in the way that it is possible for the Continent and Virtuous, so too the latter Character Types are able to Trust themselves. Extending this to relations with others, it follows that Friendship between Good persons and between lovers of the Good will be the friendships capable of sincere Trust. That is to say, you may Trust that a lover of Pleasure will betray you or leave you if they find some different Pleasure to pursue; however, that is not the kind of Trust we are seeking in a Friend. Thus, it seems that Friendship in terms of the Good is Naturally the best and highest Friendship and that one of the excellences of that type of Friendship is sincere Trust.

§18 *Teleological Eudaimonia: Happiness as Human Destiny*

It is primarily for heuristic purposes that we make the distinction between *Eudaimonia* as "supervenient" and "teleological." Traditionally this kind of distinction is just the attempt to further distinguish Aristotle from Plato. However, given our discussions of Natural Law and Divine Justice, it is not immediately clear that Plato's *Eudaimonism* should not be characterized as "Teleological." We will return to clarify this point last in this section. For now, we will characterize the manner in which Aristotle's *Eudaimonia* is teleological. What we intend to emphasize with "teleological" is that *Eudaimonia* for Aristotle is the Natural completion or perfection of the individual in regard to its Natural Functions. Recall, because Aristotle sees the city as conditioning an individual's flourishing and Happiness, he understands *Eudaimonia* to necessarily include family and material goods. In other words, whereas Plato's version of *Eudaimonia* tended to emphasize one's—solitary—relation to divinity, Aristotle emphasizes humans as "social animals," by nature and Happiness as the excellent, that is, virtuous, fulfillment of Natural Functions.

Thus, as Aristotle's *Rhetoric* indicates, *Eudaimonia* is: (1) that to which the entire species of humans naturally strives as a fulfillment in terms of completion or perfection; (2) a continuous and complete or perfect activity; (3) the total inclusion of one's life including their relationships with others, that is, friends, and material belongings. Though the last idea reminds us of the quote from Solon and §4 above, we still maintain that Happiness is possible in this life. Recall for Aristotle, "Happiness is an activity; and activity plainly comes into being and is not present at the start like a piece of property" (1169b30). Finally, we may identify four primary features of Aristotle's notion of *Eudaimonia*: (a) the primacy of Character, (b) the primacy of habit, (c) the centrality of Prudence, and (d) the centrality of flourishing. Aristotle's is a Character ethics, in that, particular actions are important insofar as they influence the Type of Character we become by performing them. Thus, we are concerned for Self-Mastery, not the mastery of rules. By developing our moral sensibility we may become a moral virtuoso in that we consider the right aspects of the situation at the right time and in the right way—this relates back to what we called the "phenomenological reading" above. Happiness, then, rests on top of these conditions, when they are fulfilled, and, therefore, it is possible to sustain Happiness as the excellence of human existence by sustaining a Virtuous Character by cultivating our habits in regard to Wisdom.

In this way, according to Aristotle "Living well or badly does not depend on one's fortunes; rather, human life has an additional need for these things, as we said, but virtuous activities are sovereign over happiness, and contrary activities are sovereign over the contrary state." (1100b8–10). Thus, "moral luck" is not of primary significance, if of any significance at all, for Aristotle. For

> there are certain external advantages, the lack of which sullies supreme felicity, such as good birth, satisfactory children, and personal beauty: a man of very ugly appearance or low birth, or childless and alone in the world, is not our idea of a happy man, and still less so perhaps is one who has children or friends that are worthless, or who has had good ones but lost them by death. (1099b1–5).

Yet, echoing the Virtue of Fortitude and the striving of the Great-Souled Person, integrity means "not deviating from one's nature" (Rhetoric, 1390b21–23), and, in this way, it is our birthright as humans to self-actualize, and be Happy. This final thought may, in fact, be the differentiating factor between Aristotle and Plato.

Hence, for both Plato and Aristotle *Eudaimonia* supervenes as the highest excellence of human life. Further, they both understand it as necessarily involving the continuous activity of contemplation. Ultimately, they are, of course, both still philosophers. Though they both think of *Eudaimonia* as deriving from a kind of self-perfection and excellence, the primary difference— were we to attempt to call them both "teleological"—is that Plato's soteriology seems to span multiple incarnations. Thus, Plato's preoccupation with Divine Justice contrasts with Aristotle's concern for Natural Function, despite the clear moments of teleological and soteriological overlap.

3

Ancient Greek "Socratic" Wisdom Schools: Cynicism, Hedonism, Skepticism, Stoicism

"The unexamined life is not worth living."[14]
~Socrates

§1 Chapter Overview

They are called the Socratic Schools because each in their own way attempts to emulate the life they believed Socrates lived, and they are called the Wisdom Schools because each in their own way put forth an ethics for how to achieve the Good Life, that is, the best human life, as evidenced by the characteristics of the Great-Souled person and *Eudaimonia*. Thus, though there is overlap regarding goals toward, and evaluations of various aspects of life, they may also be clearly differentiated. The Socratic Wisdom Schools are often contrasted with the "Sophists" who held Convention to be Justice. If we wish to widen the lens, we may even consider the followers of Plato and those of Aristotle as comprising two more schools to add to the list.

In regard to the term "school," in some cases it is meant to refer to an actual school, such as Plato's Academy. However, in this chapter it is most often used more generally to refer to a "school of thought." In other words, per the latter use of the term, *you* may "belong" to one of these schools of thought, despite the fact that the original schools have long since been closed. Moreover, as we will see, Hedonism and Skepticism actually each divide into two different schools of thought. Hence, technically this chapter will briefly introduce six (6) different schools. This book contains an Appendix which provides charts comparing these schools regarding various ethical principles.

Lastly, note the use of the following terms: "individualism," "utilitarianism," "intellectualism," and "voluntarism." The term "individualism" in this section is simply intended to convey the opposite of "collectivism." Despite living in communities, the stereotype of the wise person or sage as reclusive or, at least withdrawn, from the pursuits of a political life is accurate. Though the ancient Greek Wisdom Schools may be differentiated in terms of their different understandings and approaches to the Good Life, it seems there were two issues regarding which they were in agreement. First, they seem in agreement that a life lived away from, or outside of, the hustle and bustle (*à un rythme d'enfer*) of political life is to be preferred, that is, leisure is supposed to be, at least, a catalyst to Wisdom.

However, it should be noted the Cosmopolitanism of the Stoics, for example, given their understanding of Natural Law, conceived of humanity in terms of a "natural fellowship of mankind." At the same time, Panoramic Wisdom is an accomplishment of the Virtuous individual, and what the Great-Souled person strives for seemed to consider the solitary individual a sufficient condition for Happiness. This is contra-Aristotle's emphasis, of course, on the *polis* and political life. Second, they seem in agreement that in some circumstances suicide may be the best action to perform. In regard to the term "utilitarianism," here it simply means following a path guided by satisfaction and usefulness; "pragmatism" is a close synonym here.

Lastly, though the contrast between "intellectualism" and "voluntarism" will receive a deeper treatment in the next chapter, the basic idea here is that the former emphasizes the primacy of the intellect over the will, and the latter emphasizes the primacy of the will over the intellect. However, it is important to note that in this Ancient Historical perspective, the Will is not understood, as it later will be, to have a separate status from the intellect and appetites. Basically, theories which suggest that the appropriate *logos* is the primary determining feature in regard to ethics tend toward intellectualism. Thus, roughly the distinction maps onto the difference between Plato and Aristotle. Moreover, this is the reason discussing Freedom of the Will is so difficult and important regarding the Ancient and Medieval periods. Perhaps the best we can hope for is a fusion of horizons, that is, concerning our own worldview and historical perspective. Generally speaking, the Cynics and the Hedonists seem more pragmatic than the Skeptics and the Stoics; however, the Cynics seem more intellectualistic than the Hedonists. Though Stoicism may seem like a feat of the Will for us, the Stoics are perhaps the most intellectualistic of all the schools, given their Fatalism and nearly total Determinism.

Cynicism

§2 *Nature over Convention: Askēsis & Cosmopolitanism*

The perhaps most famous of the cynics was Diogenes of Sinope (c. 412–323 BC). Because of the way he lived, he is often called "the dog philosopher." However, Cynics honor Antisthenes (c. 445–365 BC) with having "founded" the Cynic school when he began providing lectures free to the public at the "Cynosarges," a public gymnasium. Cynicism refers, then, to an interpretation of Nature which emphasizes Freedom as self-sufficiency. Because Cynics consider your only possession to be your mind, they understood Freedom to include anticonventionalism. Wisdom, reason, and doubt, then, are good—and help one lead a Good life—insofar as they can be used to maintain your Natural state of self-sufficiency.

Their anticonventionalism made them resist public life and the pursuit of conventional goals, for example, owning a home or luxurious external goods. Some commentators have referred to them as the first "Hippies" of the Western Tradition. They are attributed the position of "Cosmopolitanism," because they considered themselves citizens of the world, rather than some particular city. In other words, they thought of the earth as their home and cities as propped up on belief in conventions and political power, rather than the forces of Nature. Thus, being able to withstand being homeless may be seen as a kind of Virtue to them. It is as if to rely on the city is to pervert one's Natural State, as if sleeping in a bed were a sign of weakness.

Hence, they followed a path of *Askēsis*, which is not necessarily directed at asceticism; rather, it is directed at "toughness" and "desensitization," making oneself rugged enough to live a Natural human life, and once adjusted to that life, recognizing it is the Good Life, i.e. the best life a human can live. Moreover, the etymology of the word Cynic refers us to *kunikos*, which is Greek for "dog-like." This name seems quite fitting, then, since it reflects the Natural style of living. In fact, having acquired this viewpoint, some Cynics, treating the city as if it were the wilderness, were not opposed to urinating or even masturbating in public places. Hence, the sense in which the Conventional public tended to find Cynics, for example, laying around the city streets, to be annoying like undomesticated dogs.

§3 *Freedom: Autarkeia, Eleutheria, Parrhēsia*

The Cynics believed they were born free, despite whatever city or parents through which Fate happened to bring them into the world. Thus, the ancient Greek term "*eleutheria*" refers to the Freedom or liberty which they believed was their Natural birthright. Further, the term "*autarkeia*" refers to the ideal of self-sufficiency, which one may attain through *askēsis*. Finally, the term "*parrhēsia*" refers to the ideal of frankness or honesty that exemplifies Freedom of speech. In other words, self-sufficiency entails not being dependent on Convention or political favor in such a way that one would need to speak dishonestly to sustain a livelihood. These three terms, then, characterize the essence of the Cynic understanding of Freedom.

In fact, as if striving to be a Good Friend to all the world, when asked: "What is the best thing in the world?" Diogenes replied, "*Parrhēsia*." (Laertius, VI, §69). And, there are two anecdotes regarding Diogenes which may help convey the Cynic ethic and lifestyle. First, philosophers have long told the story of when Diogenes—who lived at the same time as Aristotle—met Alexander the Great. According to the (allegorical) story, Diogenes was sitting in an outside cubbyhole, perhaps reminiscent of a small cave, and basking in the sun, when Alexander appeared. As the story goes, Alexander said to Diogenes, "Ask any boon of me you like." And, Diogenes replied, "Stand out of my light." (Laertius, VI, §28). Of course, the story is potent because, given Alexander's power, Diogenes seemingly could have acquired anything he wanted. Thus, perhaps because he thought Diogenes did not realize who he was, Alexander announces himself and his rank noting, "I am Alexander the Great King," to which Diogenes responded, "I am Diogenes the Cynic," that is, "the dog." (Laertius, VI, §60).

Lastly, there is the story of the supposed interaction between Diogenes and Plato. As the story goes, "Plato saw [Diogenes] washing lettuces, came up to him and quietly said, 'Had you paid court ... you wouldn't now be washing lettuces,' and [Diogenes] with equal calmness answered, 'If you had washed lettuces, you wouldn't have had to pay court...'" (Laertius, VI, §69). The idea of "pay court" here means participate in whatever political activities necessary to acquire a livelihood. Whereas given his lifestyle Plato preferred more of an aristocratic existence than Diogenes, it is also the case that the Cynics disagreed with Aristotle's sense of Equality. That is, the Cynics are often referred to as "equalitarians," as the story regarding Diogenes and Alexander the Great reflects, they considered all humans equal. Recall, Aristotle may have assented to potential Equality, but not to the thesis that we are all actually equal.

Hedonism

§4 *Types of Hedonism: Cyrenaic & Epicurean*

The term "Hedonism" comes from the ancient Greek term for Pleasure, that is, *hēdonē*. There are two main schools of Hedonism, the Cyrenaic and the Epicurean. These schools differ in regard to the type of Pleasure they deem most worthy to pursue, that is, lower and higher Pleasures respectively. In both cases the goal may be said to be—maximize Pleasure and minimize pain. The Cyrenaic School was founded by Aristippus (c. 435–356 BC), and though there may be some controversy regarding their actual practices, traditionally we hold that they were less discriminating regarding Pleasure than the Epicureans.

> 'Philosophy was good,' Aristippus is reported to have said, 'to enable the philosopher, supposing all laws were abolished, to go on living as before.' Thus the Socratic justification of law as useful, and thereby pleasurable, came ultimately to undo the law which it had served to justify. Because utility was the basis of law, it might serve *in lieu* of the law. Law was a mere convention, said the Cyrenaics: 'right and wrong existed by custom and enactment, not by nature.' (Barker 1906, 60).

Thus, the Cyrenaics believed the Highest Good to be Pleasure, and the Good Life a life lived maximizing Pleasure and minimizing pain. Further, they did not think the law Natural enough in comparison with the Nature of Pleasure and pain, to require Temperance and Fortitude.

The Epicurean School was founded by Epicurus (c. 341–270 BC). Epicurus taught in his garden just outside Athens. Hence, the Epicureans are sometimes called the "garden philosophers." Epicurus, like the Cyrenaics, was a materialist. So, though, as we will see, he believed in different qualities of Pleasure, he still considered the higher quality Pleasures to be material in Nature. He took the pursuit of Pleasure and avoidance of pain to be our most Natural engagement with existence. The Epicureans believed anyone who examined their own preferences and those of children would see that the pursuit of Pleasure and avoidance of pain is most Natural. However obvious this may seem to you, notice that it functions as a kind of counterargument against the Cynics, whom we noted "train" themselves to endure less Pleasure and more pain.

§5 *Ataraxia: Positivism, Individualism & Contractarian-Justice*

Due to his materialism, Epicurus has a non-spiritualistic understanding of *Eudaimonia*. Hence, Epicureans primarily identify *Eudaimonia* with *ataraxia*, which translates to "tranquility." This may be compared with the *autarkeia* of the Cynics, and the "self-possession" of the Great-Souled person noted in Aristotle. Now, because Epicureans are materialists, they understand this tranquility in terms of its material constituents, that is, as we shall see, they understand self-sufficiency and tranquility in terms of self-satisfaction. This means they do not believe there is anything beyond what our human senses can encounter, and such a philosophical position regarding experience and existence is called "Positivism." Thus, Happiness for the Epicureans involves the pursuit of Pleasure and avoidance of pain which leads one to sustain a state of *ataraxia*, thereby, understood as a material state of the body.

Given their understanding of Happiness, the Epicureans also adhered to a philosophy of individualism and self-sufficiency; however, it clearly differs from the Cynics. Moreover, whereas the Cynics could think of our Natural state in terms of Justice, how might Epicureans understand Justice? As noted above, since law is rooted in Convention and the value of law is its usefulness or utility, the Hedonistic understanding of Natural Law and Natural Justice extends only as far as reciprocity. In this way, contracts are advantageous to secure agreements for increasing Pleasure and reducing harm and pain to the extent individuals in a community deem fit and, ultimately, regarding the senses and the body. In this way, Epicureans hold that it is Naturally in our self-interest to pursue peace through contracts so that we may obtain some amount of security which would allow for Hedonistic self-sufficiency and tranquility, that is, *ataraxia*. Notice, again, Hedonistic individualism is different from the "rugged" individualism of the Cynic.

§6 *The Dynamics of Pleasure & Types of Desires: Food, Sex & Fame*

Regarding the dynamics of Pleasure, Epicureans distinguish between "moving" and "static" Pleasure. When you are in the process of satisfying a desire, then Pleasure is said to be "moving," for example, when you are eating food or engaging in a sex act. Further, once you have satisfied the desire for which you were experiencing moving Pleasure, then the feeling of satisfaction refers to "static" Pleasure. In this way, Epicureans believe that you are always already somewhere on a spectrum of unsatisfied, satisfying, or satisfied desires. Since Epicureans consider unsatisfied desires to be "painful," then the ideal is to stay close to the satisfied end of the spectrum. Lastly, because it is possible to feel regret over the past and anxiety toward the future, both of which Epicureans consider to be "painful," we may notice a kind of *askēsis* even in Hedonism. That is to say, "psychological training" for a Hedonist would amount to embracing maxims such as "You only live once," and "To regret is to add a second stupidity to the first."[15] Thus, perhaps the best Hedonists are the forgetful and those most easily able to lie to themselves. And, from the materialist perspective, we hear one of the celebrated Epicurean maxims: "Death is nothing to us."

Epicurus distinguishes between three types of desires: (1) Natural and necessary desires, (2) Natural but non-necessary desires, and (3) "vain and empty" desires. First, Natural and necessary desires include desires for things such as food and shelter. Epicurus thinks that these desires are easy to satisfy, difficult to eliminate, and bring great pleasure when satisfied. They are necessary for life, and they are Naturally limited: if you are hungry, your desire can be satisfied by a limited amount of food. Second, a Natural but non-necessary desire is the desire for luxurious food or luxurious shelter. Third, vain desires include desires for power, wealth, fame, and so on. These are more difficult to satisfy precisely because they do not seem to have a Natural limit. Also, these desires are considered non-natural, since they tend to arise due to interaction with others and not naturally, that is, on their own.

Lastly, it is worth emphasizing two insights. First, notice that since you can eliminate pain by controlling your desires, from some angles Hedonists may look similar to Cynics and Stoics. Second, notice how the idea of Natural limit may refer to a kind of Natural Justice. That is to say, we can only eat so much food, before we become sick. We can only engage in so many sex acts before we become exhausted and in pain; however, the desire for "Likes" on social media is limitless. If you do not eat food you will die. You will not die if you do not engage in sex acts. You may waste your life, if you spend too much time on social media.

Thus, we risk losing Freedom and becoming a slave to desire, if we do not Master the process of desire, and for the Hedonist that means maximizing Pleasure and minimizing pain.

Skepticism

§7 *Types of Skepticism: Academic & Pyrrhonian*

The term Skeptic comes from the ancient Greek "*skepsis*," which means inquiry or examination. In order to appreciate the Skeptic Wisdom School it is important to briefly state its relation to Plato. The "Academy" was, of course, the name of Plato's (Wisdom) School, and at the time of Plato's death, Aristotle expected to become the new schoolmaster. However, instead Plato's nephew Speusippus (c. 408–339 BC) took over the Academy. Subsequently, the Academy seemed to begin teaching views different from those we tend to attribute with Plato. It is sufficient for our purposes to make two points. One, the Academy became increasingly Skeptical, and two, ideas about the Highest Good began to take on Neo-Platonic characterization, for example, consistent with Plotinus' (c. 205–270 AD) Neo-Platonism found in the *Enneads* (*The Nines*). Of course, Aristotle went on to found his "Peripatetic school" at the Lyceum in Athens, and Plato's Academy eventually experienced a tension between its identity as a Skeptic Wisdom School or a Stoic Wisdom School.

Because Plato's Academy was engaged in debates with the other Wisdom Schools, these vibrant debates influenced the ancient Greek Skeptics of Plato's Academy in two essential ways. First, the debates helped the Academic Skeptics state the tenets of their Wisdom School in opposition to the School of Epicureanism and Stoicism. Second, exposure to the views of Stoicism ultimately threw the Academy into a kind of crisis regarding its identity, and it subsequently split into different factions. Ultimately, as will be discussed just below, the Academy embraced a Skepticism which many simply considered Stoicism. This is the Greco-Roman Wisdom School of Academic Skepticism adopted by Cicero (106–43 BC), a.k.a. Ciceronian Skepticism.

Now, Aenesidemus (who lived during 1st century BC) was a member of Plato's Academy as it was leaving its phase of high Skepticism. Therefore, in order to return to a purer form of Skepticism, Aenesidemus left the Academy and revived the ancient Wisdom School founded by Pyrrho of Elis (c. 360–270 BC) and, therefore, known as Pyrrhonian Skepticism. Most of what we know about Pyrrho comes from Sextus Empiricus (c. 160–210 AD). However, it is important to note that Pyrrho participated in Alexander the Great's "Indian Campaign," and it is believed that during his time in India, Pyrrho was exposed to the ideas and practices of Hinduism and Buddhism. For our purposes, whatever influence these ideas and practices may have had on what amounted to Pyrrhonian Skepticism, Western Skepticism is associated with "doubt." Therefore, were we to identify a kind of *askēsis* training or techniques constituting the ethics and practice of being a Skeptic, such training or techniques will be characterized in terms of the use of doubt.

Because the Pyrrhonian type of Skepticism may be characterized as "extreme," from the first-person perspective of being a Pyrrhonian Skeptic, supposing the goal of such a Skeptic were to sustain a kind of psychological state through the use of doubt, then it would behoove such a person to doubt the truth of the claim that they use doubt as a method. Thus, Pyrrhonian Skepticism can be extreme. However, Academic or Ciceronian Skepticism is not so extreme. For example, they would be willing to admit that they use a method of doubt to pursue Wisdom and to preserve *ataraxia*, that is, tranquility. Ultimately, by comparison to the other Wisdom Schools, we may say that Skepticism considers doubt to be therapeutic, and Skeptics believe the truth of Nature cannot be known as it is in Itself. Recall, this last point seems like a gesture back toward Plato and away from the Natural. Hence, there may be a kind of "opening" back onto the Divine to be found here in the Skeptic Wisdom School.

§8 *Ataraxia: Swaying in the Clearing of Aporia*

This and the next section, then, refer to the practices of ancient Skepticism proper, that is, Pyrrhonian Skepticism. A few observations regarding the relation between Skepticism and the other Wisdom Schools may be helpful. If we consider the ideals of individualism and the different emphases thus far regarding *Eudaimonia*, Skepticism may make more sense. First, notice how it is possible to feel lonely even in a crowd, for example, at work or as a stranger in a new city. In this way, notice how it may be possible to isolate our own perception of a situation as the determining factor regarding our *feelings* about the situation. Technically, we are always already alone. Though we may at different times be in closer proximity to other bodies, one is always alone with one's self.

Second, just as the Cynics emphasized self-sufficiency and the Hedonists emphasized tranquility, as self-satisfaction, in regard to the Wise person's experience of *Eudaimonia*, the Skeptics seem to emphasize the "Contemplative" aspect of the self-sufficiency and tranquility which traditionally characterize *Eudaimonia*. Further, they seem to understand *ataraxia* in terms of "freedom from disturbance," and this Freedom seems to be understood along more spiritual and psychological lines, that is, not as it was understood by the Hedonists or the Cynics. Though, the feature that perhaps most distinguishes Skepticism as a Wisdom School, and especially in contrast to Stoicism, is what was meant by the suggestion that "suspending judgment" is "necessary." (Laertius, IX, §3). The ancient Greek term of "suspending judgment" is *epochē*, and Classic sources identify it as the essential element to Skepticism (cf. Laertius, IX, §8).

Keep in mind that we want to understand what is meant by the Skeptic suspension of judgment, that is, *epochē*, so that we may see the Skeptic understanding of tranquility as the essential dimension of *Eudaimonia* by way of achieving and sustaining the excellence of contemplation. On the one hand, in terms of the Structural Model, we may say that when a human has an experience that experience is comprised of the *phantasia* produced by the bodily senses which constitute the human's perception. The role of judgment, then, is to appropriately apply a *logos* to the *phantasia*. Thus, you experience the judgment that what you are perceiving is Socrates walking toward you on the shore. The question is, then, do you affirm or deny the truth of that judgment? Suspending judgment would mean you neither affirm nor deny the truth of the judgment. On the other hand, we will discuss three ideas for the sake of coming to understand the Skeptic *epochē*. First, we will use the metaphor of a picture changing inside its frame. Second, we will use the idea of what we may call "the clearing." Third, we will use the idea of listening to music through headphones.

In regard to the metaphor of a picture changing inside its frame, we can understand *epochē* as analogous to the activity of keeping our awareness on the frame. By keeping our awareness on the frame of the picture, it is as if we don't get "carried away" by the changing images inside the frame. In regard to the idea of "the clearing." If we think that mind must have a clear space in it for the content to be able to continuously flow through it, then we want to keep our focus on the clearing. Think of the experience of wishing to express some thought to a friend, but you have forgotten the thought; so, you say, "wait a moment, *it'll come to me.*" As thoughts come to us, that is, come and go, we want to sustain an awareness on the clearing in which thoughts come and go; the "space" through which thoughts "flow." Lastly, have you ever been alone in a room listening to music through headphones? Imagine that you are listening to some music, and you are so "into" the music that you are dancing along with it. Now, when you take the headphones off, notice the difference between the silence of the room and the experience you were having listening to the music. The silent room is the frame of the picture.

By suspending judgment, Skeptics can achieve and sustain *ataraxia*, that is, tranquility. It is as if no matter what images and thoughts enter into the frame, we can continue to recognize that they are just a part of the "magic lantern" show; they are just a part of this play of images and thoughts which continuously flow through our experience. By not "attaching" to any of the content, we remain tranquil. Plato used to say that "perplexity" is good. Not because you are confused; rather, because when you experience perplexity you become aware of your relation to the content of your experience. Otherwise you might just rush right by it, judging it for what it is, and not noticing the play of *phantasia* and ideas before you. The Greek term to describe that point of being stopped is "*aporia*." Were a vehicle moving on a path suddenly unable to go further, they would say, "*aporia*," that is, impasse. Thus, Skeptic techniques to achieve *epochē* function as a kind of *askēsis* toward achieving the contemplative self-sufficiency and tranquility associated with the *Eudaimonia* of the Wise person. All that remains, then, is to briefly examine the famous "Ten Modes" associated with Pyrrhonian Skepticism.

§9 Skeptic Askēsis: Modes for Suspending Judgment and Sustaining Tranquility

The following ten (10) modes are supposed to be thoughts we may use to achieve a suspension of judgment, that is, *epochē*.

1) Think of how two different species in the situation you are in would experience the situation differently. Were you and a cat both experiencing the presence of the same object, the cat would not experience it in the same way as you, so why do you expend so much energy believing it is exactly as you experience it to be?
2) Even within the same species, humans have enough physical and mental differences that we may be able to ask the same question, and suspend our judgment that we know exactly how what we are experiencing is.
3) We can think of how the senses differ from one another. The example that comes from Pyrrho is that honey may seem good to the tongue but not to the eye. When you are looking at someone's "highlight reel" on social media, remember the *phantasia* appearing to you depend on your trusting the experience of your eyes. Why not shift to touch and realize that the truth of the situation is that you are just sitting touching a machine and dreaming about the lives other people might be living.
4) Try to keep in mind that your present state of well-being influences your experience, that is, being hungry, angry, lonely, or tired influences how you experience circumstances.

5) This mode depends on remembering that certain perceptions depend on your point of view, the position from which you are viewing (e.g., are you standing on your head, sitting down, and so on?), and the distance from which you are viewing.
6) Think of how in order for us to have a coherent experience there must be a combination and "mixture" of all sorts of factors, both external and internal. This will help us not lose sight of the picture frame.
7) Remember that external objects appear differently to us depending on factors such as their quantity, motion, and temperature. In this way, we see the rain on the sidewalk just as if it were snow or dry, and the same when it is dry, that is, we see it as though it could be covered with water or snow. Whatever happened in the moment prior, we may see this moment as though it never happened, this is a kind of forgiveness and stopping the force of the hate which surrounds us.
8) We are told this mode is "the one based on relativity." Thus, since everything is in relation to something, we suspend judgment regarding what the Thing in Itself is, that is, we do not attempt to judge its true Nature.
9) When we make a judgment, we determine just one of the many relations a thing has; therefore, no judgment will be able to give us the thing's true Nature.
10) These modes are essentially "Cultural Relativism." By keeping in mind that different cultures from our own would experience this moment differently than we are experiencing it, we are supposed to be able to keep from being carried away by impressions and *phantasia* and our judgments about what the body is currently going through.

These "Ten Modes," then, are supposed to help us not be dragged down by *pathos* or led astray by an inappropriate *logos*. For example, when you encounter an attractive person, you may say to yourself—That person may have a quality of attractive comeliness about them; however, that person's soul is most likely ugly and in disarray. Entering that person's psychic space may entrance me into the *logos* which they follow, and that *logos* may result from their chaotic grasping at whatever they can, or care to, hear of *logoi*, in the attempt to justify their viciousness.

Stoicism

§10 *Stoicism: Corporealism, Determinism & Spirit*

There is a direct lineage between Cynicism and Stoicism. The Cynic Crates of Thebes (c. 365–285 BC) is known as the teacher of Zeno of Citium (c. 334–262 BC), and it is Zeno of Citium who is remembered as the founder of the Stoic school. Zeno lectured at a place called the "*Stoa poikilē*" which translates as "the painted porch." Hence, the Stoics are sometimes referred to as the "porch philosophers." The teacher-student lineage credited with completing the formation of Stoicism moves from Zeno to his student Cleanthes (c. 330–230 BC) and on to the most famous student of Cleanthes, Chrysippus, a.k.a. Chrysippus of Soli, (c 279–207 BC). Each of these individuals succeeded each other as the head of the Stoic Wisdom School founded by Zeno. The more famous of the philosophers counted among the Stoics were—the "tutor" to Emperor Nero, Lucius

Annaeus Seneca, a.k.a. Seneca, (c. 1 BC–65 AD), the slave Epictetus (55–135 AD), and the Emperor Marcus Aurelius (121–180 AD).

Stoic philosophy is comprised of three parts. Stoicism is ultimately an Ethics; however, it is informed by the method of their Logic, and grounded in their understanding of Physics. Thus, Stoic "Corporealism" refers to the belief that, according to their Physics, only "bodies" exist. This is essentially materialism; however, they do believe there are some "incorporeals," that is, non-bodies, which—though they do not exist—subsist in that which does exist. These are: void, place, time, and "the sayable."

In terms of their Logic, there are two principles *determining* the corporeal world. The first is the "passive" principle of material, and the second is the active formal principle. In regard to their Physics, they held that there are four elements—earth, water, air, and fire. Therefore, they understood the active principle in terms of air and fire working on *the mud* of earth and water. They conceived of the mixture of air and fire as a warm breath, or *pneuma*, breathing life into inanimate (i.e., non-souled) material. Thus, it is as if human existence is a by-product of the "World Soul" bringing order to material (recall the discussion of Celestial Be-ing in the Plato chapter). Lastly, in terms of their Logic, this breath of life is *Logos*. That is to say, it is Reason, because it is that which is ordering the material dimension, the presence of embodied rationality is its very presence.

Now, in terms of their Ethics, this *pneuma* is Spirit, that is, the breath of God, who is understood to be a "craftsman-like fire." In this way, because the human body is subject to the order-ing of God as this fire orders the material dimension, the presence of rationality is Logically fully determined, and in terms of Ethics it is our Fate. Thus, Stoic intellectualism refers to the idea that the Stoic Sage is one who can use the rational capacity of the soul to recognize the movement of reason in the world. The only freedom involved here, then, would be whether we correctly judge the ordering of the World as we experience it. Like Plato's Myth of Er, if "what is coming toward you" (cf. Scalambrino 2015a) is Fated, and it is fully determined in the physical dimension with the only part you can control is how you relate to the *pathos* it provokes, then the best life will be the one which appropriately controls *pathos*.

The aspect of this judgment which corresponds with "Freedom of the Will," then would be our freedom to either affirm or deny the judgment formed by the *logos* present in our soul in relation to the *Logos* forming the World. Moreover, this *Logos* forming the World is also order-ing Nature, and, therefore, is the Natural Law. Notice, for the Stoics, it is both the Natural and the Divine Law. Hence, Stoic Ethics seeks to develop a relation to one's already determined place in the Cosmos, that is, Fate, along with the development of rationality for the sake of appropriately judging one's experiences, and "appropriate" here means in accordance (harmony) with the Natural Law.

§11 *Natural Law: Pantheism & Katalepsis*

Because "appropriate" judgment means in accordance with Natural Law, we will briefly discuss this Stoic understanding of judgment, that is, *katalepsis*, with some concluding remarks regarding Natural Law. The next section will discuss the relation between Stoic Ethics, Skepticism, *Eudaimonia*, and Stoic *askēsis*. The Stoics were considered "pantheists," since they recognized the omnipresence of God, as fiery Spirit, in Nature. Thus, to be in harmony with the order-ing to which God fatefully subjects us, we must appropriately judge our experiences.

INTRODUCTION TO ETHICS

As we mentioned above, though Cicero studied in Plato's Academy and a Skeptic Wisdom School carries his name, he actually identified with Stoicism to fill-in what he considered gaps in the later Academic Skepticism regarding, for example, politics and Natural Law. Cicero seems to have considered Stoicism as an attempt to synthesize Plato and Aristotle. Thus, two metaphors which come from Cicero—that of flames and seeds—are helpful for explaining the Stoic position regarding Natural Law and human Natural endowment, that is, human souls are sparks temporarily separated from the Great Flame (World Soul), and that Nature not being able to teach us directly gave us the seeds for us to cultivate. In this way, it is as if the intellect is a "Divine Spark."

Further, discussing the founder of the Stoic Wisdom School, Zeno, Cicero recounts the Stoic understanding of *katalepsis*,

> he would display his hand in front of one with the fingers stretched out and say 'A visual appearance is like this'; next he closed his fingers a little and said, 'An act of assent is like this'; then he pressed his fingers closely together and made a fist, and said that that was comprehension (and from this illustration he gave to that process the actual name of *katalepsis*, which it had not had before) ... (Cicero 1967, 2.145)

It is as if the "gripping," or getting a grip, on the order of Nature with the *logos* with which one's soul is judging constitutes a soul in harmony with reality. Therefore, because an individual's *logos* may or may not accurately reflect reality, the metaphor of the mind as a mirror of Nature emerged. The second piece, then, is the "Choice" of the individual to accept the judgment reflected by the mirror of the mind or not. Stoic intellectualism still did not conceive of a "Free Will," rather, the individual could either choose to "assent" to the formed judgment or not. Epictetus provided an excellent summary statement at §31 in *The Stoic Manual*:

> Concerning piety toward the gods, know that this is the main thing: have right beliefs about them—that they exist, that they run the world well and justly; and you have been appointed to obey them and to resign yourself to whatever happens and to follow willingly because you are led by the best judgment. Thus you will never blame the gods nor accuse them of unconcern. However, this [Stoic attitude] can never come about unless you withdraw yourself from things not up to us and place good and evil exclusively in the class of things up to us. (Epictetus 1998).

Similarly, §50 in regard to the Natural Law: "Whatever principles are set before you, follow them as laws, the dishonoring of which would be impious. But don't worry about what anyone says about you; for this is not at all up to you." (Epictetus 1998). In this way, and because the Stoics were pantheists, the judgment is not only related to Natural Law but also Divine Judgment.

Notice how one person's judgment may be more accurate than another's and, therefore, may be employed as a more accurate mirror. Thus, when the Stoic Seneca wrote *On Mercy* it was supposed to function like a kind of textbook to instruct the proper way to rule the city, and this gave rise to an entire genera of literature known as "Mirrors for Princes" or "Mirror of the Prince" writings. The most famous example is, of course, Machiavelli's *The Prince*, which we will briefly address in subsequent chapters. It is important to note that the idea that a book of philosophy may influence your *logos*, and, thereby, help you relate differently to your

Fate, follows from Plato's Analogy of the City and the Soul. Moreover, through *katalepsis*, the Stoic Sage was supposed to be able to discern the truth of the real reason behind every chain of events.

On the one hand, because the *Logos* behind every chain of events was God, for the individual able to hear a *logos* revealing the *Logos* the Panoramic Wisdom would have been considered tantamount to viewing reality—to whatever extent possible—as if "through the eyes of God." Thus, the idea of Providence emerges, that is, that the Stoic Sage may know "the end of all things," adding eschatology to teleology and soteriology. On the other hand, since rationality is constitutive of being human, everyone is supposed to have a kind of rational "common sense," and this contributes to the Stoic belief in a Natural "fellowship of mankind." For their cosmopolitanism also meant that we are all "under" one God.

In this way, and as related to the Cynics, the Stoics may be seen as also concerned with obtaining Freedom and tranquility by aligning their lives with Nature. A major difference, of course, being that the Stoics did not reject Convention, in that it too may be considered a result of human judgments in regard to the unfolding of Providence. Further, as we shall see pertaining to the Stoic prescription regarding the proper relation to desire, to reject Convention may work against tranquility and self-sufficiency. Hence, Stoics practiced a reasoned form of "indifference," that is, *apatheia*, or resistance to passion (*pathos*) to achieve the tranquility and self-sufficiency associated with *Eudaimonia*. Moreover, as we will see in the next chapter, as it was eloquently characterized in Heinrich Rommen's *The Natural Law*:

> The metaphysical natural law of Plato as well as the more realistic one of Aristotle formed the high-water mark of moral and natural-law philosophy in Greek civilization. Stoicism, on the other hand, in a remarkable eclectic synthesis of single principles drawn from many philosophers, furnished in its system of natural law the terminology or word vessels into which the Church Fathers were able to pour the first conceptions of Christian natural law and to impart them to the world of their time. (1998, 10).

Before examining Augustine, Aquinas, and Duns Scotus regarding this claim, we will conclude this chapter with a brief examination of Stoic *apatheia* and *askēsis*.

§12 *Stoic Askēsis & Relation to Desire: Apatheia & Ataraxia of the Sage*

In this brief section we will look at a few passages from *The Stoic Manual*, that is, the *Enchiridion*, written by Epictetus. Ultimately, the Stoic prescribed relation to desire is that we neither pursue nor avoid based on *phantasia*, rather we accept, that is, assent to an accurate judgment (*katalepsis*) of, the situation which Fate has determined for us. It is interesting to compare the Skeptics and the Stoics regarding judgment and *ataraxia*, that is, tranquility. Whereas the Skeptics advocated for the contemplative tranquility deriving from suspending judgment, the Stoics advocated for the contemplative tranquility associated with accurately judging reality and accepting it based on its relation to Fate and God, that is, given the tranquility of *Eudaimonia's* harmony with Natural Law and Divine Justice.

To conclude, consider the following seven (7) instances from The Stoic Manual, which may be referred to as a kind of Stoic *askēsis*. These passages are suggestive of the cultivated indifference, that is, *apatheia*,

INTRODUCTION TO ETHICS

and tranquility (*ataraxia*) of the Stoic Sage: (1) Harmonic Visualization; (2) Locus of Control; (3) the Stoic version of the "Headphones Example"; (4) Appropriate Dignity; (5) Fatalism; (6) Negative Visualization; (7) Rational Emotive & Cognitive Behavioral Therapy.

(1) Harmonic Visualization: The Target Analogy, that is, every arrow aims at some target. We hear from Epictetus, "As a target is not set up for the purpose of being missed, so nothing in the world is intrinsically evil." (Epictetus 1998, §27). Further, Epictetus tells us: "Don't seek for things to happen as you wish, but wish for things to happen as they do, and you will be free from disturbance." (Epictetus 1998, §8). Thus, everything is already in harmony, and we should harmonize with it.

(2) Locus of Control: Where do we locate the power controlling us? According to Epictetus: "If someone were to hand over your body to just whomever happened along, you would be outraged. Why aren't you outraged at the fact that you turn over your own mind to whomever happens along—if he insults you and you let it upset and trouble you?" (Epictetus 1998, §28). To this we might add, if they sexually attract you and seduce you from your purpose. Further, "If you want to make progress, shun these sorts of reasoning: 'If I neglect my affairs, I shall have nothing to live on'; 'if I don't punish my slave he will be good for nothing.' For it is better to attain freedom from sorrow and fear and then die of hunger than to live lavishly in vexation. It is better for your slave to be bad than for you to be unhappy … he is not so well off that your tranquility should depend on him." (Epictetus 1998, §12).

(3) The Stoic version of the Headphones Example: Recall that we may recognize there is an experiential world, a "life-world" for each individual, which though structurally constituted the same, that is, the Structural Model insofar as we are human, is experienced differently in terms of the *phantasia* and the individual's ability to *katalepsis*. Therefore, according to Epictetus:

> We can learn the will of nature by considering the matters about which we don't disagree with one another. For instance, when somebody else's miserable slave breaks a cup, you are ready right away to say "So it goes." But realize that when it is yours that gets broken, you ought to behave the same way you did when it was someone else's. Apply this to more important matters as well. Somebody else's child or wife has died; there is no one who would not say "That's life." But when his own child or wife dies, it is "Alas, woe is me!" We ought to remember what we feel when we hear the same thing about other people. (Epictetus 1998, §26).

(4) Appropriate Dignity: This may be understood as the Stoic teaching in regard to the appropriate *logos* toward being Great-Souled:

> Do not pride yourself on superiority that is not your own. If a horse in its pride should say, "I am a fine horse," that could be tolerated. You however, when you boast "I have a fine horse," should realize that you are boasting about the excellence of a horse. What then is your own? The use of impressions [*phantasia*]. So, make use of your impressions in accord with nature, and then take pride; for your pride will be in a good thing that is your own. (Epictetus 1998, §6).

Further, "If someone brags because he understands the books of Chrysippus and can explain them, say to yourself: 'If Chrysippus had not written unclearly, this fellow would have nothing to brag about.' But what is it that I want? To learn nature and to follow her..." (Epictetus 1998, §49).

(5) Fatalism: According to Epictetus: "Remember that you are an actor in a drama such as the playwright wishes it to be. If he wants it short, it will be short; if long, long. If he wants you to play a beggar, play even that capably; or a lame man, or a ruler, or a private person. For this is yours, to play the assigned role well. Casting is the business of another." (Epictetus 1998, §17).

(6) Negative Visualization: Stoics advocate that we: "Let death and exile and all dreadful appearances be before your eyes every day, and most of all, death; and you will never deem anything trivial, nor desire anything excessively." (Epictetus 1998, §21). Epictetus has been accused of "lethal high-mindedness" for suggesting the following:

> As for everything that delights your mind or is useful or beloved, remember to describe it as it really is, starting with the smallest thing. If you are fond of a pot, say "it is a pot that I am fond of." For then, if it breaks, you will not be upset. If you kiss your child or your wife, say that you are kissing a human being. Then if they die you will not be upset. (Epictetus 1998, §3).

Further, Seneca suggested that we visualize each day as our last, and suggested the Sage could visualize every moment as the last.

(7) Rational Emotive & Cognitive Behavioral Therapy: The following from Epictetus has been cited by the founders of RET & CBT as the origin of those forms of therapy. We should recognize the value of the following without mistakenly falling into a kind of Subjectivism regarding human experience:

> It is not things that upset people but rather ideas about things. For example, death is nothing terrible, else it would have seemed so even to Socrates; rather it is the idea that death is terrible that is terrible. So, whenever we are frustrated or upset or grieved, let us not blame others, but ourselves—that is, our ideas. It is the act of a philosophically ignorant person to blame others for his own troubles. An educated person blames neither anyone else nor himself. (Epictetus 1998, §5).

Remember to look to the charts in the Appendix I for a comparison of the "Socratic" Wisdom Schools regarding various key issues differentiating their visions of the Good Life.

4

The Catholic Revolution: Augustine, Aquinas, Bonaventure, and Duns Scotus

"For it is not the hearers of the law who are righteous before God, but the doers of the law who will be justified. For when those who do not have the law, by nature do what the law requires, they are a law to themselves … They show that the work of the law is written on their hearts, while their conscience also bears witness, and their conflicting thoughts accuse or excuse them on that day when … God judges the secrets of men."[16]
~Romans 2:13-17

§1 *Chapter Overview*

To begin, it is important to note that this chapter approaches Christianity and Catholicism from a philosophical perspective. The point of this chapter, then, is to provide a reading of "Catholic Ethics" for the sake of comparison with the other ethical theories discussed. This is not the first time Catholicism has been depicted in terms of a philosophical theory of ethics. For example, the Catholic Priest Lucien F. Longtin, through the National Catholic Educational Association, produced *An Introduction to Catholic Ethics* (2003). From a philosophical perspective and due to its immense importance in establishing the catholic, that is, universal, Christian Church, Catholicism and some of its chief philosophical proponents (a.k.a. "Church Doctors") deserve a chapter. It is interesting to note that—philosophically speaking—Christianity may be compared to the Socratic Schools. Just as Skeptics were aware of Christian teachings, so too when Paul entered cities to preach Christianity, he was debated by Epicureans and Stoics (cf. Acts 17:18–32). The following two chapters will present, then, different readings of Christianity and its outright rejection by various philosophers who have protested against Christianity in general and Catholicism in particular.

The primary idea that sets the Catholic Church apart from other denominations of Christianity is that the Catholic Church is believed to be the continuation of the Church established by Jesus of Nazareth. There is, of course, much more which could be said; however, for our purposes, we will simply note that "Christ" means the "anointed one." Hence, when the divinely inspired prophets whose claims constitute Holy Scripture predicted God's incarnation for the salvation of humans, "the Christ" refers to the incarnation and the series of events fated, that is, predetermined by God, surrounding the incarnation (cf. Athanasius 2016). Though an introduction to ethics book is not the place to explicate the Scriptural foundations of the following claims, it may be helpful to make the following two notes toward articulating the foundation of Catholic ethics. Given the sense in which Catholic ethics transposes a number of the earlier ancient Greek concepts into the Christian Worldview and emphasizes a number of concepts not previously weighted as heavily, it seems appropriate to refer to the changes brought about by the Catholic Church as "Revolutionary" in the history of the Western Tradition.

First, and this will be more fully discussed in §5 below, philosophically the question of the "first" in any series seems logical enough to be a question for Natural wonder. So, it becomes possible to inquire regarding the first man, and where and how he lived. This is ultimately a "State of Nature" question, since it asks about the *original* natural state of humans. Of course, Christianity tends to affirm the Myth (in the technical sense of the term) of the Garden of Eden. This is an optimistic State of Nature narrative in that the Garden was described as a paradise. Further, "Adam" is considered the "first man." Now, generally speaking in regard to the lapsarian account, after "The Fall" in which Adam and Eve gained "knowledge of Good and Evil," a downward slide into civilization began. The fault of Adam and Eve is known as Original Sin, and all of their blood progeny carried the guilt of their Original Sin.

Thus, just as the ancients made blood "sacrifices" to appease the gods and to ask for blessings or for a safe journey (cf. Girard 1979), the question arises how can humans atone for the Fall? The idea is that the only sacrifice which could atone for such a grievous fault would need to be made by God Himself. Further, it was predicted by the Divinely Inspired (notice how the word "inspiration" invokes breath as in being filled by the Spirit) prophets that God would "send" His only Son, and in this way it is understood that the blood of Jesus (the) Christ counts as a sacrifice to atone for the sins of mankind. The Crucifixion, then, of Christ is believed to have opened a New Testament, that is, a new Contract, between God and humans. Notice, as in the phrase "last will and testament," the term "testament" refers, for example, to the arrangement someone makes for their *property* after they have died. Hence, in this way, so long as humans meet the requirements of the new Contract (New Testament) with God, since Adam and Eve did not meet the requirements of the Old Contract, humans may be considered the Property of God; being the Property of God ensures eternal life, then, as God will eventually gather all His Property and "bring it home" to Heaven. This may be seen as a literalization of "entry" into the "register" of Divine Justice through Personhood, that is, assignment in the register as the property of God.

The second note to make as a general introduction, is to point out a number of the pieces which follow from the above narrative that add or change the ancient Greek conception of "after life" or what happens to the soul after the body's death. First, notice there is the question of "why" God would make a sacrifice to atone for our sins, and this question should be placed beside the question of "why" would God create us to begin with? Second, the above narrative seems to suggest God can "*be* more than one place at the same time." This will lead to an account of "the Holy Trinity," for explanation. Third, the narrative clearly claims that God can and does "intervene" in the human world, and this will lead to a more complicated understanding of God's Will and a conception of Miracles. Fourth, the idea that humans are God's Property—though technically also in Plato, for example, the *Phaedo* argument against suicide—ties together the human and the Divine in terms of Natural *Law*, which thereby makes ethics absolute in regard to salvation. Finally, the fifth idea is that the Divinely Inspired prophets by predicting the Apocalypse, which literally means the uncovering of God's Presence, adds the element of "eschatology" to the philosophical aspects of teleology and soteriology mentioned previously.

Now, because many of these topics will be discussed below and specifically from the perspective of Augustine, Aquinas, or Duns Scotus, we will only briefly respond to the above pieces of the second of the two notes with which we are introducing the "Catholic Revolution" in ethics. First, as heard in 1 John 4:8 and John 3:16, the account of "why" is that "God is Love," that is, human be-ing is constituted by God's Love, and the New Testament is, then, binding in terms of Love. Second, just as God's Love emanated "out" from God as the Holy Spirit (of God) and incarnated the Christ, so too the Holy Trinity is understood to account for the Three Persons (think of the importance of Personhood throughout this book) of God, that is, the Father, the Son, and the Holy Spirit. Whereas the Stoics thought of God as a Craftsman-like Fire, it is as if—in retrospect—they were coming to understand the Holy Spirit. We should note the relation between the beginnings in *Genesis* of the Myth of the Garden of Eden, on the one hand, and, on the other hand, the Plato passage from *Timaeus* noted in the Plato chapter's discussion of Celestial Be-ing and the Stoic understanding of the *Logos* breathing God, as the Craftsman-like fire, over the water. Further, recall the idea related to Orpheus and Plato's Charioteer, noted by Marsilio Ficino.

> Love is the power that produces harmony in all things. This leads into a discussion of love as the master of the arts… What artists or craftsmen in their various crafts seek to achieve is a state of love. (Warden 1982, 102).

Finally, the "gods," plural, come to be Celestial Be-ings, that is, Heavenly Beings, with the Highest Go(o)d "outside" the system of Be-ing in which all other beings are found; thus, God is omnipresent "inside" the System as the Holy Spirit, historically and eschatologically as Jesus Christ, and "outside" the System as the One God, the Creator of Heaven and Earth.

Third, there are numerous accounts of Jesus performing Miracles, and this has been a point of contention among the more "scientifically" minded who protest Christianity in general and the Christian Creation Myth specifically. Philosophically speaking, the idea that God intervenes in the progress of human history is not unique to Christianity, so we will briefly only look at its relevance for ethics. The basic idea may even be thought of in terms of the popular and contemporary notions of "Synchronicity" and the "Law of Attraction," that is, by establishing an appropriate relation to God, there may be Divine Intervention behind the seemingly mundane events, for example, bringing together or tearing asunder worldly bonds between souls. Fourth, the idea that humans are God's Property makes a number of ideas suddenly coherent. For example, consider the ideas of Law, Property, and Forgiveness. From the perspective of the Trinity, because God incarnated and was sacrificed for our sins, it is now through the "inwardness" of the Holy Spirit and a *Personal* (think in terms of Divine Justice from Plato) relation to the "living Christ" that we may attain salvation. Like Aristotle's Continent Character Type, to acknowledge we have mistreated God's Property is to be able to ask for Forgiveness, and God's Love as attested to in the New Testament will grant us Forgiveness. Thus, the Sacraments function not only as initiation but also as confirmation of our willingness and our belief, (which is better characterized by the term "fidelity," from the Latin *Fides*, and translated as Faith).

Hence, thinking of the problem we discussed in Plato about how the soul can persist after disembodiment, at the time of the Second Coming of (the) Christ, it will not only be the Apocalypse, that is, the unveiling of the Omnipotence and Omnipresence of God, but also the full conclusion of the Garden of Eden's First Man by the Last Man, Christ.

Finally, in regard to the fifth idea which adds the notion of eschatology to the philosophical aspects of teleology and soteriology, the philosophical issues raised regard God's Foreknowledge of human Fate, that is, Providence and Predestination. To examine these issues thoroughly would take us too far away from our purpose of introducing Catholic ethics; however, the basic idea revolves around the questions: (1) If God knows what is going to happen to us before it happens, then how are we supposed to understand it, that is, our Fate, and relate to it? This question is sometimes asked—If God knows we are going to Sin, and Sin is bad for us, then why does God allow us to Sin? Moreover, this question is intimately related to another question (we will briefly address both questions below)—If God is Love, then how could God send souls to the eternal damnation of Hell? For now, the second question around which Predestination revolves: (2) If God already knows who will be saved and who will not be saved, then is it possible to do anything to save yourself? This is, of course, closely related to questions regarding the relevance and possibility of Grace, that is, to put it simply—be-ing in God's Good Graces.

In regard, then, to the major concepts which the Catholic Revolution adds to the philosophical history of the Western Tradition, we may note five (5):

(1) A stronger conception of Free Will;
(2) A clearer understanding of Intention;
(3) A concept of Sin;
(4) A concept of Conscience;
(5) A different understanding of the Highest Good
   a. in terms of the Trinity,
   b. in terms of a different soteriology, that is, no more reincarnation, just Heaven or Hell,
   c. in terms of a more focally-unified understanding of the Super-Natural, which shifts daimon to guardian angel and demon to tempting demon.

As we will see, then, the Stoic reading of Natural Law and the Roman developments regarding Property Law are carried forward in a kind of synthesis of the more Naturalistic Aristotle with the more Divine Plato through the New Testament and the Catholic Revolution in ethics. As Rommen describes the impact of Christianity on Natural Law:

Christianity, however, contains three ideas of decisive importance… [1] the idea of the supermundane, transcendent, personal God as Lawgiver in the absolute sense, [2] the idea of Christian personality, whose eternal goal transcends the state, the law, and the mores of the polis, and [3] the idea of the Church as the institution charged with the salvation of mankind standing alongside and, in matter of faith and morals, above the will of the state. Such ideas had in the long run to affect the whole problem of natural law. (Rommen 1998, 30).

Hence, for our purposes, it is as if the ambiguity and tension between the Natural Law's governance of Civil Duties and Divine Justice are resolved by the Church's authority over the State. However, as we already know, in the subsequent chapters we will examine the separation between Church and State and the "scientific" development (both critical and positive) of the Christian heritage in the Western Tradition, regarding ethics.

§2 *Theological Virtues*

Just as we noticed that the Virtues related to Natural Function in Aristotle supervene and such supervenience provides its own benefits, for example, the Congruence and Pleasure experienced by the Virtuous Character Type and the Panorama of Wisdom gained through Prudence and Justice, so too Catholic ethics suggests there are Virtues beyond the Natural Virtues which seem to pertain to one's use of God's Property. These, then, are the Super-Natural Virtues or Theological Virtues: Faith, Hope, and Love. The perennial definition comes from Thomas Aquinas:

> additional principles must be given by God to man by which he can thus be ordered to supernatural happiness. … These additional principles are called theological virtues: first, because they have God as their object, inasmuch as by them we are rightly ordered to God; secondly, because they are infused in us by God alone; and finally, because these virtues are made known to us only by divine revelation in Sacred Scripture. (*Summa Theologica*, I–II, q. 62, a. 1)

Notice, these Virtues are Graces, or gifts to us from God, so we must rely on God to give them to us, though they also require us to be Willing to receive them. Further, having them allows for Super-Natural Happiness. We will discuss this more in-depth just below; however, clearly this is a kind of Happiness beyond the Natural Happiness discussed by, for example, Aristotle.

§3 *From the Transcendentals to the Trinity*

There are two goals for this section. First, what are the "Transcendentals," and how do they influence our understanding of the Highest Good, especially in light of Plato's discussion of the form of the Good in Itself as the condition for the possibility of all that is Good? Second, how may we use a philosophical understanding of the Transcendentals to comprehend the need to posit God as "outside" the system, as mentioned in §1.

The term "Transcendentals" comes from the Latin "*transcendere*," that is, "*trans*" for "across" and "*scandere*" for "to climb," meaning to "climb over or beyond." Just as "Transcend" means to "surpass the usual limits," the Transcendentals "climb over" and surpass the usual categories of reality. For example, Beauty and Goodness are two of the Transcendentals. Were we to categorize all of reality, we would find that there are certain types of, what seem like, categories that must be higher than categories, however, since they "climb across" the other categories. A house is not a sandwich; however, a house *is one* house and a sandwich *is one* sandwich. Thus, is-ness or being and one-ness "climb across" the categories of being a "this" or a "that." It is also the case that Goodness and Beauty "climb across" the categories of reality. Hence, it is as if these Transcendentals go "beyond" the categorization of reality, and, as a result, they are believed to be attributes of God. God Is; God is One; God is Good; God is Beautiful. There's more to say, but since this is ethics and not metaphysics, we'll stop here.

The final thought is that this helps us think of God as "outside" the system of all reality or all of God's Creation. Yet, because it is the very emanation of God's attributes—like rays of the Sun—which create reality, then God is also "inside" the system. This thought connects back up with our earlier discussion of the Trinity. Since it seems to be a difficult thought to comprehend, let us emphasize it once more: God is both "inside" and "outside" reality. For example, by being outside of reality, God would be able to see all of time in a single glance.

§4 *Providence, Predestination, and Grace*

In this section, we merely want to understand the meaning and interrelation between the terms which constitute its title. Thus, "Providence" from the Latin *prōvidēre*, like providing, the term refers to God's ability to foresee what to us (inside the system) will be the future. This, of course, raises the question of Fate and Freedom. The metaphysical problems are called "the problem of God's Foreknowledge" or "the problem of future contingents." Is everything Determined already and, thereby, Fated? Or, are we somehow Free to choose, at least to some extent, the outcome of our lives? Though we are not God, some Divinely Inspired humans have participated in the ability to see, as if from the Celestial point of view. If everything is Fated, then we are Predestined or not for Heaven or Hell, that is, despite how we live or what we believe or what ethics we have. This is the problem related to Predestination. Because some people believe our lives are Predestined, their soteriology suggests we can only be saved by the Grace of God. Of course, how God makes such decisions is a Mystery.[17]

Briefly, then, a number of conclusions may be drawn regarding material from earlier in this book by thinking about God's relation to Providence, Predestination, and Grace. Within a Predestined system, the goals of Self-Perfection, that is, Self-Realization and Self-Knowledge, seem to rely on God's Grace. That is, the Natural Virtues would suddenly seem to depend on the Super-Natural Virtues, and these on the Grace of God. We will return to this question in the next section; however, what we can at least say, is that suddenly relations with others seem like a veil covering what is really one's own relation to God, and the same with society, that is, participating in the hustle and bustle (*à un rythme d'enfer*, as they say in Paris) of political life, would be like an illusion or veil over the true meaning of one's actions. As one political theorist articulated it:

> A distinction must be made between civil society … (i.e. in the sense of political and cultural hegemony of a social group over the entire society, as ethical content of the State), and on the other hand civil society in the sense in which it is understood by Catholics, for whom civil society is instead political society of the State, in contrast with the society of family and that of the Church.[18]

At the personal level, the following quote from "Mother Teresa" excellently captures an encouragement to view one's life with one's relation to God and one's own salvation as most primary.

People are often unreasonable, irrational, and self-centered—Forgive them anyway.

If you are kind, people may accuse you of selfish ulterior motives—Be kind anyway.

If you are successful, you will win some unfaithful friends and some genuine enemies—Succeed anyway.

If you are honest and sincere people may deceive you—Be honest and sincere anyway.

What you spend years creating, others could destroy overnight—Create anyway.

If you find serenity and happiness, some may be jealous—Be happy anyway.

The good you do today, will often be forgotten—Do good anyway.

Give the best you have, and it will never be enough—Give your best anyway.

In the final analysis, it is between you and God. It was never between you and them anyway.

§5 *The State of Nature: Introducing Sin & Evil*

There are two (2) main ideas we want to gain from this section. First, what is the difference between the "pre-Fall" State of Nature, that is, the Garden of Eden, and the "post-Fall" State of Nature? Second, how are we to understand Sin and Evil, in terms of the Structural Model discussed in previous chapters? Because we will elaborate on each of these ideas across the parts of the chapter designated explicitly to Augustine, Aquinas, and Duns Scotus, here we will simply state the answer to these questions with a sufficient degree of generality to orient us, before examining the different specific characterizations found in the history of Catholic ethics.

Recalling Aristotle's Four Causes, we may say that the Material and Efficient Causes map onto the body and its motor force, respectively. Further, the Formal and Final Causes map onto the human understanding of objects, properties, and situations, or states of affairs, and the purposes for which humans interact with objects, properties, and states of affairs, respectively. In this way, it would be as if in the pre-Fall State of Nature, that is, the Garden of Eden, because humans did not yet have "Knowledge of Good and Evil," all of the Four Causes would have been in Harmony with God. Hence, when humans interacted, whatever control they enjoyed over their own motor forces, there would have been no deviation from a godly or pious understanding of Nature. Thus, the Garden of Eden would have been a State of Innocence.

The post-Fall State of Nature, then, in terms of the Four Causes would seem to point to a disruption in the Harmony of Formal and Final Causes. Put generally, it would be as if the human "internal" *logos* was no longer Naturally in Harmony with the "external" *Logos* permeating Nature. Humans were suddenly able to understand Nature in terms of their own Judgments, that is, with different *forms* of interpretation. Though, the most damning, as it were, aspect of the Fall, in terms of Christian soteriology may be characterized as the newly acquired capacity with which humans can determine their own purposes, that is, Final Causes. Though we will not take up the idea here, notice how this splits the once unified Natural and Divine Law of Paradise into the Natural Laws of Physics, the Natural determinants of Civil Law, and the Moral Law. Whereas the Natural Laws of Physics pertain to the embodied survival of humans, the Moral Law pertains to punishment and reward.

This is precisely how to understand the introduction of Sin and Evil, on the one hand, into the world, according to Christianity, and, on the other hand, into the vocabulary and ethical Worldview persisting from the ancient Greek philosophers through the Western Tradition. That is to say, we may imagine that humans could still make "mistakes" in the State of Nature. For example, it seems Natural to slip on rocks, stub toes, or step on something jagged, and so on. However, they would have handled such adversity in Paradise innocently. However, Sin belongs to the deliberate choosing of an action understood in an evil way or performed for evil purposes. Thus, it even makes sense to personify what was the momentum of habit in Aristotle as a kind of "devil" tempting us to understand Nature in ways contrary to its Natural Function and Purpose.

Since we will look at this more closely below, let us consider this sufficient after making one further note. That is, the context in which we are supposed to understand the appropriateness of the human *logos* and judgment in regard to Nature is in terms of God's Property. Thus, we were originally in Harmony with the appropriate way to interact with God's Property (we ourselves being a part of it), and after the Fall, humans were not. Consider the following two quotes, which will help contextualize our discussions below. First, Augustine noted, "However great and good your natural gifts are, it takes true piety to make them pure and perfect; with impurity they merely end in loss and pain." (Augustine 1958, Bk II, §29). Second, according to John Finnis' excellent *Natural Law and Natural Rights*, following the explication by Hugo Grotius (1583–1645 AD) regarding how "Roman lawyers" understood the relation between Justice and Personhood, Justice is understood as a "moral quality," and when that quality is perfected, it is understood in a threefold way.

> (i) power (*potestas*), which may be power over oneself (called liberty: *libertas*) or power over others (e.g. *patria potestas*, the power of a father over his family); (ii) ownership (*dominium*) ...; and (iii) credit, to which corresponds debt (*debitum*). (Finnis 2001, 207).

§6 *Natural Law & Justice: From the Garden of Eden to Just War*

It is possible, then, to understand the revelation of the Decalogue, that is, the Ten Commandments, as God's revelation of the now Moral Law to assist—recall our discussion from the Introduction chapter regarding Divine Command Theory—and restore order to the State of Nature, disrupted by the Fall. Thus, in his discussion of Natural Law, Rommen provides a distinction between the "primary" Natural Law, that is, the "moral norms" relating to the worship of God and which were written on the first Tablet, and the "secondary," which was written on the second. The first Tablet contains the first three Commandments, and Rommen notes the "secondary natural law" is "(i.e. the last seven of the Ten Commandments), is a consequence of original sin." (Rommen 1998, 39). The Ten Commandments (according to the *Catechism of the Catholic Church*, listed on the Vatican archives website) are listed here:

1. "I am the Lord your God, you shall not have strange gods before me.
2. You shall not take the name of the Lord your God in vain.
3. Remember to keep holy the Lord's Day.
4. Honor your father and your mother.
5. You shall not kill.
6. You shall not commit adultery.
7. You shall not steal.
8. You shall not bear false witness against your neighbor.

9. You shall not covet your neighbor's wife.
10. You shall not covet your neighbor's goods."

Reading the Commandments as, at least to some extent, enforcing Property Rights notice how the quality of *dominium* or Kingdom follows. Just as the first Tablet orders humans in regard to Divine Justice, the second Tablet orders humans in regard to Civil Justice. Thus, it serves as a kind of reminder that once the two were in Harmony. Further, it has been understood to justify the use of violence, as a kind of extension of the Efficient Cause of God's Will, to bring into order those aspects of God's Kingdom which delight in Sin and Evil. Thus, we will see Augustine's notion of Just War, as the righteous infliction of violence and killing.

§7 *From the Daimon to Agent Intellect to Conscience as Divine Illumination*

As we have already seen, Plato clearly had an understanding of Celestial Beings, and the notion of a Daimon, as mediating between humans and gods, which also may be seen as a kind of Divine Being. In Aristotle we saw the notion that a potentiality may be actualized by some agent. Combining these ideas, that is, depersonalizing the daimon and thinking of its activity in terms of psychological faculties, led to the Christian notion of "Conscience." In this section, we will provide a general statement, followed by the distinction between Augustine and Aquinas regarding the identity of Conscience.

The idea that the "Law may be written in our Hearts," is thought to signify "the inward operation of the Spirit of truth; for Christianity plainly teaches us that, without such an influence, there can be no acceptable obedience to the moral law of God." (Gurney 1880, 39). Hence, the Law written in the Heart points in a twofold way. First, it points to the Grace of God, that is, God gave us the potential to act rightly by inscribing the Spirit of His Will in our Hearts. Second, it points to the sense in which Conscience activates in relation to the Heart. That is to say,

> The law written on the heart is a divine illumination; the conscience is a natural faculty, by which a man judges of his own conduct. It is through the conscience that the law operates. The law informs the conscience. The law is the light; the conscience is the eye. The light reveals the beauty of any given object: the eye "bears witness" to that beauty; it beholds and approves. (Gurney 1880, 39).

Thus, it is worth noting that the internalization of the Moral Law, which is Divine, relates to the activity of—what in Plato was called the voice of (Socrates') Daimon—an internal "voice" acknowledging conformity of one's actions with the Moral Law. Whereas Augustine thought Conscience was the Voice of God, Aquinas thought of the voice of Conscience as developing out of human rational capacities.

§8 *From Eudaimonia to the Super-Natural Happiness of Beatitude: Angelic Subsistence*

There are just two observations we want to make in this section. First, with the Catholic Revolution in Ethics comes a shift in the understanding of *Eudaimonia*—it becomes Beatitude. Again, this may be articulated in terms of a synthesis of Plato and Aristotle. On the one hand, recall, Plato understood *Eudaimonia* in relation to the Wheel of (re)incarnation, and thus to the "after-(this)-life" regarding the journey of the soul. On the other hand, Aristotle understood the *ataraxia* of a Contemplative Life, regarding one's Natural Functions, to characterize the excellence of *Eudaimonia*.

Now, Beatitude refers to "viewing the Face of God." And, there is significant debate as to how or when such an activity would be possible. For example, can this be accomplished to some extent—perhaps by Sages—while still alive, does it require death, or does it require a post-Apocalyptic reality? In either case, Catholic ethics replaces *Eudaimonia* with Beatitude, while retaining its connection with Natural Function, that is, soteriology as teleological. That is to say, the post-Fall human is supposed to desire to return to the State of Nature, that is, Paradise, situation in which we witnessed the beauty of God constantly.

Second, as Augustine famously declared regarding Plato's Wheel of (re)incarnation, the Cross stops the Wheel (cf. Augustine 1958, Bk 12, §21). In other words, after the God incarnated and was sacrificed to re-bridge, as it were, the human connection to God, Christians are no longer supposed or allowed to believe in reincarnation. The thought now is that disembodied souls either go to Heaven or to Hell at the end of life. This leads to a number of questions, only two of which we need answer for our purposes. We will examine Aquinas' answer to the question: How and why would an all Loving Good God send souls to Hell? And, how are we to understand the kind of be-ing humans have in Heaven? In regard to the second question, we called this Celestial Be-ing in the Plato chapter, and here we can understand it as the kind of spiritual subsistence enjoyed by Angels. In other words, it is as if Angelic beings occupy the dimension between humans and God, in that they do not require material embodiment. It is thought that their subsistence involves Beatitude, that is, continual gazing at the Face of God.

Augustine: Intentionalism

"Pray as though everything depends on God;
work as though everything depends on you."
~Augustine

§9 *The Fall & Roman Law: From Family Innocence to the Guilty City*

As the story usually is told regarding Augustine, responding to the fall of Rome in 410 AD, as it was sacked by the Goths, he understood what was happening as a kind of "War" between God's Kingdom and Man's Kingdom. Thus, he wrote his highly influential book *The City of God*. It is in regard to this work along with *On Free Will, On the Trinity,* and his *Confessions* that we may see elements emerging from out of Plato, Aristotle and the Socratic Schools toward the formation of Catholic ethics. In fact, taking Aristotle's Character Types as a point of departure may be an efficient way to see Augustine's disdain for the City of Man. Whereas Aristotle's teleological account speaks of the city as the natural and necessary culmination of family politics through which humans may thrive, a Platonic concern for Divine Justice returns in Augustine's account, de-necessitating the progression from family to city.

Recall from the above discussion of Aristotle's Character Types, becoming virtuous is tantamount to "Self-Mastery," and to be Master of one's self is—philosophically—the most important sense of Freedom. That is, to truly be free, we must free ourselves from animalistic tendencies toward Vice. Thus, we perfect the powers of our soul by allowing the Natural Harmony involved in the "higher" powers ruling the "lower" ones. We can think about this anew with Augustine, then, in that communities in Paradise perhaps more resembled Plato's utopia in which everyone thought of everyone else as brother and sister and mother and father. However, after the Fall, there is a move toward the centralization and hierarchy of the city. One of the features which distinguishes Augustine from Aquinas, and contributes to the general characterization that he be primarily associated with Plato and Aquinas with Aristotle is that Augustine sees political life as a vain distraction from living a godly, pious life. Aquinas thinks a life of politics may be lived virtuously. Hence, for Augustine, the city represents decline from the Garden and the attempt to build a Kingdom of Man. Moreover, he understood War against such corruption to be perfectly in Harmony with God's Will.

§10 *Theodicy: Providence & Predetermination in Harmony with Free Will & Intention*

Augustine provides us with the general structure of the concerns which constitute the study of Theodicy, and in providing his resolution to these concerns brings a stronger conception of Free Will and an emphasis on the first-person perspective, that is, the interiority of subjectivity, into the Western Tradition. The basic idea is that God's sacrifice of "His only Son" bridges the gap and brings a New Testament with God. Augustine reads this as indicating that we absolutely need God to accomplish Self-Perfection. We may be Virtuous; however, we need God's Grace to achieve the Self-Realization, Self-Knowledge, and Self-Ownership associated with Self-Perfection.

Philosophically, this pulls back toward Plato from Aristotle, again, because Virtue is no longer Sovereign, usurped now by Fate (this time as Predestination determined by God) specifically in regard to God's Judgment to grant us His Grace. A key piece from which Augustine draws a number of conclusions is the idea that humans are created "in the image of God." (Genesis 1:27). Just as with Plato we were able to articulate a relation between *logos* in the human soul and *Logos* permeating reality, Augustine seems to do this with Will. In this way, God Wills certain events to occur, and so do humans. We saw the Stoic Intellectualism highly emphasize the importance of matching our *logos* with the predetermined, that is, Fated, *Logos* of reality. Interestingly, Augustine adopts something of this Stoic concern for Harmony in the face of Fate as he is confronted with God's Providence and human Predestination. Augustine needs to show how humans can be guilty and how God remains omnibenevolent and Just.

He accomplishes this with the notions of Free Will and Intention. Though God intends for us to be Happy, it is still possible, given our Free Will, for us to choose evil. Thus, we slide into the question, why is there evil to choose, and we find that evil results from our Intention when we perform an action. We may now be able to see the parallel with Stoicism. For the Stoics events are pre-determined, for Augustine events are Pre-Destined. Stoic *katalepsis* is concerned to appropriately identify the reality of the event occurring, so as to accept reality as it really is. For Augustine, Freedom of the Will is Freedom to choose. The idea is that, supposing the event is completely determined, humans must still choose the action which constitutes their contribution to the event. Here is where Intention comes in, just as we briefly indicated in Aristotle; having the right Intention determines how the performance of the action influences the momentum of the habit structure and, thereby, the constitution of one's Character. Now, supposing evil to be its own punishment, then the idea is that the Providence and Predestination associated with God's Justice may determine the event with which we are confronted; however, even the punishment is supposed to be good in that it sustains and restores us to Harmony with God. Yet, evil enters in when the human Intention is "perverse" and the Will chooses the event not in accord with the Providence of God.

The event is *absolutely* Good; however, evil may be present in the soul of the agent performing the action. This is in the form of a perverse Will, and in order to explain the perverse Will, the notion of Intention is used. For, evil is not *efficient* (think Efficient Cause), rather evil is *deficient*, and that deficiency is accounted for in terms of the interiority of the subject. It is worth quoting Augustine at length, then, regarding *pathos*,

> The important factor in those emotions is the character of a man's will. If the will is wrongly directed, the emotions will be wrong; if the will is right, the emotions will be not only blameless, but praiseworthy. The will is engaged in all of them; in fact they are all essentially acts of will. For what is desire or joy but an act of will in agreement with what we wish for? And what is fear or grief but an act of will in disagreement with what we reject? We use the term desire when this agreement takes the form of the pursuit of what we wish for, while joy describes our satisfaction in the attainment. In the same way, when we disagree with something we do not wish to happen, such an act of will is fear; but when we disagree with something which happens against our will, that act of will is grief. And in general, as a man's *will* is attracted or repelled in accordance with the varied character of different objects which are pursued or shunned, so it changes and *turns into feelings* of various kinds [emphases added]. (2003, Bk XIV, §6).

Hence, "the character" of the Will refers to its "directedness," and this directedness is an agent's Intention. We will see how this idea evolves below. For now we want to examine Augustine's statement of Intention from his *On the Trinity* Book XI, §2.

When Augustine discusses vision, moving through an analogy with the Trinity, he distinguishes between (1) the visible object, (2) the activity of seeing, and (3) "the power that fixes the sense of sight," that is, in Latin *animi intentio*. (2002, 61–62). On the one hand, the directedness of Intention accounts for the Free Willing of evil, is associated with the Spirit in the Trinity, and also accounts for the habitual instantiation of an Incongruent and possibly even Vicious or wicked Character Type (cf. Aristotle 2009, 1111a1 & 1111a20). On the other hand, Augustine is quite clear as to what Self-Perfection entails regarding evil. He explains,

> For this reason [regarding what was said about *pathos* above], the man who lives by God's standards, and not by man's must necessarily be a lover of the good, and it follows that he must hate what is evil. Further, since no one is evil by nature, but anyone who is evil is evil because of a perversion of nature, the man who lives by God's standards has a duty to "perfect hatred" toward those who are evil; that is to say, he should not hate the person because of the fault, nor should he love

the fault because of the person. He should hate the fault, but love the man. And when the fault has been cured there will remain only what he ought to love, nothing that he should hate. (Augustine 2003, Bk XIV, §6).

This, again, shows not only Augustine's explicit avowal of War against the unjust, it suggests we have a Duty to War against the unjust. In Book IV he suggests to Kingdoms without Justice are "like criminal gangs." And,

There are however certain exceptions to the law against killing, made by the authority of God himself. There are some whose killing God orders, either by a law, or by an express command to a particular person at a particular time. In fact one who owes a duty of obedience to the giver of the command does not himself "kill"—he is an instrument, a sword in its user's hand. For this reason the commandment forbidding killing was not broken by those who have waged wars [standing] on the authority of God, or those who have imposed the death-penalty on criminals when representing the authority of the State in accordance with laws of the State. (Augustine 2003, Bk I, §21).

Hence, Augustine provides us with a view of killing as Natural and in Harmony with Divine Providence (cf. Augustine, *City of God*, BK V).[19]

Aquinas: Dominican Intellectualism

"The things we love tell us what we are."[20]

~Aquinas

§11 *Intellectualism: Synderesis*

Intellectualism in general is the belief that reality is a kind of Divine Intellect. In terms of Natural Law, then, it holds that the laws of reality are laws because of the structure of the Divine Intellect. In this way, we can see how human intellect by participating through rationality in the activity of Divine Intellect is able to grasp the principles from which reality was formed. In Aristotle this was characterized as the Natural Inclination of the intellect toward the Good, that is, the natural interest of Reason to discover first principles. In the Stoics this looked like the contemplative state allowing for true *katalepsis*, that is, judgment of reality.

Aquinas is credited with developing the notion of the activity called "*synderesis*." Aquinas was not the first to use the term; however, he extensively developed our understanding of it. As one Aquinas commentator expressed it:

Synderesis is a disposition by virtue of which men are enabled to grasp the most general principles of morality. It has exactly the same relation to basic moral principles as intellectual intuition (*intellectus* in one of the senses of the word) has to the first principles of speculative reasoning. Aquinas describes such a mental disposition (*habitus intellectivus*) as being midway between pure potentiality and complete actuality. (O'Connor 1967, 43).

Thus, *Synderesis* seems to refer to a kind of intellectual virtue, yet sometimes Aquinas uses the terms *instinctus* and *inspiratio*, that is, instinct or inspiration, so it seems *synderesis* is open to different interpretations, including in terms of the Catholic priest Bernard Lonergan's discussion of *Insight*; and, we will examine how it looks in terms of the distinction between the Dominican Intellectualism reading and the Franciscan Voluntarism reading from Aquinas and Bonaventure, respectively.

According to Aquinas, and sounding a good deal like ideas innate to the intellect by way of its rationality, we have a natural understanding of some things "prior to rational analysis," therefore Aquinas concludes,

> There must be naturally sure principles governing our practice just as there are governing thought. … Hence the principles our nature imparts to us in practical matters do not belong to a special power but to a special habit, there by nature, *synderesis*. (Aquinas 1947, Pt. I, Q. 79, A. 12).

On the one hand, we may understand Aquinas here as providing a more Intellectualistic reading of Augustine's notion of intention. Notice Aquinas' statement of the Target Analogy:

> [T]wo things are required for a good act of choosing. The first is that the act of intending the end be good, and this is effected by moral virtue, which inclines the appetitive power toward a good that is consonant with reason, i.e. toward a fitting end. The second is that the person correctly perceive the means to the end, and this cannot happen except through reason's correctly deliberating, judging, and commanding… (Aquinas 1947, Pt. I, Q 58).

On the other hand, an important function of *synderesis* is "to provide these principles which serve as the major premises" of the Practical Syllogism, which, of course, associates *synderesis* with our discussions of Prudence and Practical Action found in the ancient Greek philosophers. In this way,

1. "By *synderesis*, we know the general principles of morals;
2. reason supplies the "minor premise" of the syllogism,
3. and conscience consists in the application of the facts to the particular act under consideration. In general, the form of the practical syllogism is as follows:
Major Premise (from *synderesis*): X is right (or wrong).
Minor Premise (from reason): This is a case of X.
Conclusion (from conscience): This ought to be done (or avoided)." (O'Connor 1967, 43).

In terms of making an error in our moral judgments, *synderesis* is supposed to ensure, "since *synderesis* is infallible," that we cannot err regarding first principles, though "we may very well go wrong over the minor [premise], and so conclude, *erroneously but conscientiously*, that something ought to be done which ought not to be, or *vice versa*." (O'Connor 1967). Finally, to ask what these first principles might be or say seems natural. The answer which comes generally, though not without controversy among Catholics, is that these first principles are the Ten Commandments. Notice, then, it seems natural that Augustine would have thought of conscience as the "Voice of God" in the interiority of the soul.

§12 *Theodicy & Providence: On the Relationship between God and Hell as Punishment*

There are two (2) questions to which we want to hear Aquinas' answers regarding in this section. Both of the questions pertain to the study of Theodicy. First, Why would an Omnibenevolent God, that is, if God is Love, send sinners to the eternal damnation of Hell? Second, regarding God's Omniscience and Omnipotence—If God knows the future, if God knows what is Fated to us, then why does God not stop us from sinning? As we will see, the answer to that question is intimately related to the answer to the previous question. Yet, we should also ask regarding our Freedom in relation to God's Omniscience and Omnipotence—If God knows what we will do in the future, then are we even Free to not sin? That is, as articulated by Cicero, if God cannot be wrong about the future, then it would seem we cannot change or freely choose what He knows we will do and what He knows will happen to us.

Recall, Divine Providence means God's ability to foresee the future, and Predestination is the Christianized way to refer to the events that have been Fated to us, i.e. aspects of our life determined by God, which we cannot change. We have already seen Augustine's treatment of these puzzles in §10. Now, according to Aquinas,

> Divine providence imposes necessity upon some things; not upon all, as some [e.g. the Stoics] formerly believed. For to providence it belongs to order things toward an end. Now after the divine goodness, which is an extrinsic end to all things, the principle good in things themselves is the perfection of the universe; which would not be, were not all grades of being found in things. Whence it pertains to divine providence to produce every grade of being. And thus it has prepared for some things necessary causes, so that they happen of necessity; for other contingent causes, that they may happen by contingency, according to the nature of their proximate causes. (Aquinas 1947, Pt. I, Q 22, A. 4).

Though the above is essentially straightforward, we will clarify a couple terms. In regard to "every grade of being," this does not mean that being is "lacking." Being is full actuality. If something actually is, then we don't say that it could have more actuality. Though, one could be *actually* ignorant at one moment, and then *actually* knowledgeable in the next moment. Hence, one's degree of Self-Perfection seems to belong to Providence.

Next, "proximate cause" refers to a kind of secondary cause or causation. John Calvin notoriously criticized Catholic philosophy for believing in secondary causation. Yet, Aquinas' idea here is that God is responsible for the first causation of generating our be-ing, however, our human nature and Self-Perfection are responsible for Sin. The distinction between primary and secondary causation also helps Aquinas formulate his understanding of the Freedom of God's Will.

> For the divine will has a necessary relation to the divine goodness, since that is its proper object. Hence God wills His own goodness, necessarily. ... Hence, since the goodness of God is perfect,

and can exist without other things since no perfection can accrue to Him from them, it follows that His willing things apart from Himself is not absolutely necessary. (Aquinas 1947, Pt. I, Q 19, A. 4).

In this way, "Since then God necessarily wills His own goodness, but other things not necessarily ... He has free choice with respect to what He does not necessarily will." (Aquinas 1947, Pt. I, Q 19, A.10). This points directly, then, to the Mystery of God's Grace. That is, because God is free to bestow His Grace upon whomever He likes, the puzzle of Predestination becomes merely academic.

Finally, we may answer the questions. We are Free to sin, though God knows what we will do. This resolves the puzzles of God's Omnipotence and Omniscience, so the puzzle of God's Omnipotence and Omnibenevolence remains. That is, on the one hand, why would an all-powerful God who could stop us from sinning and, thereby, going to Hell, not stop us (?); especially keeping in mind God's Omnibenevolence. On the other hand, if God is Love, and His Omnibenevolence entails wanting Goodness for us, then why does God send souls to Hell? In an astonishingly logical response, Aquinas claims it is because it is fully in keeping with God's Omnipotence and Omnibenevolence that He gives souls what they desire (cf. Scalambrino 2015b). Thus, souls who desire sin are allowed to sin, and their sinning leads them—along the path they want—to Hell. At the same time, recalling the Mystery of God's Grace, God can and does save some souls from eternal damnation against their Will.

Bonaventure & Duns Scotus: Franciscan Voluntarism

§13 *Voluntarism: Miracles & the Will of God*

We will find the following two explications regarding Intellectualism and Voluntarism will be helpful. On the one hand, "The terms 'intellectualism' and 'voluntarism' classify theories of moral psychology and of ethics according to whether primary importance is placed on the intellect or the will in human agency." (Hoffmann 2010, 414). On the other hand,

> there are two basic approaches to keeping God essential to morality. One is now usually called "voluntarism." Voluntarists hold that God created morality and imposed it upon us by an arbitrary fiat of his will. He is essential to morality, therefore, because he created it and can always, in principle, alter it—as he seems to do on those rare occasions, such as his commanding Abraham to sacrifice Isaac... On the other approach, often called "intellectualism," God did not create morality. When he gives us moral commandments, his will is guided by his intellect's knowledge of eternal standards. He is nonetheless essential to morality because his providential supervision ensures that we live in a morally ordered world. (Schneewind 1998, 8–9).

Thus, as Catholic Voluntarists, the Franciscans can philosophically *account*, that is, provide a *logos*, for Miracles by being able to coherently explain Divine Intervention. This is also why Protestant Voluntarists, for example, Hobbes, will feel the need to so vehemently attack Catholic claims about Miracles, since they hope to affirm Voluntarism, especially that "God created morality and imposed it upon us by an arbitrary fiat of his will," without such direct Divine Intervention as that found in Miracles.

Franciscan Voluntarism ushers in Divine Command Theory, then, in order to solve the puzzle that the content of Divine Laws does not seem to justify its being a Law. According to the Franciscans, it is God's Commanding it that makes it a Law. Regarding human agency, Bonaventure (1221-1274 AD) "holds that free decision encompasses both reason and will." (Hoffman 2010, 415). Further, Freedom belongs primarily to the Will in that "reason's control of the lower powers of the soul depends on the 'command' (i.e. the control) of the will, and the will is not bound to follow the dictate of reason unless it is a 'definitive judgment.'" (Hoffman 2010). Notice the "created in God's image," then, aspect of the argument. Just as God's Will ultimately determines, so too, regarding human agency, Will ultimately determines. Were this not the case, then similar to having a deficient account of God's altering from His own Commands in terms of Miracles, it becomes difficult to account for how humans can sin and why they are to be held responsible for sinning. According to Duns Scotus (1266-1308 AD),

> if some power were exclusively appetitive … [it] could not sin. … for it would be powerless to seek anything other than what the intellect would show it. … But this same power, having been made free … could moderate itself in willing. … from the fact that it could moderate this, it is bound to do so according to the rule of justice it has received from a higher will. … a free will is not bound in every way to seek happiness. (Duns Scotus 1968, 471, quoted in Schneewind 1998, 23).

This insight into Divine Justice, of course, significantly increases the understanding of Free Will in the Western Tradition. Moreover, it will be out of this understanding that Consequentialism, discussed in the next chapter, will develop its justification. For, on the one hand, suddenly, it may be the case, for example, that the means we Will may be appropriate—despite being sinful—insofar as the ends they manifest are Good. On the other hand, if Freedom of Will is not inherently evil in itself—remember God too has Freedom of Will—, then for some ethicists rational calculation seems to need to involve the balance of punishment involved, as a kind of risk calculation.

§14 *Theodicy & Beatitude: Future Contingents*

To conclude this chapter, we will briefly look at two final thoughts. First, Scotus' Voluntarism is famous for holding that if anything is Good other than God, it is only because God Willed it to be Good. Of the more pronounced innovations for Catholic ethics regarding Aquinas's notion that God Will's His own Goodness, involves Beatitude, so we will look at the essential distinction between them. Borrowing from the work of Anselm (1033-1109 AD), Scotus provides the first non-Eudaimonistic articulation of Happiness, that is, Beatitude, by locating the Natural desire to see God in human *pathos* or affection. Second, we will look at the Franciscan Voluntarist reading of future contingents insofar as they relate to Theodicy through the topics of Providence and Predestination. Since we have stated the puzzle and the problems associated with Providence and Predestination a number of times already, we will here simply report a response to the puzzle associated with Duns Scotus.

In regard to Beatitude, recall Aquinas understood humans to have a "natural desire" to see God. The standard interpretation of what he meant suggests it refers to a "naturally elicited desire that follows on knowledge of God's existence." (Feingold 2010, 11). The idea is that "there is a threefold division of appetite in creatures," which coincides with Aristotle's tripartite division of the soul; they are:

> *natural appetite*, *sensitive appetite*, and *rational appetite*. Rational appetite or will is aroused on the basis of intellectual knowledge; sensitive appetite is excited by sense knowledge; and "natural appetite" always flows from a given form without any knowledge whatsoever in the subject of the inclination. (Feingold 2010, 12).

Finally, the act of "willing" to see the Face of God is "elicited" or "drawn out" by the Intellectual awareness of the source of Goodness (cf. Feingold 2010, 13). However, Dun Scotus disagrees with the idea that an "elicited" act of will is Natural. Hence, Scotus understands the natural desire for Beatitude in terms of the Self-Perfection and Self-Realization of the Will, that is, the Natural Inclination the Will has "toward its own perfection, just as in the case of other things that lack a free appetite." (Scotus, *Ordinatio* IV, d. 49, q. 10, n. 2, quoted in Feingold 2010, 48). This is the essential distinction between Duns Scotus, then, and Aquinas regarding the origin of Beatitude.

In regard to Scotus' articulation of future contingent events, Scotus seems to have understood the idea that God could see all of time in an instant as referring to God's ability to see all possible events and all their possible consequences, and so on at once. In regard to the Providential question whether the events God sees are true or not, Scotus holds that they are neither true nor false until God assents to them with Divine Will. Thus, notice, again the "created in the Image of God" theme seems to have returned insofar as God's relation to His Divine Intellect and Divine Will sound much like Augustine's clarifications to the Stoic account, with the Franciscan Voluntaristic Free Will replacing Intention.

5

The Protestant Reformation of the Catholic Revolution I: Machiavelli & Hobbes

> "[I]f any two men desire the same thing,
> which nevertheless they cannot both enjoy,
> they become enemies."[21]
> ~Thomas Hobbes

§1 *Chapter Overview: Realism & Consequentialism*

Both the Italian Niccolò Machiavelli (1469–1527 AD) and the Englishman Thomas Hobbes (1588–1679 AD) were concerned to apply methods more scientific than the deductive-analytic methods found in the work of philosophers discussed in previous chapters. In this way, we identify both of these thinkers with the notion of "Realism." In this instance, "Realism" contrasts with "Idealism," and simply means a concern to focus on the actual efficient causes producing change in the world, rather than on understanding situations in terms of their ideal articulation. Both Machiavelli and Hobbes are considered "political philosophers." Whereas Machiavelli popularly tends to be associated with a pragmatic politics or "Realpolitik," we will also examine the role of integrity in his understanding of Virtue. Further, whereas Hobbes is popularly characterized by materialism, mechanism, and the idea of a Social Contract, we will also examine the sense in which his Voluntarism influenced the re-formation of the Voluntarism disseminated by the Catholic Revolution in the Western Tradition.

Consequentialism is, of course, a kind of ethics that emphasizes the consequences of actions in determining their value, and the Realism of Machiavelli and Hobbes lends itself to a Consequentialist understanding of value. Further, in terms of the Traditional Political Interpretations of Justice, the Consequentialism of Machiavelli and Hobbes situates them in the Utility school of thought. Though it may be tempting to associate them with the Order school of thought, insofar as they are both interested in political power for the sake of establishing political Order; they are not attempting an articulation of Order in terms of Rationalism, that is, these philosophies do not bring about the Natural rational order, they work on the Natural chaos with Power to stabilize it.

The seventeenth century is the Great Divide between the age in which all political and social concepts bear the decisive impress of the religious and universalist tradition, and an era in which the political idea of nationalism, secular and parochial, becomes dominant and creates its own symbols [e.g. other than those of the Church] for the integration of human thoughts and emotions. Out of this crisis the second Renaissance emerged, more permanent and far deeper-reaching than that of the fifteenth century. In the seventeenth century brutality of life and violence, disregard of social responsibility and humanitarian sensibility prevailed (Kohn 1967, 187).

As a result of the "crisis" just noted and the need to stabilize chaos, lest life be "nasty brutish and short," Machiavelli and Hobbes provide innovative readings of Prudence, Virtue, and the appropriate conduct with regard to the State of Nature or, at least, a state of War.

"Sovereignty" is a key term when discussing these two philosophers, which for our purposes refers to an authority within some country or territory. Insofar as the sovereign rises from within the territory in question, then the idea sovereignty involves a notion of autonomy, that is, after seizing power the sovereign may impose whatever laws (as commands) they deem fit. There are two thoughts to emphasize here as they have influenced the re-formation of the Western Tradition. *First*, any individual in the territory wishing to seize power must engage in the traditional virtuous development of Natural dispositions, such as Self-Realization and Self-Knowledge. Thus, in regard to their ethical theories of conduct, Machiavelli and Hobbes are described as self-centered or universally egoistic, and in regard to Traditional Political Interpretations of Justice, (despite centering on Utility over Order or the Mystico/Religious) their Consequentialism is egoistic rather than Utilitarian. Further, in regard to Virtue, that is, virtuous develop of one's Natural constitution, their conceptions differ from prior discussions in that they seem to advocate for the Sophist positions against which Plato's arguments were the very establishment of the Western Tradition. For example, what a Machiavellian approach to the Ring of Gyges would entail should be obvious. Hence, as we will see, by directing what counts as virtuous activity toward establishing sovereignty, an inversion takes place in regard to Plato's Analogy of the City and the Soul.

Whereas Plato's analogy is direct, the Realism of Machiavelli and Hobbes calls for a distinction to be made. On the one hand, as we saw with Aristotle, Happiness of the citizen may depend on the Happiness of the city. However, just as the citizen needs to be virtuous to realize its inherent Goodness, in order for the city to be Good, much chaos and violence must be overcome, and as we noted with Augustine and his notion of Just War, overcoming the chaos and violence requires greater violence (cf. Aristotle 1995b, 1276b16). Thus, on the other hand, the individual who would contribute to the Goodness of the city needs to be prepared and Willing to perform actions associated with the Vicious Character Type. Though these actions may be Just from the perspective of the city (thinking of the Analogy of the City and the Soul), from the perspective of the individual, the individual would be "putting their soul at risk." That is to say, one runs the risk of becoming Personally "a tyrant" though one may be wielding political power in accordance with what is Good and Just for the city.

The *second* thought to emphasize as it has influenced the re-formation of the Western Tradition generally regards the Realpolitik reading of dominion, that is, the kingdom building which naturally coincides with

Self-Perfection for the sake of sovereignty, and specifically as it relates to the separation between Church and State. Though we will see this manifest with what may be characterized as increasing hostility to the presence of the Church in the political sphere across the Modern period of the Western Tradition differently in Machiavelli and Hobbes, the basic idea remains the same. That is, for the sake of the Good of the city, a separation may be justified between the Church's political influence and the doctrine of the Church. Paradoxically it seems as though one may need to be Vicious toward the former in order to be regarded Virtuous according to the latter. Of course, it must be kept in mind that all of this is from the perspective of the individual becoming autonomous for the sake of the Good of the city, that is, from the perspective of the sovereign. In fact, this may also all hold true in regard to Just War and the idea of extending or establishing (according to the doctrine of the Church) the Right-ful Dominion of God's Kingdom. This is the complexity of the kind of "ends justifies the means" philosophy which historically emerged and was exemplified through Machiavelli and Hobbes.

Machiavelli: Kingdom Making is the Art of War

§2 *The Masculinity of Virtue & The Necessary Relation between Justice and Violence*

As recollected by Aquinas' discussion of the etymology of the Latin term *virtus*, the term "Virtue" has its roots in notions of manhood, strength and power (Aquinas 1947, Pt. I, Q. 55, A. 2). Thus, Machiavelli's notion of *Virtù* emphasizes a masculine ethics. For example, following the lead of Plato's education of philosopher-kings found in the *Republic*, Machiavelli advocates "hunting" both literally and as a metaphor for learning dialectics of philosophical argumentation as good training for those who would be sovereign, that is, "Princes" (cf. Plato 1997k, 410d; cf. Plato 1997l; cf. Benner 2009, 116–24).

> You should therefore know there are two ways to fight: one while respecting the rules, the other with no holds barred. Men alone fight in the first fashion, and animals fight in the second. But because you cannot always win if you respect the rules, you must be prepared to break them. A ruler, in particular, needs to know how to be both an animal and a man. (Machiavelli 1995, 54).

Recalling a story from the ancient Greeks describing how Achilles, among others, was said to be raised by Cheiron the centaur:

> What they intended to convey, with this story of rulers' being educated by someone who was half beast and half man, was that it is *necessary* [emphasis added] for a ruler to know when to act like an animal and when like a man; and if he relies on just one or the other mode of behavior he cannot hope to survive. (Machiavelli 1995).

As we will see, this philosophy of Viciousness (beast-like behavior) factors into Machiavelli's notion of "Superhuman Prudence." Moreover, we must keep in mind that in sustaining a Kingdom is understood as holding and acquiring more Property.

It was a Natural truism for Machiavelli that "you cannot escape wars, and when you put them off only your opponents benefit." (Machiavelli 1995, 11). In Chapter Five of *The Prince*, he advocates for "demolishing" conquered cities and "lay[ing] them to waste." Not only is this Machiavelli's endorsement of preemptive legal violence, that is, Just War, it also shows his philosophical strategy of accentuating any trace of Vicious behavior in Aristotle's Great-Souled Person and attributing it to "Superhuman" Virtue. He tells the following story to illustrate his moral:

> The Romans always looked ahead and took action to remedy problems before they developed. They never postponed action in order to avoid war ... Thus, they wanted to have a war with Philip and Antiochus in Greece, so as not to have one with them in Italy. At the time they could have avoided having a war at all, but this they did not want. They never approved of the saying that nowadays is repeated *ad nauseam* by the wise: "Take advantage of the passage of time." Rather they relied on their strength [*virtù*] and prudence [*prudenza*], for in time anything can happen... (Machiavelli 1995).

Notice, two additional aspects. Machiavelli is reinscribing a notion of Wisdom here, especially in terms of Practical Wisdom or Prudence, by suggesting what is Prudent is *not* that which "the Wise" counsel. This is part of the larger theme for Machiavelli of the Great-Souled Person as a "man of action" and perpetrator of Prudence-driven preemptive violence. For he believes,

> It will always happen that he who is not your ally will urge neutrality upon you, while he who is your ally will urge you to take sides. Rulers who are unsure what to do but want to avoid immediate dangers, generally end up staying neutral and usually destroy themselves by doing so. (Machiavelli 1995, 69).

The Great-Souled Sovereign, as it were, must have courage that leans toward "recklessness," so as to be preemptive (which neither legally nor strictly "self-defense") but tempered by Prudence to avoid self-destruction.

Machiavelli "argued that it was irresponsible and morally wrong to apply to political action the moral standards that are appropriate to private life and to personal relations: standards of friendship and of justice." (Hampshire 1978, 49). Notice, the "morally wrong" claim. In fact, out of Machiavelli's consequentialism may be articulated a self-centered obligation to be ruthless for the sake of the community and for the sake of expressing one's power-to-rule.

> If one refused to be ruthless in pursuit of objectives in public policy, and refused to use deceit and guile as instruments of policy, one betrayed those who had put their trust in the man who represents them. Deceit and violence and the breaking of promises and undertakings are normal in the relations between states... (Hampshire 1978, 49–50).

Interestingly, in regard to the Analogy of the City and the Soul, it is as if "ruthlessness" is required to bring the Kingdom into, and hold it in, Harmony (cf. Hampshire 2001). Hence, it seems for Machiavelli only the Great-Souled Sovereign would be capable of such autonomy and Kingdom building.

§3 Necessity & Virtue: Fate, Providence, Fortune & Autonomy and Prudence

Keeping in mind that Machiavelli's *Fortuna* has been translated as Providence, and it refers to necessary and uncontrollable events, which also allows it to be rendered as Fate, Fortune not only refers to wealth at any given time but also existential aspects of one's life; thus, the Wheel of Fortune, which is the Middle Ages version of the ancient Wheel of (re)incarnation and the torturous Wheel of Ixion in the Underworld. Machiavelli explains,

> I am not unaware of the fact that many have held and still hold the view that the affairs of this world are so completely governed by fortune and by God that human prudence is incapable of correcting them, with the consequence that there is no way in which what is wrong can be put right. (Machiavelli 1995, 74).

He continues,

> So one may conclude that there is no point in trying too hard; one should simply let chance have its way. This view has come to be more widely accepted in our own day because of the extraordinary variation in circumstance that has been seen and is still seen every day. (Machiavelli 1995).

Finally, he concludes,

> Nevertheless, since our free will must not be eliminated, I think it may be true that fortune determine one half of our actions, but that, even so, she leaves us to control the other half, or thereabouts. (Machiavelli 1995).

In this way, Machiavelli advocates for the Virtues of Prudence and Fortitude in response to both good and bad Fortune.

Compare this briefly with what we noted regarding the Great-Souled Person. For in Aristotle's *Rhetoric* he notes "the young and the great-souled" are among those who "deem themselves worthy of goods they do not possess" (1388a38). The difference being that the Great-Souled person actually is worthy of great things and Honor. At the same time, the Great-Souled Person will not be excessively joyed at receiving Honor for being Great-Souled, because—keeping in mind Panoramic Wisdom and a discernment of relations in accordance with Justice— Great-Souled persons accept what to their minds should belong to them already and "because others are not able to give them anything greater in tribute" (Aristotle 2009, 1124a5-9). Hence, the Great-Souled Sovereign would not be overly taken by either good or bad Fortune—being Stoic in regard to Fortune.

Now, despite Machiavelli's comments regarding Providence, God, and the Church, it has been suggested,

> There is no serious assumption of the existence of God and divine law; whatever our author's private convictions, an atheist can read Machiavelli with perfect intellectual comfort. Nor is there piety

toward authority, or prescription—nor any interest in the role of the individual conscience, or in any other metaphysical or theological issue. (Berlin 1958, 37–38).

Yet, it is clear that Machiavelli advocates for some kind of Integrity. Notice the following four (4) clarifications regarding his use of the term *virtù*, that is, Virtue.

1. Not pragmatism: "Machiavelli's *virtù* [sic] does not involve pragmatic adaptation to whatever standards are found in various environments, regardless of whether agents judge the standards as reasonable."
2. Not simple industry: "*virtù* is not just any form of hard work, or any robust force imposed in the name of order. The sheer energetic force of an agent's will may temporarily impose restraints [, but the control must be sustained to count as Virtue]."
3. Requires Self-Discipline: "Machiavelli's *virtù* does not involve the unconstrained exercise of free will [self-discipline is in its heart]."
4. Requires Authenticity: "Virtuous imposing involves taking pre-existing necessities seriously, and authorizing some as conditions for further building." (Benner 2009, 166). "Authenticity," here, refers to an agent's capacity to "take hold of" the existential aspects of their present life situation "in their own way," that is, mindfully and not simply as may be expected by the herd.

Finally, *fortuna* and *virtù* "are always antithetical forms of causation for Machiavelli." (Benner 2009, 167). That is to say, "Agents who rely on *virtù* rely primarily on their own resources. Machiavelli associates *virtù* with self-reliance, independence, and self-responsibility, and *fortuna* with causal resources that are not an agent's own." (Benner 2009). Moreover, Machiavelli warns against clinging too much to the Wheel of Fortune, and the different between these types of reliance have been linked to Machiavelli's "extraordinary" and "ordinary" modes of Sovereignty. It is here, then, where what may be seen as Machiavelli's synthesis of Plato's Analogy of the City and the Soul with Aristotle's Great-Souled Person takes place insofar as the "extraordinary" mode of Sovereignty applies to both the individual and the manner in which they govern a Kingdom.

§4 *Dirty Hands & Clean Gloves: Authority & Dissimulation*

Focusing primarily on chapters seventeen and eighteen, in regard to the Prince as Sovereign, Machiavelli asks the infamous question: "Is it better to be loved than feared?" Machiavelli warns, "be careful about being compassionate." (Machiavelli 1995, 51). In fact, hearkening back to the inversion of Aristotle's Character Types, he notes ultimately "it is more compassionate to impose harsh punishments on a few than, out of excessive compassion, to allow disorder to spread, which leads to murders or looting." (Machiavelli 1995). For example, "Cesare Borgia was thought of as cruel; but this supposed cruelty of his restored order to the Romagna, united it, rendered it peaceful and law-abiding." (Machiavelli 1995). Indeed, "a ruler ought not to mind the disgrace of being called cruel." (Machiavelli 1995). Hence, he answers his own question:

> one ought to be both loved and feared; but, since it is difficult to accomplish both at the same time, I maintain it is much safer to be feared than loved, if you have to do without one of the two. For of

men one can, in general, say this: They are ungrateful, fickle, deceptive and deceiving, avoiders of danger, eager to gain. As long as you serve their interests, they are devoted to you. They promise you their blood, their possessions, their lives, and their children, as I said before, so long as you seem to have no need of them. But as soon as you need help, they turn against you. (Machiavelli 1995, 51–52).

The difference between being feared and being hated, a condition Machiavelli is keen the Prince avoid, is that citizens will hate you if you deprive them of their property without making it appear Just. Machiavelli advises, "Whenever you have to kill someone, make sure you have a suitable excuse and an obvious reason" (Machiavelli 1995, 52).

The paradoxical aspect of how the Sovereign must be versus how the Sovereign should appear, is often characterized in terms of the "Dirty Hands" problem. Integral for the later example of the "Coventry Blitz," the Problem of Dirty Hands asks: Should a Sovereign act immorally if doing so would achieve great goods for his Kingdom? At the point of Machiavelli in the history of the Western Tradition it may still seem reasonable to point out—following Augustine—that if human concerns are ultimately directed at the Kingdom of God, then it is not worth the trade-off for "great goods" directed at the Kingdom of Man. Yet, at the same time, this may mean something like accepting death, and the time of the Great-Souled ancient Greek martyrs continues to distance itself from us.

Machiavelli's solution to the Problem of Dirty Hands seems to be Dissimulation; that is to say, he speaks as though he considers lying to be a Virtue (*virtù*) when performed by the Prince. What is more, it is remarkable to recall what was considered from the perspective of the Self-Perfection and Self-Realization of the individual "Incongruence." It was suggested that Incongruence refers to "a discrepancy between the actual experience of the organism and the self picture of the individual insofar as it represents that experience." (Rogers 1957, 96). However, here it becomes a practical skill in the sense that one project and manage a false image of one's true self—as if Machiavelli were emphasizing the relation between Persona and Personhood. Often the notion of Image Management has been associated with the use of social media in contemporary society, for example, profile pictures. Yet, the point here is that Dissimulation is considered highly valuable. Machiavelli explains you should *seem* "to be compassionate, trustworthy, sympathetic, honest, religious, and indeed, be all these things; but at the same time you should be constantly prepared, so that, if these become liabilities, you are trained and ready to become their opposites." (Machiavelli 1995, 55).

Hobbes: Leviathan as an Immortal Clockwork Kingdom of Man

§5 *Voluntarism Conceives Natural Law as Positive Law*

What seems to be needed to grasp the depth of the initial insight upon which Thomas Hobbes' *Leviathan* stands is the notion of Voluntarism. Recalling the distinction between Intellectualism and Voluntarism, the question becomes some version of: *Are the Laws of Nature the way they are because God could not make them any other way, or are the Laws of Nature the way they are because God Willed them to be that way, instead of any other way he could have Willed them to be?*[22]

Of course, if we side with the former, then we decide in favor of Intellectualism, and if with the latter, then in favor of Voluntarism. Now, by siding with Voluntarism, it is as if Hobbes suddenly gains the ability to conceive of God as though God were some kind of—thinking of Machiavelli here—Celestial Prince. It follows, then, for Hobbes that he may decide not to place his trust in God. As we will see by the end of this chapter, what that means is that he must remain a kind of enemy of God and at War with God, that is, by remaining in a State of Nature in relation to God and, to quote Dostoyevski, by "refusing the ticket" into God's Kingdom.

Voluntarism "makes" Natural Law into Positive Law because it no longer treats Natural Law as necessary. Rather, what made Natural Law into *the Law* is that God posited it, that is, Willed it to be as it is; though, since he could have Willed it differently, Natural Law is no longer considered necessary in the sense of unchangeable. "Man sins, therefore, because and only so far as a positive law, by which he is bound, stands over him." (Rommen 1998, 53). Hence, as we will see, it is as if Hobbes may be seen advocating a kind of "civil disobedience" against the posited Law of God.

On the one hand, as a lawyer, perhaps Hobbes believes he knows how Law works well enough to bring the case for Freedom against God. For example, consider the following two passages from Chapter 20 of *Leviathan*. First, regarding the idea developed from Plato and established by the Catholic Church that we are the Property of God, that is, in regard to God's Kingdom or Dominion and God's rightful rule over humans; Hobbes notes:

> Dominion is acquired in two ways: by generation and by conquest. The right of dominion by generation is that which the parent hath over his children, and is called Paternal. And is not so derived from the generation as if therefore the parent had *dominion* over his child because he begat him, but *from* the child's *consent*, either express or by other sufficient arguments declared [emphases added]. (Hobbes 1994, 128).

On the other hand, Hobbes' Voluntarism reveals him as a "subjectivist" and someone who believes "that obligation only stems from self-interest." (Mill 2001, 119). Ultimately, what makes Hobbes an exemplar of Voluntarism is that almost everything hinges on "voluntary consent." Thus, commenting on the Myth of the Garden of Eden, Hobbes claims:

> that of *Genesis*: "Ye shall be as gods, knowing good and evil." (Genesis 3:5). And verse 11. "Who told thee that thou wast naked? hast thou eaten of the tree, of which I commanded thee thou shouldest not eat?" For the cognizance or judicature of *good* and *evil*, being forbidden by the name of the fruit of the tree of knowledge, as a trial of *Adam's* obedience, the devil to inflame the ambition of the woman, to whom that fruit already seemed beautiful, told her that by tasting it they should be as gods, knowing *good* and *evil*. Whereupon, having both eaten, they did indeed take upon them God's office, which is judicature of *good* and *evil*, but acquired no new ability to distinguish between them aright. And whereas it is said that, having eaten, they saw they were naked, no man hath so interpreted[23] that place as if they had been formerly blind, and saw not their own skins; the meaning is plain, that it was then they first judged their nakedness (wherein it was God's will to create them)

to be uncomely, and by being ashamed, did tacitly censure God himself. And thereupon God saith Hast thou eaten, etc. as if he should say, doest thou that owest me obedience, take upon thee to judge of my commandments? Whereby it is clearly (though allegorically) signified that the commands of them that have the right to command are not by their subjects to be censured, nor disputed.

Thus, by the end of this chapter, we will see that it is as if Hobbes suggests humanity not consent to the commands of God; and, rather, create a Kingdom of Man to be ruled by the commands that humans judge to be best, that is, a *Leviathan* against God.[24]

§6 *The State of Nature: Meat Machines at War*

Perhaps the concept most immediately associated with Hobbes' is that of the State of Nature. Given Hobbes commitment to a philosophy of materialism and mechanism, humans in the State of Nature have been given, by some commentators, the memorable and illustrative characterization of "Meat Machines."[25] Hobbes is notoriously pessimistic about the State of Nature; that is, he refers to it as a War of everyone against everyone (Hobbes 1994, 80). For in the State of Nature there is only one Right, and that is the Right to protect yourself, that is, to Self-preservation; each individual has "the liberty … to use his own power, as he will himself, for the preservation of his own nature…" (Hobbes 1994, 223–4). Contemporary French philosopher Gilles Deleuze (1925–1995 AD) tells us Hobbes' greatest innovation in the history of the Western Tradition was to ensure that the "principle of consent (pact or contract) [became] the principle of political philosophy, and replaces the rule of authority." (Deleuze 2005, 260).

Whereas the Western Tradition prior to Hobbes placed emphasis on the Ideal of the Sage or Wise Person and in teleological and soteriological terms, Deleuze characterizes Hobbes as completing the undermining of the "authority of the Wise." Further, according to Deleuze, Hobbes articulates a conception of Natural Law "thoroughly opposed to" the "natural law of Antiquity." Thus, Deleuze presents four (4) characteristics of Natural Law as understood by the ancient Greeks, so that he may contrast Hobbes' "four basic theses" against the ancient Greeks. We have put them in list form to facilitate clarity and memorization, as needed.

The characteristics Deleuze associates with the "natural law of Antiquity":

1. "It defines a being's nature by its perfection, within an order of ends (thus man is 'naturally' reasonable and sociable).
2. It follows that the state of nature is not, for man, a state preceding society, even in principle, but rather a life in conformity with nature in a 'good' civil society.
3. What is then primary and unconditional in such a state are 'duties'; for natural are only potential, and always require an act of reason to determine and realize them in relation to ends they are [naturally] to serve.
4. This itself grounds the authority of the wise man; for the wise man is the best judge of the order of ends, of duties that follow from it, and of the offices and actions that it falls to each to exercise and carry out. One can foresee the use Christianity would make of this conception of natural law: law would become inseparable from natural theology and even Revelation." (Deleuze 2005, 258–9).

Now, the following theses are associated with Hobbes' re-formation of the Western Tradition, which "transform the philosophical problem of right precisely by taking the body as their mechanical and dynamical model." (Deleuze 2005, 259).

1. "The law of nature is no longer referred to a final perfection but to an initial desire, to the strongest 'appetite'; detached from the order of ends, it is deduced from appetite as its efficient cause.
2. Reason, from this viewpoint, enjoys no privilege: the fool tries no less than a reasonable being to preserve in his being; and desires or actions born of reason exemplify this effort no more than do the desires or passions of the fool.
    a. nobody is born reasonable …
    b. nobody is born a citizen …
    c. nobody is born religious …
3. What then is primary and unconditional is power or right. 'Duties,' of whatever sort, are always secondary relative to
    a. affirmation of our power,
    b. to the exercise of our power,
    c. the preservation of our right.
   And power is no longer referred to an act that determines and realizes it in relation to an order of ends.
4. It follows that nobody has the authority to decide my rights. Everyone in the state of nature, whether wise man or fool, judges what is good or bad, and what is necessary to his preservation. … And if it comes about that we are led to renounce our natural right, this will not happen through the recognition of the wise man's authority, but through our own consent to this renunciation…" (Deleuze 2005, 259–60).

Like machines, then, though made of flesh and bone, in the State of Nature humans pursue what they desire and avoid that to which they are averse. Good and bad, Good and evil are merely the determinants of an individual's desire.

§7 Natural Right & The Social Contract: The Innocence of Existence in the Chaos of Freedom

The term Hobbes uses to refer to the civil situation after the State of Nature is "the Common Wealth." This is a telling term if we think about the relation between the Kingdom established by God and the Kingdom established by humans, especially in terms of Property. Of course, as Hobbes' narrative goes, the State is a voluntary association, rather than a Natural, that is, organic, organism. Thus, the City, State, or Kingdom (given different historical periods in the Western Tradition) results from the *agreement* of "families" (think Aristotle) to band together into, ultimately, a Kingdom, and, thereby, in some sense at least, the *wealth* of the Kingdom is that which is held in *common* by its members. In terms of Property, this does not mean simply money but also the genes, the talents, the beauty, and so on, of the citizens who *voluntarily* belong to the Kingdom.

INTRODUCTION TO ETHICS

In the State of Nature, Hobbes notoriously claims that there is no Justice, and there is no Property. As brutal as this next statement may sound, it needs to be noted: this means you do not own your own body in the State of Nature. Hence, the only thing stopping anyone from doing anything they want to your body is your own power to repel them or your power to persuade others to help you repel them. For since there is no such thing as Justice in the State of Nature, there is no such thing (according to Hobbes) as unlawful carnal knowledge or even no such offense as "rape." However, supposing you would not want to be restrained and spend your life subjected to whatever depraved fancies your captors could conjure, then you most likely have an interest in acquiring powerful Friends. This idea of banding together for the Self-preservation of the group is the basis, then, of the idea of a Social Contract, since such "mutual transferring of right" is called a "Contract" (Hobbes 1994, 82).

This is also the reason why Hobbes thinks that Aristotle's suggestion that a Rule of Law may replace the Natural rule by men is seditious, that is, "the crime of saying, writing, or doing something that encourages people to disobey their government." (Merriam-Webster 2016). For the laws of nature are each twofold in that, on the one hand, they impose a moral requirement, and, on the other hand, they carry the disclaimer that releases a subject from the requirement if others fail to meet it; thus, with an obviously pejorative intention, the commentator calls the twofold structure of Hobble's laws of nature "the Copper Rule," as opposed to the Golden Rule. (Kavka 1986, 344). This leads some to see Hobbes as the first theorist to characterize the State of Nature as a kind of Prisoner's Dilemma. We will discuss this in just a moment. For now, note that the positive Nature of the Laws of Nature situate one's relation to them as Prudential, though not necessary. Put more technically, Laws of Nature are "assertoric hypothetical imperatives ... the fixed end for which they prescribe practically necessary means—namely the preservation of oneself and the avoidance of injuries—is an egocentric end ... laws of nature do not have a distinctively moral character." (Watkins 1973, 55–56). This has significant consequences regarding how to characterize Rights and Duty as ethical terms.

Following his determination of the Laws of Nature as positive, Hobbes makes a further distinction which may be considered re-formative in regard to the Catholic Revolution in the Western Tradition.

> *jus*, and *lex*, *right* and *law* ... ought to be distinguished; because Right, consisteth in liberty to do, or to forbear; whereas Law, determineth and bindeth to one of them: so that law, and right, differ as much as obligation, and liberty; which in one and the same matter are inconsistent. (Hobbes 1994, 79).

Thus, in his commentary on this passage John Finnis suggests Hobbes has accomplished a significant shift in our thinking about Rights. He notes,

> Pushed as far as Hobbes' purposes, this contrast between law and rights deprives the notion of rights of virtually all its normative significance. Hobbes wishes to say that one has most rights when one is in the "state of nature," i.e. a vacuum of law and obligation, since "in such a condition, every man has a right to everything; even to one another's body." But we could just as well say that in such a condition of things, where no persons have any duty no to take anything they want, *no one has any rights*. (Finnis 1980, 208).

We want to be sure to notice two key features out of the above passages. First, both Rights *and* Duties are based in voluntary Contract. Second, to be at liberty in regard to some Sovereign authority is to be in a State of Nature, that is, relation of War. In the context of the submission to the Sovereign given his power to protect you, recall Hobbes' characterization in terms of violence regarding a power sufficient to bring humans out of a State of Nature, that is, someone who can "shock and awe" to win the hearts and minds. Hence, according to Hobbes, just as we have no Duties to those with whom we are not in a Contract, we are also at liberty to do as much as our power allows, which means we and they are still "natural enemies" and at War.

Finally, in regard to these last two points. On the one hand, we gain the Right of Property through our Consent to be governed by the Sovereign, since it is the Sovereign's constitution of a Kingdom which determines the environment and bodies to be Property to be owned. On the other hand, Hobbes' characterization of a Free Will as an unimpeded "last appetite" or desire prior to the "decision" to act, recalls the idea of humans as meat machines, that is, mechanically processing their relation to Pleasure, pain, and Liberty. Yet, this conception of Free Will—which sounds more like the Stoics than Augustine—makes it seem for Hobbes that humans would Naturally side with the Kingdom of Man over the Kingdom of God, since it is the Kingdom of Man that provides us with safety and security now, as opposed to the Church's promise of safety and security in some other place or after-life. In some ways, this sounds like Hobbes is merely affirming the Fall from the Myth of the Garden of Eden; however, quite subtly it also may sound as though he is suggesting Self-Realization and Self-Perfection—insofar as it may pertain to Civil, rather than Divine Justice, and the Kingdom of Man, rather than the Kingdom of God—is best understood in terms of being an "enemy of God."

§8 *The Separation of Church and State: The Distinction between Submission and Subjection*

We can now name the distinction which Hobbes seems to have accomplished, that is, the difference between submission and subjection.[26] Put simply, whereas "submission" is involuntary, "subjection" is voluntary. As a result, the "meat machine" stands always already in a relation of submission to God, insofar as the Laws of Nature hold it in existence. However, whether we wish to call it "mind," "soul," "will," "Civil Personhood," or something else, Hobbes seems to believe this aspect must be Voluntarily *subjected* either to the Kingdom of God, according to God's terms, or to the Kingdom of Man, in terms of the Sovereign *Leviathan*.

Further, Hobbes' position seems clear. That he repeatedly refers to the "Church Fathers" as "seditious" shows his allegiance with the Monarchy against any entities who—in not respecting the Monarch's power—would try to dissuade the Sovereign's subjects to pledge allegiance to a different Kingdom. Suddenly the Stoic and Christian "Cosmopolitanism" begins to look as if they don't respect the boundaries of the Common Wealth. Must one be either an enemy of one Kingdom or the other? Or perhaps be a Cynic?

Thus, Hobbes levies the accusation that from "Duns Scotus and Thomas Aquinas, was born the theology which they call scholastic, [which is] a hodge-podge of Aristotle's philosophy and Sacred Scripture." (Hobbes 1994, 473; cf. Kantorowicz 1957). Leviathan is filled with disparaging remarks about the Church and Church Fathers, as if they are simply agents of another political entity among others, vying to usurp the Sovereign's rule. See especially the entire concluding "Part IV" of *Leviathan*, which Hobbes titled "Of the

Kingdom of Darkness," and which is a clear reference to the Kingdom for which he takes the actual historical proponents of the Christian Church to be advocating. Notice, in this context, he charges, a kind of sedition against the Church in that they have taught *"that there is no other rule of just and unjust except the dictates of the Roman church, that kings are not to be obeyed further than is permitted by the Roman church, and kings themselves ought to obey the Roman pontiff like sheep* [emphasis in original]." (Hobbes 1994, 473; cf. Byron 2015, 20–21). What is more,

> It is not only in matters of justice that Hobbes thinks that God is incomprehensible to us. Almost no language applied to God can be literal. ... When we call God "good," we are only expressing an indefinite admiration for him. Admiration is also expressed when we speak of God as existing, [etc.]... With such language we are not describing anything; we are honoring God by expressing our feelings of fear and hope [(cf. Hobbes 1994, 237)]. All of this is quite in line with the Lutheran and Calvinist view that God is beyond our intellectual grasp. (Schneewind 1998, 96).

Hobbes treats Voluntarism as if it were an advertisement for the Kingdom of Man. Noting, the "justification of affliction" is not always determined by sin, that is, an individual's actions; Hobbes invokes the example of Job. Rather, the justification of afflicting suffering is ultimately determined "from God's power," and this idea secures the characterization of Voluntarism for Hobbes' philosophy (Hobbes 1994, 236–7).

For the sake of space, we will not work out the entirety of the matrix here; however, to facilitate discussion, we will mention that one should not just entertain the idea of a "Prisoner's Dilemma" among the populace of a State of Nature, and subsequently in a Common Wealth, given the positivity of Law, but also one should consider the Prisoner's Dilemma as it interfaces with Pascal's Wager. The idea here being that the either/or option in the Kingdom of Man may still be a decision in the face of the either/or option *between* the Kingdom of Man and the Kingdom of God. Ultimately, this complexity does not seem to escape Hobbes who seems comfortable with the moniker "enemy of God." (cf. *Leviathan* chapters 31.2 & 31.6).

6

The Protestant Reformation of the Catholic Revolution II: Hume & Utilitarianism

> "for there is nothing
> either good or bad,
> but thinking makes it so…"[27]
> ~Shakespeare

§1 Chapter Overview

Philosophically speaking, the ethical theories discussed in this chapter fit the description of "protesting" against both the ancient contributions to the Western Tradition and also the Catholic synthesis of the ancient contributions in regard to God. The first philosopher, David Hume, is standardly described as the "greatest atheist of the Modern period" and as a "Modern skeptic." Of course, you don't receive such a label unless what you have to say is considered to have some significance and/or made some significant impact. In many ways, Hume was "before his time" in that he laid the Naturalistic and atheistic groundwork for, and in many cases more clearly articulated a coherent position than, many of the contemporary theories with the same goals (e.g., the theories of Sigmund Freud). One further title which we may confer upon Hume is that his philosophy, perhaps better than any other (at least in the Early Modern period), most concisely and clearly provides an articulation of and justification for Nihilism.

The versions of Utilitarianism stemming from Jeremy Bentham and John Stuart Mill follow from Hume's theorizing in many ways. They explicitly share the goal with Hume that they intended to use the Modern scientific method to make progress in ethics. Thus, Utilitarianism is often thought of as the modern scientific version of Hedonism and Consequentialism. Moreover, it is probably safe to say that the default position for critical-ethical-thinking in contemporary America tends to be Utilitarianism. That is to say, the influence of Christianity notwithstanding, if you were to ask most people to ethically evaluate an action, they would tend to immediately consider the Consequences of the action. Of course, we now know that this is just one approach to considering the action and situation in which an action takes place. Further, with an eye to the Consequences, they would tend to inquire specifically about the Pleasure and pain caused by the action.

Hume: Influencing Motives of the Will

"Reason is, and ought only to be, the slave of the passions,
and can never pretend to any other office
than to serve and obey them."[28]
~David Hume (1737)

§2 *The Role of Judgment in Action: The Path to Nihilism*

David Hume (1711–1776 AD) in his Treatise of Human Nature set out to criticize rationality-based ethical theories. As the above epigraph clearly states, Hume sees *logos* as in the service of *pathos*. "Every rational creature, it is said, is obliged to regulate his actions by reason; and if any other motive or principle challenge the direction of his *conduct*, he ought to oppose it, till it be entirely subdued, or at least brought to conformity with that superior principle." (1874, Bk II, §3.3). He set out, then, "In order to show the fallacy of all this philosophy, I shall endeavor to prove *first*, that reason alone can never be a motive to any action of the will; and *secondly*, that it can never oppose passion in the direction of the will." (Hume 1874, 193).

In this way, describes the role of judgment in action in terms of two types of activity, that is, reason can "speculate" and "calculate." According to Hume, "The understanding exerts itself after two different ways, as it *judges* from demonstration or probability; as it regards the abstract relations of our ideas, or those relations of objects of which experience only gives us information." (Ibid) Thus,

1. Reason can help us calculate the distribution of our resources.
2. Reason can help us speculate regarding what might happen if we choose some specific course of action.
   a. When our speculations suggest our future actions may result in pleasure or pain, then we may judge one course of action better than another; however, the impulse to choose a particular course of action does not come from reason.

Hence, Reason neither gives rise to action, nor prevents any action. For Hume, Reason does not control Will.

§3 *Dynamic Tension of the Passions: The Will Unmotivated by Reason*

Of course, if Reason does not control the Will, then how do humans make decisions? If all deliberation is wishful thinking motivated by *pathos*, then what determines the Will. According to Hume,

"A passion is an original existence… When I am angry, I am actually possessed with the passion, and in that emotion have no more a reference to any other object, than when I am thirsty, or sick, or more than five feet high. It is impossible, therefore, that this passion can be opposed by, or be contradictory to truth and reason; since this *contradiction consists in the disagreement of ideas, considered as copies*, with those objects which they represent." (Hume 1874, 195)

Thus, "passions can be contrary to reason only, so far as they are accompanied with some judgment or opinion…" Therefore, "it is only in two senses that any affection can be called unreasonable:

1) when a passion, such as hope or fear, grief or joy, despair or security, is founded on the supposition of the existence of objects, which really do no exist.
2) When in exerting any passion in action, we choose means sufficient for the designed end, and deceive ourselves in our judgment of causes and effects."

For, "Where a passion is neither founded on false suppositions, nor chooses means insufficient for the end, the understanding can neither justify nor condemn it." (Ibid). In sum,

"Since a passion can never, in any sense, be called unreasonable, but when founded on a false supposition, or when it chooses means insufficient for the designed end, it is impossible that reason and passion can ever oppose each other, or dispute for the government of the will and actions." Hence, the theory of the "dynamic tension of the passions" is needed to account for the determination of the Will. (Ibid).

Dynamic Tension of the Passions suggests that we have conflicting and what would be, rationally speaking, contradictory passions and desires. In other words, we want to satisfy desires which cannot be simultaneously satisfied. For example, we may want to sit in a classroom and learn, while at the same time wishing to spend the time sending text messages or "surfing" the internet. We may wish to "stay in shape" or be fit, while at the same time wishing to eat pastries and not exert ourselves. Thus, for Hume whatever we end up doing, that is, whatever action we perform, it is the outcome of the tension between Passions. That is to say, when you decide to do something it is because you were more Passionate about it than you were about the alternatives. Notice, the decision's Reasonableness does not determine its manifestation. As we will see, the theory of Dynamic Tension of the Passions socially leads to Conventionalism and, in terms of Justice, opens the door for Nihilism.

§4 *The Relation between Is and Ought: The Tension between Right and Good?*

As we discussed in the introductory chapter, Right is a concept that pertains to the sphere of Duty and Obligation, and Good is a concept that pertains to the spheres of Virtue or Excellence and Value. Now, because Reason does not determine the Will, for Hume, and the Dynamic Tension of the Passions is governed by Pleasure and pain, Value is understood in terms of Utility. Therefore, dynamic tension has undercut the ability to determine Obligation. For example, it does not follow that because some experience is pleasurable that you are then obliged to do anything afterward. Thus, a kind of tension emerges between the ideas of Right and Good. This is captured in Hume's infamous comments regarding the relation between "*Is and Ought.*"

First off, we want to remember that "Ought" is another term for "Should," so when someone says: "You should do X" or "You should act differently," they are invoking the concept of Ought. Now, when we have an experience there may be some objective empirically verifiable aspects of the experience, therefore, we do have some claim as to the reality of what we are experiencing. That is to say, you do experience Pleasure and you do experience pain. So, in regard to experienced situations we may say the situation "Is" some way or another. Hume's point, however, is that an "Ought" does not follow from the "Is." Because Reason "alone can never be a motive to any action of the will" and "it can never oppose passion in the direction of the will" *the motive force of the Ought is alien to the Is*. It is as if, the results of rationality are mere illusion insofar as rationality may suggest, for example, quid pro quo, that an Obligation or Duty exists based on the experience of some situation; however, since passions are neither rational nor irrational and Reason does not motivate the Will, then Reason, for Hume, is outside its jurisdiction when it suggests any subsequent actions *should* be performed.

§5 *A Naturalistic Account of Virtue: Sympathy & the Virtue of Natural Sentiments*

Given what we have seen already, it may be clear now that Hume was interested in establishing a kind of Virtue theory that was based solely in a Naturalistic Account, and, thereby, without the importance attributed to Reason by the likes of Plato and Aristotle. For clarification, the Naturalistic Account and the account in terms of Natural Function, for our purposes, differ in that Reason counts as a Natural Function, whereas Naturalistic may be understood as including only the attributes of our physical Nature.

Thus, Hume distinguished between what he called Natural and Artificial Virtues. In order to understand his distinction, we first need to understand his "Elements of Virtuous Action." According to Hume a situation which calls for possible Virtuous action may be analyzed into the following elements: an Agent, a Receiver, and a Spectator. Notice, we may think of these elements as spanning any number of individuals. That is, it is possible to think of these elements spanning three (3) individuals in a situation or more or even one (1) individual comprised of these elements. Hence, the Agent is the efficient cause or individual who is performing the action, the Receiver is the individual who receives the action from the Agent, and the Spectator refers to the individual witnessing the Receiver receive the action from the Agent. For example, someone can witness themselves lying to themselves or to others, and so on.

Now, Hume used these elements in conjunction with the notion of sympathy to distinguish between Natural and Artificial Virtues. In other words, when a Spectator witnesses a Receiver receive an action from an Agent, if the Receiver is able to sympathize with the Pleasure received by the Receiver, then the action refers to a Natural Virtue. If the Spectator is not able to sympathize with the Pleasure received by the Receiver but is able to acknowledge the Goodness in terms of its Utility, then the action refers to an Artificial Virtue. Hume's Natural Virtues are—Benevolence, Meekness, Charity, and Generosity; his Artificial Virtues are—Justice, Keeping Promises, Allegiance, and Chastity.

Notice that this seems to "flip" the distinction between Moral and Intellectual Virtues in Aristotle. Whereas Aristotle held the Moral Virtues—which, recall, are associated with the body—require training to be Good and can be destroyed through excess, Hume seems to hold that these Virtues are Naturally Good and cannot be destroyed by excess. Further, Aristotle's Intellectual Virtues, by being associated with rationality itself, were naturally directed in terms of Goodness; however, Hume sees these Virtues as deriving their Goodness from Utility based, ultimately, on Convention. Finally, it seems as though Aristotle might say, regarding Hume's characterization, that it seems to take the internal relations of the Structural Model which constitute the Vicious person to be that of humanity in general. For example, recall in regard to the intemperate person, in the *Nicomachean Ethics*, he noted "thought by itself moves nothing" (1139a36). The idea was that the right thoughts should have become associated with the appropriate desires as individuals were molded.

§6 *Convention vs. Contract & Public Interest*

As discussed in previous chapters, if a philosopher denies the mythico/religious grounding of Justice, then the general characterizations of the traditional political interpretations of Justice left to them are Order and Utility. We saw that Order needs determined, and it may be determined by power (i.e., non-divine command) or agreement. If we stretch this into a spectrum linking with Utility, then it is as if agreement may be in Order (e.g., rationally or due to Obligation) or it may derive from Utility. Hume, then, may be seen advocating for Convention over Contract, consistent with the elimination of rational import which generally characterizes him.

We just saw that keeping promises, for example, in terms of contracts, represents an Artificial Virtue for Hume. Therefore, to show how Convention, rather than contracting, may account for the bases from which to determine Justice, he invokes the example of two people in a "row boat." It is important to keep in mind that it is not a canoe. That is, the boat is such that the two individuals are seated on either side of the boat and beside each other. Now, according to Hume, if they want to move forward, then they need to both row, and their synchronized rowing would not need to originate from a Contract; rather it may be accounted for Naturalistically, in terms of the presence of the sympathetic motivations and similar determinations of Value by whomever is "in the same boat" together. This is how we are to think of Conventions generally, according to Hume, and, specifically, in relation to Contracts. Moreover, Hume's notion of Convention Contrasts, then, with the notion of a Social Contract as found, for example, in Epicurus, Hobbes and John Locke.

Further, notice how it may be easier to articulate what a "Public Interest" is from Hume's perspective of Convention, rather than the perspective of Contract. In other words, for Hume, a Public Interest is an interest of society or a supervening goal which emerges from the fact of a group of people living in close proximity, that is, being "in the same boat" together. Thus, Hume claims, "the obligation to justice is founded entirely on the interests of society." (1985, 489).

On the one hand, notice how it reminds us of Hobbes' notion that there is no Justice in the State of Nature. On the other hand, notice Hume is advocating for an informal Convention-based society and Justice, rather than basing society and Justice on a Social Contract. It follows then for Hume that the role of the government/Sovereign is "no object or purpose but the distribution of justice." (1985, 37). Hence, we are ultimately supposed to sympathize with the intuitions and desires of all, and in a spirit of constitutional democracy have concern and regard for the community, as a result. That is to say, the dynamic tension of the passions being "in the same boat" is supposed to provide the *constitution* of a society which is truly democratic and functioning in the service of Public Interest, in terms of Utility.

§7 *Relations of Ideas: Conventionalism & Nihilism*

This section provides a deeper account of Hume's Conventionalism and Nihilism in terms of the Structural Model. Basically Hume's position is a kind of positivism in that it only attributes certain reality to the empirically verifiable data of the senses. We gain ideas in an experience, then, because there are ideas which correspond with the input of sensory data from the environment. Notice that, in terms of rationality, we can relate these ideas to each other. In this way, we can form ideas based on the Relations of Ideas, and, thereby, we can distinguish between two different kinds of ideas in terms of Intensity. The first kind of ideas, since they correspond with sensory input, correspond to a more intense aspect of experience. The second kind of ideas are ideas which refer to the relations among the first kind of ideas.

Notice, given Hume's positivism and empiricism, we can be certain of the reality to which the first kind of ideas correspond; however, we cannot be certain of the reality which the second kind of ideas suggest. There are two conclusions to draw, then, from this depiction of the Structural Model. On the one hand, the second kind of ideas can be grounded in Convention. So, ultimately what will count as truth will be whatever narratives emerge from the culture which the community will use to understand the relations among the first kind of ideas. This is Hume's Conventionalism. On the other hand, if we emphasize Hume's Conventionalism in terms of the Structural Model, then notice how his Conventionalism may be Nihilism. That is, the Passions will determine which narrative becomes Convention for a community, and such will be the only determination of these higher ideas or narratives—this is directly analogous to the notion of dynamic tension in the role of judgment in action. In other words, there may be nothing of intrinsic Value insofar as even "Natural Sympathies" could be relative to different biological and geographical constitutions for humans. Interestingly, here again Hume is "before his time" in that he had already worked out a kind of "Post-Modern" logic.

Utilitarianism in General Principles of Happiness

§8 *Principle of Utilitarianism in General: Justice as Utility*

Utilitarianism borrows from ancient Greek Hedonism, Hobbes, and Hume. Utilitarianism, of course, determines Justice in terms of Utility, and Utility translates as Pleasure or Satisfaction. Utilitarianism is concerned with Conduct, not Character. It is a Consequentialist Normative Theory in that it determines what Conduct is most Valuable in terms of the consequences of the actions under consideration. It is an Objective Normative theory in that the Utility which derives from the consequences of an action are supposed to be objectively Valuable. It is difficult to characterize Utilitarianism in terms of being either Particularistic or Universalistic.

On the one hand, it is a Particularistic Normative Theory insofar as it is concerned with the consequences of particular situations, that is, it is not concerned whether the prescribed action would apply in all such cases as much as it is concerned with the particular situation at hand. Yet, in regard to the individuals involved in the situation, there is a sense in which all of the individuals will be universally treated the same, that is, as if democratically each gets only one vote. Hence, we may say it considers the features of particular situations by way of a method which is universally the same. Though the above characterization of Utilitarianism holds in general, we will examine different versions, specifically those of Jeremy Bentham and John Stuart Mill.

Finally, though "Utility" refers to Value, not Obligation or Duty, Utilitarians still speak of Right insofar as, for example, when one's life is lived appropriately in regard to Utility, then one may be Happy. Thus, humans have a Right to Happiness as a teleological and soteriological aspect of human reality. This is understood as the Principle of Utilitarianism, that is, that an action is considered Right insofar as it promotes Happiness. Moreover, "Right" here is understood to mean both "Right, not Wrong" and "Right in terms of humans seem to have a Duty to self to pursue their own Happiness." Hence, this may be seen as the Right to pursue Happiness in any way that seems best to an individual, though there will be two further principles which keep the Principle of Utilitarianism somewhat in check.

§9 *Structural Model: The "Jeffersonian Democratic" Reading*

In regard to the Structural Model, whereas Plato seemed to emphasize the Intellect over the body, and Hume seemed to emphasize the Passions over the Intellect, Utilitarians allow for the fact that both of these (what in Aristotle we called) Inclinations to the Good factor into the determination of which action is best in terms of Utility. In this way, Utilitarianism represents the further efforts of Modern philosophers to a science of living, or a scientifically grounded method for determining how humans should live. Because it is generally characterized in terms of the pursuit to maximize Pleasure and minimize pain, Utilitarianism is most often characterized as a Modern scientific version of Hedonism.

§10 *Act vs. Rule Utilitarianism*

Briefly, when we are about to perform an action, we may focus solely on the possible actions, or we may focus on the Maxims to which the possible actions refer. This is the Utilitarian way of handling Practical Syllogisms discussed in Plato and Aristotle. Just as it is possible to notice that when you perform an action you are following some Rule, for example, picking an apple in these circumstances follows the Rule that picking an apple in these circumstances is Right and Good. Rules may be understood as Maxims. Therefore, Act utilitarianism suggests we should perform the action which produces the greatest balance of Pleasure over pain. Rule Utilitarianism suggests we should perform the action which follows the Rule which would produce the greatest balance of Pleasure over pain. Rule Utilitarianism may be seen as more Universalistic than Act Utilitarianism, which, with its focus on this particular action in this particular situation, is clearly Particularistic.

Bentham's Utilitarianism

§11 *Principles Specific to Bentham: Positivism & Egoism*

Bentham's Utilitarianism is clearly positivistic and more egocentric than J.S. Mills' version. Following Hobbes' understanding of human Nature and Hume's positivism (speaking as if sense experience were the only object of knowledge for humans), Bentham's understanding of Utility seems to be rooted in sensation and quantity. He regarded Pleasure and pain as our "two great masters." Further, as we will see in his famous Hedonic Calculus, when an individual makes calculations to scientifically determine which action will produce the most pleasure, it is clear that the Calculus refers more to the individual performing it than to anyone else it may affect.

§12 *Hedonic Calculus*

Bentham identifies seven (7) features of pleasures that allow us to determine the greatness of a given Pleasure. They are listed in the order of their importance, according to Bentham's theory:

1. *Intensity* – a more intense pleasure is preferable to a weaker pleasure;
2. *Duration* – pleasures that last are preferable to those that don't;
3. *Certainty* – if the act guarantees a pleasure, that act is better than one that merely makes pleasure likely;
4. *Propinquity* – if the pleasure is far off in space or time, the act is less right;
5. *Fecundity* – the likelihood that the pleasure or pain will be followed by more pleasures or pains;
6. *Purity* – a pleasure that is mixed with pain is not as good as one that just pleasure;
7. *Extent* – the more people who will enjoy the pleasure, the better the act.

We must provide a disclaimer regarding the seventh criterion. Standard accounts suggest that the seventh should be added because Bentham's principles technically suggest it; however, rather than featuring last, as it does in Bentham's criteria, this concern features prominently for J.S. Mill. Hence, prescriptively, when we are about to perform an action, we are to use the above criteria to calculate which action is best, and, descriptively, if we wish to justify why some action is better than another in terms of Bentham' Utilitarianism, then we employ this same Calculus.

J.S. Mill's Utilitarianism

§13 *Mill's Critique of Bentham: "Better to be Socrates dissatisfied than a pig satisfied."*

The goal for this section is to understand Mill's two (2) criticisms of Bentham's Utilitarianism. Because Bentham was friends with J.S. Mill's father, James Mill, J.S. Mill was well aware of Bentham's philosophy. Rather than viewing Mill as hostile to Bentham, Mill seems to have conceived his criticisms as attempts to improve Bentham's version. For example, we find the following in Mill's *Autobiography*:

> What thus impressed me was the chapter in which Bentham passed judgment on the common modes of reasoning in morals and legislation, deduced from phrases like "law of nature," "right reason," "the moral sense," "natural rectitude," and the like, and characterized them as dogmatism in disguise, imposing its sentiments upon others under cover of sounding expressions which convey no reason for the sentiment, but set up the sentiment as its own reason. … Bentham's principle put an end to all this. The feeling rushed upon me, that all previous moralists were superseded, and that here indeed was the commencement of a new era in thought. (1960, 67).

In this way, it should be clear that Mill fully stands on the same ground, generally characterized (cf. §1 above), as Bentham. To be sure, however, the following also shows his criticism of Plato, Aristotle, and the Catholic views discussed in previous chapters:

> Conformity to nature has no connection whatever with right and wrong. The idea can never be fitly introduced into ethics discussions at all, except, occasionally and partially, into the question of degress of culpability. To illustrate this point, let us consider the phrase by which the greatest intensity of condemnatory feeling is conveyed in connection with the idea of nature—the word "unnatural." That a thing is unnatural, in any precise meaning which can be attached to the word, is no argument for its being blamable; since the most criminal actions are to a being like man not more unnatrual than most of the virtues. (1874, 102).

It is as if Mill may be suggesting here that Vice, just like Virtue, fulfils Natural Functions, and therefore we require some different criteria for blameworthiness. Moreover, as we will see in the next chapter, this idea would count as Mill's attempt to criticize Kant as well. However, in order to provide a kind of corrective for what Mill sees as the "Naturalness" of Vice, the next section discusses Mill's Liberty and Harm principles.

Mill's two improvements on Bentham's Utilitarianism involve "quality over quantity" and "the greatest good for the greatest number." In terms of the first improvement, Mill essentially rejected Bentham's Hedonic Calculus, since the criteria seem to consider Pleasure solely in terms of quantity. The suggestion was that if someone who had experienced two different kinds Pleasure would still choose one Pleasure over the other, even if they could receive an endless quantity of the former Pleasure, then the latter was of a higher quality of Pleasure. Lastly, it is as if Mill thought Bentham's last criteria should have been his first. In other words, Mill's Utilitarianism is more altruistic and other-centered than Bentham's. Mill thought the consequences we should seek from our conduct should be those that bring about the "greatest good for the greatest number," that is, the greatest extent. These then are the two improvements for which Mill advocates regarding Bentham's Utilitarianism.

§14 *Principles Specific to Mill's Utilitarianism: Liberty & Harm*

Though brief, these principles deserve their own section to emphasize not only their importance for Mill but also to remind us to not confuse them. Given the language of each, it is, in fact, easy to confuse the following two principles. First is the Principle of Liberty. Mill posited, what was at his time radical, the Principle of Liberty, which suggests you are at liberty to do what you please, that is, to pursue Happiness as you see fit, so long as you do not harm anyone else in the process.

Second, according to the Harm Principle, you only have the Right to harm another person to either defend yourself or to stop that person from harming someone else. In other words, individual members of a community, or the community as a whole, have the Right to interfere with someone's liberty in order to prevent harm. Notice, this is a justification for police force. "Harming someone" usually means using them as a means against or without their voluntary consent or producing a situation contrary to their interests. Thus, here are some examples of ways a person may be harmed:

1. Killing them (decreasing their life)
2. Wounding them (decreasing their health)
3. Slandering them (decreasing their honor)
4. Stealing from them (decreasing their wealth)
5. Infidelity regarding vows with them (decreasing their dignity)

Because the Principle of Liberty contains the word "harm," and the Harm Principle contains the word "liberty," it may be easy to confuse them. Hopefully you will be able to remember that the Harm Principle provides a justification for a community's maintaining a police force.

Criticisms of Utilitarianism

§15 *Non-Casuistical; Yet Navigating Blindly?*

The term "Casuistical" refers to the use of universally oriented theory to determine practical action. The term is often used pejoratively with the suggestion being that the particulars of a situation should matter more than a universally oriented description of the situation. Thus, Utilitarianism, especially Act Utilitarianism and Bentham's Hedonic Calculus, seem to avoid the criticism of being Casuistical. However, as the following criticisms highlight, does it avoid the criticism of Casuistry at the cost of future orientation?

Here are the standard criticisms of Utilitarianism:

1. Who should be included in the calculation?
    a. Should all the people involved truly be treated as equal, for example, shouldn't family and loved ones be treated differently from strangers?
    b. How far do the consequences extend in terms of humans?
    c. Do nonhumans count?
    d. How far do the consequences extend in time?
2. What if those involved cannot articulate what is in their best interest?
3. Is it a problem that sometimes the same kind of action will be bad and sometimes good?
4. What if inhumane treatment or heinous acts are supported by Utilitarian calculations, does it change the status of those acts as inhumane or heinous?

§16 *Criticisms: Human Sacrifice & The Utility of Promises*

The following seem to be the two (2) most potent criticisms of Utilitarianism. First, Utilitarianism may be used to justify human sacrifice. The not uncontroversial example usually given is of the "Coventry Blitz" on November 14, 1940 during World War II, in which the English city of Coventry was bombed as part of the

Nazi Blitzkrieg. The idea is that Winston Churchill as the Prime Minister of England at the time had prior knowledge that the city was to be bombed. However, had he warned the residents, then Adolf Hitler could have discerned that the Allies had "cracked" their "Enigma codes." From the November 14 bombing alone over 550 people were killed, over 850 were seriously injured with almost 400 additional people receiving less serious injuries. Insofar, then, that one is a Utilitarian and compares these numbers with the *estimated* number of lives saved by not revealing to the Nazi's that their secret communications were being intercepted and decoded, the sacrifice of those individuals was Good, that is, a Utilitarian would say the choice to sacrifice those individuals was the Right choice.

The second criticism revolves around temporal relations and making promises. Put simply, it is difficult to weigh the amount of Utility associated with keeping a promise made in the past, when one is facing a new and unforeseen situation presently in which deciding against the past promise will lead to significant Utility. Perhaps the clearest concrete example stems from the, what we might call "morally bankrupt" phrase, popular nowadays in some circles, which speaks of "upgrading" one's spouse. The idea is that you may derive significant Pleasure, that is, Utility, from being married; however, if the opportunity presents itself for you to "upgrade" to a different relationship from which it seems as though you might get more Pleasure or Utility, then it seems Utilitarianism would consider the "upgrade" Good, that is, they would advocate that you do it.

Notice, from the perspective of a primarily character-based ethics, being the kind of person that "upgrades," or even looks for "upgrades," would not be considered Good. Further, from the perspective of Personhood and Duty-based Normative Theories, it would be considered Wrong, and from the mystic/religious-based Normative Theories it may even be considered Evil. However, given the right circumstances, both Bentham's and Mill's Utilitarianism would advise the action.

7

The Kantian Revolution & The Return to the Greeks of German Idealism

> "Morality is not properly the doctrine of how we may make ourselves happy, but how we may make ourselves *worthy* of happiness."[29]
> ~Immanuel Kant

§1 *Chapter Overview*

It is difficult to overstate Immanuel Kant's (1724–1804 AD) importance in the history of the Western Tradition. Kant must be ranked among Plato and Aristotle. Kant's impact on philosophy was so immense that it has been, rightfully, said regarding philosophy in his wake: "There is a saying among philosophers, 'You can philosophize with Kant or against Kant, but you cannot philosophize without him.'"[30] Kant essentially set out to organize the discipline of philosophy by using "Transcendental Logic" to show philosophy as a coherent internally organized system, that is, a system of all possible philosophical thinking. From his effort emerged a "standardized vocabulary" and the ability to recognize the interrelatedness of philosophical problems.

Kant believed such a project to be viable, since humans are rational animals, and therefore all human thinking somehow participates in the possible patterns of rationality. Thus, by limiting the use of rationality to its specific spheres, for example, theoretical and practical, Kant revealed a system of Reason around three (3) "Critiques." His second Critique, that is, the *Critique of Practical Reason* (1788), provides us with insight into his systematically organized ethics. As we will see, and as could be expected given what has been said about rationality thus far, Kant's ethics revolve around Personhood and Good Will. Kant, importantly, returns to the notion of Natural Law and Harmony we found in Plato. Thus, Kant's ethical thesis suggests that there is a way, in terms of a practical universal *logos*, to harmonize one's self with the Natural Law. Doing so leads to Self-Realization in terms of the Natural Law, understood specifically in terms of the sphere of morality, to be the Moral Law. Hence, Self-Realization in terms of Personality and Personalty harmonize the influencing forces on the Will producing the Right action, a Virtuous character, and a Good Will. These are the ingredients that make us worthy of Happiness. Kant's response to Aristotle's concerns, which include the Solon question, that is, the relation between Happiness, material goods, and death, seems to be that Happiness ultimately requires communal effort to bring about the "Kingdom of Ends," which, with its clear soteriological and teleological aspects, sounds like a description of Heaven on earth without Christian terminology, that is, in nontheistic terms.

The proper way to understand the project of German Idealism is to relate it to Kant. Sometimes Kant is counted as the first German Idealist, and sometimes his work is deemed that which launched the project of German Idealism. Basically, as Kant neared the end of his career, there were concerns he would not be able to complete the critical project he set out to complete, that is, the systematic mapping of Reason limited to its specific spheres. So, German Idealism represents a kind of "race" among German intellectuals to see who could correctly finish Kant's project first. Now, the most famous figures associated with German Idealism are Kant (1724-1804 AD), Johann Gottlieb Fichte (1762-1814 AD), Friedrich Hölderlin (1770-1843 AD), Ludwig van Beethoven (1770-1827 AD), Friedrich Wilhelm Joseph Schelling (1775-1854 AD), Novalis (1772-1801 AD), Georg Wilhelm Friedrich Hegel (1770-1831 AD), and Arthur Schopenhauer (1788-1860 AD). Thus, the question is: Which if any of these individuals completed the Kantian project? The top three answers are: Kant, Hegel, or Schopenhauer. Hence, this chapter concludes with a very brief gesture toward both Hegel and Schopenhauer, so that we may see the thinking that was developed out of Kant's philosophy. Also, as no one can fail to miss nowadays, Schopenhauer infamously is known as the greatest (and by "greatest" is meant "biggest" or "most pronounced") misogynist of the Western Tradition. As we will see, his misogyny is consistent with his philosophy of Nature. Ultimately, German Idealism represents a post-Kantian Revolution reaffirmation of the ancient Greek roots of the Western Tradition.

Moral Psychology

§2 *The Kantian Copernican Revolution*

There is a much longer and more formal way to state the Kantian Copernican Revolution; however, for our purposes, we may simply memorize the phrase: "The mind doesn't conform to objects, objects conform to the mind." (cf. Kant 1998, Bxvi). Anyone interested in a more in-depth investigation should read Kant's *Critique of Pure Reason*. The value of this, again limited to our purpose of an introduction to ethics, is that it makes rationality a condition for the possibility (remember we used the phrase in the Plato chapter) of human experience. In this way, Kant may be seen working the same Natural Function argument as Aristotle; however, Kant has retained the "Self-Realization as entry into the register of Divine Justice" aspect from Plato, though it will take the rest of this chapter to illustrate just how Kant accomplished it. The idea is that through human rationality we participate in both a species-specific community and gain access to the rule-structure of reality as it is experienced by the species-specific community. In this way, human rationality provides us with access to the Moral Law. When we choose to act in accordance with the Moral Law, our Will is in harmony with reality, allowing us to live the best possible life for a human, that is, the life humans are Naturally structured to live.

§3 Concerning the Original Predisposition to Good in Human Nature

Just as Aristotle's Two Inclinations toward the Good coincided with his Divisions, Kant takes these two inclinations and adds the component of Personhood discussed [in] Realization. Recall, these elements were indirectly located in a system together with P[lato]. They are now, explicitly so, with Kant. Thus, Kant notes regarding the Natural human [inclination] (through "inclinations") to the Good that "We may conveniently divide this predisposition, to function, into three divisions, to be considered as elements in the fixed character and d[est]iny of man": (Kant 1960, 33). Notice, Kant's clarification that this division is "with respect to function." The three divisions are:

1. "The predisposition to *animality* in man, taken as a *living* being;
2. The predisposition to *humanity* in man, taken as a living and at the same time a *rational* being;
3. The predisposition to *personality* in man, taken as a rational and at the same time an *accountable* being." (Kant 1960).

Keeping in mind, what should be increasingly clear by now, that Kant is showing us what he takes to be the system from which Plato and Aristotle developed their ethical theories, his main difference is that he is attempting to systematically reveal that system to us. Hence, just as both Plato and Aristotle discussed the role of love and self-love in regard to excellence, perfection, and Self-Realization, Kant associates three (3) different types of self-love with these dispositions.

§4 Types of Self-Love: In terms of Animality, Humanity, and Personality

In list form, here are the three (3) types of self-love Kant associates with the Natural predispositions to the Good. Keep in mind that though there is a Natural hierarchy involved, each type of self-love participates in love and in the Good.

1. "The predisposition to *animality* in mankind may be brought under the general title of physical and purely *mechanical* [deterministic] self-love, wherein no reason is demanded."
2. "The predisposition to humanity can be brought under the general title of a self-love which is physical and yet *compares* … [i.e.] we judge ourselves happy or unhappy only by making comparison with others. Out of this self-love springs the inclination *to acquire worth in the opinion of others.*"
3. "The predisposition to *personality* is the capacity for respect for the moral law as *in itself a sufficient incentive of the will.*" (Kant 1960, 34).

Notice, just as Aristotle's animal soul is without rationality, so too Kant's animality indicates a kind of love in which "no reason is demanded." The second type of self-love stems from the rational capacity of the human. Because rationality reveals *ratios*, this type of self-love compares one's self by illuminating various ratios between it and others.

...nally, the last type of self-love belongs to Personhood and the Personalty of entry into the register of the Moral Law. That is to say, rather than compare one's self to others, it is possible to love your self in regard to your "respect for the Moral Law." This is a kind of moral self-esteem, as if being able to rest assured that you are in harmony with Divine Justice and lovable from the perspective of the Divine. It is also in this way that the "respect for the moral law" is an "incentive of the will," which is "in itself sufficient." We love ourselves for being Good.

Thus, Kant—following Plato—is critical of Hume's Naturalistic philosophy. In his *Lectures on Metaphysics*, Kant explained,

> The consciousness of the ego proves that life is not located in the body, but in a special principle differing from the body; that as a consequence this principle can continue to exist without body, and that its life is not thereby diminished but augmented. This is the sole proof that can be given *a priori*, and one drawn from the knowledge and nature of the soul comprehended *a priori* by us. (2001, 176–77).

For our purposes in regard to introduction to ethics, and not metaphysics, we want to be sure to note that just as there is an order constituting some kind of Natural Law, so too there is an order constituting the Moral Law. Further, just as our bodies are already "inserted" into the order of Nature, it is up to us through the Freedom of our Will to rise up from material Nature and see ourselves in terms of the Moral Law. We may be reminded of Plato's Charioteer Allegory; however, in either case, acting in Harmony with the provision of the Moral Law, we may then navigate material Nature with a Dignity worthy of Happiness, and live (what the ancient Greeks referred to as) the Good Life.

Original Nature

§5 *The Propensity to Evil in Human Nature & the Distinction between Propensity and Predisposition*

Kant's position regarding Theodicy can be found in his "On the Failure of All Philosophical Efforts in Theodicy" from the year 1791. Discussing the story of Job from the Old Testament, Kant distinguished between "doctrinal" and "authentic" Theodicy. Using the notion of Personhood constituted by one's relation to the Moral Law, Kant praised Job for his authentic Theodicy characterized by "honesty in openly admitting one's doubts" and "repugnance to pretending conviction where one feels none." (Kant 1791, 33). In terms of Kant's Revolution, we may say that Kant is "making room for faith" in that not everything in relation to the Divine can be known. Aspects of the Divine must always remain mysterious to humans.

In accounting for "Evil," then, in terms of Human Nature, Kant distinguishes between "propensities" and "predispositions." According to Kant, "By propensity I understand the subjective ground of the possibility of an inclination (habitual craving, *concupiscentia*) so far as mankind in general is liable to it." (Kant 1960, 35). Further, "A propensity is distinguished from a predisposition by the fact that although it can indeed be innate, it *ought* not to be represented merely thus; for it can also be regarded as having been *acquired* (if it is good), or *brought* by man *upon himself* (if it is evil)." (Kant 1960).

In a gesture that both hearkens back to the discussion of the Practical Syllogism in Plato and Aristotle and also points forward to his famous Categorical Imperative, Kant clarified:

> Here, however, we are speaking only of the propensity to genuine, that is, moral evil; for
> a. since such evil is possible only as a determination of the free will, and
> b. since the will can be appraised as good or evil only by means of its maxims,
> this propensity to evil must consist in the subjective ground of the possibility of the deviation of the maxims from the moral law. (Kant, 1960).

Thus, Kant emphasizes *the distinction between the subjective and the universal aspects of each individual human being*. With this distinction Kant is able to show that evil—think Theodicy here—is not a part of human Nature universally, as if all humans were made to be evil. Rather, the propensity toward evil belongs to the subjective aspect of each individual human, and in this way, each individual is responsible for their own evil actions, that is, we cannot use Theodicy to suggest our wrongdoings were willed by God. It is with the Freedom of our *own* Will that we cultivate and pursue propensities.

Finally, it is important to note—recalling Augustine—that Kant characterizes the ability of the Will to Harmonize with the Moral Law in terms of "*a good or an evil heart.*" (Kant 1960, 35). In a move that will be quite important for us to understand the most complicated piece of Kantian ethics, Kant uses the idea of the role of *logos* or the Practical Syllogism to connect the Will, the Moral Law, and the Heart. In other words, recall that the universal part of the Practical Syllogism was called a "Maxim" or "Code of Conduct," and we even saw something similar with Rule Utilitarianism in that when you perform an action, it can be said that the action follows some Rule. Thus, for Kant, *an individual's ability to adopt the Moral Law for the determination of one's Maxims in the Practical Syllogisms guiding action reveals the extent to which the individual's Will has harmonized with the Moral Law.*

Kant clarified that "Every propensity is either physical, i.e. pertaining to the will of man as a natural being, or moral, i.e. pertaining to his will as a moral being." (Kant 1960, 36). Hence, when one is able to adopt the Moral Law for determining the Rules, Maxims, or Codes of Conduct which one follows, then one is simultaneously self-realizing in terms of the Moral Law and Harmonizing one's Will with the Moral Law. Further, because the ability to Harmonize one's Will with the Moral Law indicates a Good Heart or Goodness of the Heart, it follows that this is also how one "makes" one's Will Good. Thus, striving to be a Person by Willing as a "moral being" indicates progress toward the self-perfection of one's Self-Realization, Goodness in the Person's Heart, and acting with Good Will.

§6 *Types of Imperatives: What is Natural Law?*

An imperative is a formula for, that is, a statement of, a Command, and Kant divides imperatives into those which are *hypothetical* and those which are *categorical*. Whereas hypothetical imperatives "represent the practical necessity of a possible action *as a means* to achieving something [emphasis added]," Kant tells us the "categorical imperative would be that which represented an action as objectively necessary of itself, without reference to an other end." (Kant 2002, 25). In this way, hypothetical imperatives are formulas which function as means to an end, and a categorical imperative would be a formula which functions as an end in itself. Thus, "pick up that litter" functions as a means to an end, whereas the command to "be good" is an end in itself. Notice, hypothetical imperatives still aim at some Good, (cf. the Target Analogy), it is just that what they consider to be Good is Good as a means to some other end.

Kant characterizes the imperatives further in terms of purpose and principle. Hypothetical imperatives take some action to be Good "for some possible or actual purpose," the principles of which Kant calls "problematic" and "assertoric" respectively. In contrast, "The categorical imperative, which declares the action to be of itself objectively necessary without reference to some purpose, i.e. even apart from any other end, holds as an apodictically practical principle." (Kant 2002, 26). To clarify his terminology, "problematic" judgments regard the merely possible, "assertoric" judgments involve what is actual, and "apodictic" judgments are necessary (cf. Kant 1998, A 70/B 95).

In what may be seen as a direct attack on the Principle of Utility and Consequentialist ethics, Kant notes that following Rules as a means to the end of Happiness makes those Rules hypothetical and assertoric. Yet, the Categorical Imperative "has to do not with the matter of the action and what is to result from it, but with the form and the principle from which the action itself follows; and the essentially good in the action consists in the disposition, *let the result be what it may* [emphasis added]." (Kant 2002, 27). Moreover, according to Kant, "This imperative may be called the imperative *of morality*." (Ibid).

It may be helpful to point out that what Kant is doing here may be characterized in terms of Hobbes' re-formation of the Catholic Revolution. That is to say, it is as if Kant is attempting to give rationality the status of Nature again, while acknowledging an element of the Will is still involved in a process of Consent. In other words, just as you can deny the Law of gravity, but will ultimately *submit* to its "commands" and suffer the consequences of being its "enemy," so too you may deny the rational structure of reality, but will suffer the consequences of doing so. Kant is, of course, not a Consequentialist; however, there are still consequences to actions and those consequences may be understood as rewards or punishments. *Subjecting* one's self, through the Will, to the Unconditional Moral Law may lead to the best life possible for a human, i.e. the Good Life, beyond what may be found simply in a Kingdom of Man, as if such a division between the Kingdom of Man and the Kingdom of God neither relied on rationality to be established nor could be fully understood as distinct; hence, Kant's Revolution—as we will see by the end of this chapter—culminates in terms of a Kingdom of Ends.

As previously noted, Kant uses the Categorical Imperative to Harmonize the Will with the Moral aspect of the Natural Law. Here is the sense in which Kant's ethics as one of Duty and Obligation emerges.

> Everyone must grant that a law, if it is to hold morally, that is, as a ground of obligation, must carry with it absolute necessity ... *therefore the ground of obligation here must not be sought in the nature of the human being or in the circumstances of the world in which he is placed*, but *a priori* simply in concepts of pure reason; and that any other precept, which is based on principles of mere experience—even if it is universal in a certain respect—insofar as it rests in the least part on empirical grounds, perhaps only in terms of a motive, can indeed be called a practical rule but never a moral law [emphasis added]. (Kant 1960, 57).

Notice Kant equates empirical principles with hypothetical commands, and rules them out as unable to meet the criteria of absolute necessity. The Natural Law is both universal and necessary. As an analogy, consider how the Law of Gravity *necessarily* holds for all of us, that is, *universally*. In this way, just as we are "obligated" to abide by the Law of Gravity as pertaining to the physical part of the Natural Law, so too we are obligated to act according to Maxims, Rules, or a Code of Conduct which pertains to the Moral part of the Natural Law.

Were we to think of Kant's discussion here in terms of Plato and the Stoics or even Christianity, it would be possible to think of Kant as making the suggestion that by finding the appropriate *logos*, we may appropriately harmonize our Will with the universal *Logos* and the universal Will. This would be both in terms of Natural Law and Divine, Moral, Justice. Consider Kant's comments in this regard:

> Since the universality of law in accordance with which effects take place constitutes what is properly called *nature* in the most general sense (as regards its form)—that is, the existence of things insofar as it is determined in accordance with universal laws—the universal imperative of duty can also go as follows: *act as if the maxim of your action were to become by your will a universal law of nature.* (Kant 2002, 31).

Thus, it would be as if Kant were saying that by following the Categorical Imperative (which we will discuss momentarily), we can rationally ensure our Will's functioning in accordance with the universal higher Will, whether we call that Celestial Be-ing, that is, the Will of humans regarded as Moral beings, a craftsman-like fire, the Holy Spirit, or simply the Will of Divine Justice.

§7 *The Natural Human Obligation to be Morally Excellent: Virtues as Duty-Based*

Before discussing the Categorical Imperative, the purpose of this section is simply to look at Kant's characterization of Virtue, as if in terms of Divine Function, as based in Duty. From his work *The Metaphysics of Morals*, in the section titled "The Doctrine of Virtue," Kant divides "duties to oneself" according to "what is formal and what is material," suggesting the former are "limiting (negative) duties" and the latter are "widening (positive duties to oneself)." (Kant 2012, 174). Kant then explains,

> Negative duties *forbid* a human being to act contrary to the end of his nature and so have to do merely with his moral *self-preservation*; positive duties, which *command* him to make a certain object of choice on his end, concern his *perfecting* of himself. Both of them belong to virtue, either as duties of omission or as duties of commission, but both belong to it as duties of virtue. (Ibid).

As if emphasizing the physician analogy we discussed in our Plato chapter, Kant associates Virtue with "moral health." Regarding the duties of omission or commission the "first belong to the moral health of a human being as object of both his outer senses and his inner sense, to the *preservation* of his nature in its perfection." (Kant, 2012, 174). Further, the "second belong to his moral prosperity, which consists in possessing a *capacity* sufficient for all his ends, insofar as this can be acquired; they belong to his *cultivation* (active perfecting) of himself." (Kant 2012, 174–5). Thus, in this way,

> The first principle of duty to oneself lies in the dictum "live in conformity with nature," that is, *preserve* yourself in the perfection of your nature; the second, in the saying "*make yourself more perfect than mere nature has made you.*" (Kant 2012, 175).

Whereas the above division of Duties to oneself was "objective" the following list of virtues and vices—reminiscent of Aristotle's *Nicomachean Ethics*—derive from a "subjective" division of Duties to oneself.

Thus, "There will be a *subjective* division of a human being's duties to himself, that is, one in terms of whether the subject of duty (the human being) views himself both as an animal (natural) and a moral being[,] or only as a moral being." (Ibid).

In regard to "impulses of nature having to do with man's animality:

> Through them nature aims at
> (a) his self-preservation,
> (b) the preservation of the species, and
> (c) the preservation of his capacity to enjoy life, though still on the animal level only. —
>
> The vices that are here opposed to his duty to himself are:
> [a] *murdering himself,*
> [b] the unnatural use of his *sexual inclination,* and
> [c] such *excessive consumption of food and drink* as weakens his capacity for making purposive use of his powers." (Ibid).

In regard to "a human being's duty to himself as a moral being only (without taking his animality into consideration) consists in what is *formal* in the consistency of the [M]axims of his [W]ill with the *dignity* of humanity in his person.

> It consists, therefore, in a prohibition against depriving himself of the *prerogative* of a moral being, that of acting in accordance with principles, that is, inner freedom, and so making himself a plaything of the mere inclinations and hence a thing. —
>
> The vices contrary to this duty are
>
> [d] lying,
> [e] avarice,
> [f] and false humility (servility).
>
> These adopt principles that are directly contrary to his character as a moral being (in terms of its very form), that is, to inner freedom, the innate dignity of a human being, which is tantamount

to saying that they make it one's basic principle to have no basic principle and hence no character, that is, to throw oneself away and make oneself an object of contempt. —

The virtue that is opposed to all these vices could be called love of honor, a cast of mind far removed from ambition. But it will appear prominently later on, under this name." (Kant 2012, 175).

Placed in list form, the above extended quote from Kant speaks for itself. However, be sure to notice, generally, the sense in which the above is a gesture toward systematizing the content of the earlier chapters regarding the ancient Greek roots of the Western Tradition, and, specifically, the sense in which Kant has determined Moral Excellence to be a Duty.

§8 *The Categorical Imperative: The Supreme Principle of Morality in the Analogy of the City and the Soul*

Given all that has been said thus far in this chapter, we have finally reached a point at which we can discuss Kant's formula for determining if one is acting appropriately. It is, of course, called "The Categorical Imperative," and it is notorious for baffling individuals who wish to be introduced to Kant's ethics. What we must realize immediately is that Kant actually provides three (3) different formulations of the Categorical Imperative, that is, in terms of the principle of the law of nature, the principle of ends, and the principle of autonomy. Kant tells us the formulations are equivalent. Though, before we can look at the latter formulations, we need to get clear on the first. Therefore, the majority of this section will be devoted to understanding the first formulation; moreover, Kant tells us it is by way of this formulation that we should "proceed in moral appraisal."

Recalling the Analogy of the City and the Soul from Plato's *Republic*, there was a direct analogy from the ability of the individual to hear the *logos* of Divine Justice to the ability of the Philosopher-King to be a Good lawmaker. Though Kant does not explicitly state it, this is precisely the pattern at work behind the different formulations of the Categorical Imperative. According to Kant, then, there is "only a single categorical imperative," it is:

act only in accordance with that maxim through which you can at the same time will that it become a universal law (Kant 2001, 31).

Or put in the first-person: "I ought never to act except in such a way that I could also Will that my Maxim should become a universal law." (Kant 2002, 15). Now, before looking at Kant's examples, consider the Categorical Imperative as it relates to our previous Practical Syllogism discussions. There we noted that the appropriate *logos* refers to the universal premise, or Maxim, involved in the Practical Syllogism. Thus, Kant believes he has provided the test we may use to determine if the Maxim in our Practical Syllogism is in conformity with the Moral Law.

Hence, when we are attempting to decide which action to perform in a situation, we recognize the particulars in the situation and when we notice the Maxim, Rule, or Code of Conduct out of which our action is to follow, then we apply the Categorical Imperative. If it turns out from applying the Categorical Imperative that we cannot Will that our Maxim be universal law, then we are not acting from Duty to the Moral

Law. This is the case, of course, since the Moral Law, like the Natural Law, is necessary and universal. So, on the one hand, if your Maxim can not be Willed universally, then the action you would perform from such a non-universalizable Maxim would not be in Harmony with the Moral Law. On the other hand, if your Maxim is in Harmony with the Moral Law, then you may be acting with a Good Will.

The following four examples all come from Kant's discussion of the Categorical Imperative:

1) "Someone feels sick of life because of a series of troubles that has grown to the point of despair…" (Kant 2002, 31). According to Kant, were such a person to commit suicide, the Maxim, Rule, or Code of Conduct he would be following would be something like: "from self-love I make it my principle to shorten my life when its longer duration threatens more troubles than it promises agreeableness." (Kant 2002, 32). However, Kant suggests "that maxim could not possibly be a law of nature and, accordingly, altogether opposes the supreme principle of all duty." (Ibid). In sum, we might say that were this Maxim to be Willed universally, humans would cease to survive; therefore, it cannot be in Harmony with the Moral aspect of the Natural Law.

2) "Another finds himself urged by need to borrow money. He well knows that he will not be able to repay it but sees also that nothing will be lent him unless he promises firmly to repay it within a determinate time." (Kant 2002, 32). According to Kant, were such a person to borrow money, the Maxim he would be following would be something like: "when I believe myself to be in need of money I shall borrow money and promise to repay it, even though I know that this will never happen." (Ibid). However, Kant suggests "I then see at once that it could never hold as a universal law of nature," for were everyone to Will thus, then no one would ever lend again. In sum, we might say that were this Maxim to be Willed universally, humans would cease to trust anyone else's promises, everyone knowing that promises are not made to be kept—according to this Maxim, were it universalized; therefore, it cannot be in Harmony with the Moral aspect of the Natural Law.

3) "A third finds in himself a talent that by means of some cultivation could make him a human being useful for all sorts of purposes. However, he finds himself in comfortable circumstances and prefers to give himself up to pleasure than to trouble himself with enlarging and improving his fortunate natural predispositions." (Kant 2002, 32). However, Kant suggests this could not be Willed as universal law or Natural Instinct. In sum, we might say that were this Maxim to be Willed universally, humans would cease to develop their natural capacities, and because Kant sees the development of one's capacities to be Natural, he believes such a Maxim could not be in Harmony with the Natural Law.

4) Finally, someone "for whom things are going well while he sees that others (whom he could very well help) have to contend with great hardships, thinks: what is it to me? let each be as happy as heaven wills or as he can make himself…" (Kant 2002, 33). However, Kant suggests "a will that decided this would conflict with itself, since many cases could occur in which one would need the love and sympathy of others…" (Ibid). In sum, we might say that were this Maxim to be Willed universally, humans would no longer help each other; therefore, it cannot be in Harmony with the Moral aspect of the Natural Law.

Were we to articulate a name for the Duties which may correspond, then, to each of the above situations, they may be: "preserve your life"; "be truthful"; "assure your own happiness"; "to be beneficent." Thus, were individuals to follow the maxims in Kant's previous examples, they would not be in conformity with the just listed Duties, and they would be alienated from themselves. That is, a kind of Incongruence would manifest internally for each.

Lastly, by working through the above examples, Kant arrives at a second formulation of the Categorical Imperative. He characterizes this formulation in terms of the "principle of ends," and before explaining the third formulation and the interrelation between the three, the following general remarks will prove helpful. The three (3) formulations, then, of the Categorical Imperative are:

1) The Principle of the Law of Nature: "Act only in accordance with that maxim through which you can at the same time will that it become a universal law" (Kant 2002, 31).
2) The Principle of Ends: "So act that you use humanity, whether in your own person or in the person of any other, always at the same time as an end, never merely as a means." (Kant 2002, 38).
3) The Principle of Autonomy: "The principle of every human will as a will giving universal law through all its maxims." (Kant 2002, 40).

Thus, we can see from the term "autonomous" itself, that is, it includes the ancient Greek "auto" and "nomos," that the autonomous Will is a "self law-giving" or "self legislating" Will. Such a Will is one that has achieved its perfection in Freedom.

Whereas the principle of the law of nature, that is, the first formulation of the Categorical Imperative emphasized the *form* of the Supreme Principle of Morality, the principle of ends emphasizes its *matter*. Thus, Kant calls the third and final formulation of the Categorical Imperative the Supreme Principle of Morality itself. It is as if the efficient and final causes are expressed in the third formulation, and, therefore, coincide with the Supreme Principle itself. This makes sense if we realize that, in Kant's words, the Supreme Principle of Morality is the "Autonomy of the Will." In other words, a Will in conformity with the Moral Law relating to the material of its deliberations as ends, and not means, accomplishes its Self-Perfection as its very purpose. Hence, the Autonomous Will is both efficient cause of Moral Goodness and the fulfillment of its own purpose, that is, the achievement of Moral Goodness and Freedom. In this way, Kant's section on Happiness will discuss the Freedom of the Will, the Kingdom of Ends, which is seen by moving from the Soul to the City in the Analogy of the City and the Soul, and the differentiating factor distinguishing the perfection of the Will in the Morally Excellent Person, that is, the Virtuosity of Will as Goodness of Heart.

Happiness: Good Will, Goodness in the Heart, & The Kingdom of Ends

§9 *Freedom/Autonomy of the Will: What is a Good Will?*

In criticism of both Aquinas and the Naturalism vs. Evil debate, Kant tells us "the source of evil cannot lie in an object determining the will through inclination [cf. Aquinas' four principles of moral action], nor yet in a natural impulse, it can lie only in *a rule made by the will for the use of its freedom, that is in a maxim.*" (Kant 1960, 17). In this way Kant seems to undercut Hume's attempt to make passion sovereign. That is to say, the question—as Hume seemed to take it—is not between whether passions are evil or not. Were this the question, then Hume could argue that because they are Natural, we should either not consider them evil or shift the burden to Theodicy. However, Kant is suggesting here, in a move that Nietzsche will especially emphasize later, that the question is not whether Original Nature is evil or not; the question is how do we relate to it and what do we do with it?

Using the word "dignity," while sounding as if describing the Great-Souled Person, Kant characterizes Duty in terms of Freedom:

> although in thinking the concept of duty we think of subjection to the law, yet at the same time we thereby represent a certain sublimity and *dignity* in the person who fulfills all his duties. For there is indeed no sublimity in him insofar as he is subject to the moral law, but there certainly is insofar as he is at the same time lawgiving with respect to it and only for that reason subordinated to it. (Kant 2002, 46).

As one commentator put it, "The laws of the kingdom of ends are the laws of freedom, both because it is the mark of free citizens to make their own laws, and because the content of those laws directs us to respect each citizen's free use of his or her own reason." (Korsgaard 2006, xxv). Hence, the same move we noticed just above, that is, that evil is determined in regard to one's maxim, shows us how Goodness is determined in regard to the Will. Kant explains,

> But since it may well be that … man as a species is neither good nor bad [i.e. regarding Hume's Nihilism], or at all events that he is as much the one as the other, partly good, partly bad. We call a man evil, however, not because he performs actions that are evil (contrary to law) but because these actions are of such a nature that we may infer from them the presence in him of evil maxims. (Kant 1960, 16).

Having located the determining feature of evil in human Maxims, Kant is able to make the connection between Freedom and Goodness in the Will. That is, someone with evil maxims—to use the ancient Greek phrase—is a Slave to appetites, that is, one has not achieved Self-Mastery.

In this way, Kant couples Freedom and Necessity by noting that the Will is always Free (though it can submit itself through ignorance, etc. into slavery) and the Law (in both its Natural and Moral manifestations) is always Necessary. In regard to such conditions,

> A good will is not good because of what it effects or accomplishes, because of its fitness to attain some proposed end, but only because of its volition, that is, it is good in itself and, regarded for itself, is to be valued incomparably higher than all that could merely be brought about by it in favor of some inclination (Kant 2002, 8).

The Good Will Freely chooses to follow the Law. This leaves us with one last clarification before moving from this examination of Good Will at the level of the Soul to the level of the City. That is, what of the difference between the Will that follows Necessity due to Necessity and the Will that follows Necessity due to

Freedom? Notice, there is a direct analogy here between the Continent and the Virtuous Character Types in Aristotle, and Kant refers to this distinction as the Difference between a Person of Good Morals and a Morally Good Person.

To ensure Freedom of the Will, and thereby to ensure its highest Dignity and Goodness, Kant provides clarification regarding Duty:

(1) An action must not be simply in conformity with duty but also *from duty*.
(2) "An action from duty has its moral worth *not in the purpose* to be attained by it but in the maxim in accordance with which it is decided upon, and therefore does not depend upon the realization of the object of the action but merely upon the *principle of volition* in accordance with which the action is done without regard for any object of the faculty of desire."
(3) "*Duty is the necessity of an action from respect for the law*." (Kant 1960, 62–63)

§10 *Difference Between a Person of Good Morals and a Morally Good Person*

The distinction between a Person of Good Morals and a Morally Good Person is such a potent distinction that it receives its own section. There is much one can do with this distinction; however, for our purposes, we will merely explain it. Again, it maps onto the distinction between the Continent and Virtuous Character Types in Aristotle. Kant tells us, "For, in the case of what is to be morally good it is not enough that it *con[-]form* with the moral law but it must also be done *for the sake of the law*; without this, that conformity is only very contingent and precarious." (2002, 3). Being done for the sake of the law indicates the "respect for the Moral Law" that conditioned one's Personality. It is also the Freedom, we may say, that allows one autonomous Personalty, that is, Self Ownership.

We may go so far, then, as to say that the supervening piece for Kant would be the awareness of participation in universal Will, that is, Spirit. Here is Kant's extended and definitive statement regarding the distinction.

> There is no difference, however, as regards conformity of conduct to the moral law, between *a man of good morals* and *a morally good man* … save that the conduct of the one [former] has not always, perhaps has never, the law as its sole and supreme incentive while the conduct of the other [latter] has it *always*. Of the former it can be said: He obeys the law according to the *letter* (that is, his conduct conforms to what the law commands); but of the second: he obeys the law according to the *spirit* … 'Whatever is not of this faith is sin' … For when incentives other than the law itself are necessary to determine the will to conduct conformable to the law, it is merely accidental that these causes coincide with the law… (Kant 1960, 35–36).

Thus, without respect for the Moral Law one performs actions consistent with Good Will, without having Goodness in the Heart. It is as if conformity with the Moral Law and Duty perhaps makes us worthy of Happiness. However, it is Goodness of the Heart that may be understood as the supervening feature determining when Will is truly Good Will and the obedient Heart has been made Happy.

§11 *The Kingdom of Ends: The Starry Heavens Above & the Moral Law Within*

In his *Lectures on Ethics*, Kant credited Augustine as an influence, that is, the *City of God*, regarding the "Kingdom of Ends." (Kant 1997, 246). Kant contrasts the Kingdom of Nature with the Kingdom of Ends, and just as with the more Platonic ancient Greeks we were able to think of self-perfection regarding Natural Law as participation in Divine Justice, Kant sees the Kingdom of Ends as emerging from the Kingdom of Nature, climbing from animality and humanity to personality in regard to the Moral Law. Here is Kant's technical description from the *Critique of Practical Reason*.

> Now, nature in the most general sense is the existence of things under laws. The sensible nature of rational beings in general is their existence under empirically conditioned laws and is thus, for reason, *heteronomy*. The supersensible nature of the same beings, on the other hand, is their existence in accordance with laws that are independent of any empirical condition and thus belong to the *autonomy* of pure reason. And since the laws by which the existence of things depends on cognition are practical, supersensible nature, so far as we can make for ourselves a concept of it, is nothing other than *a nature under the autonomy of pure practical reason*. The law of this autonomy, however, is the moral law, which is therefore the fundamental law of a supersensible nature and of a pure world of the understanding, the counterpart of which is to exist in the sensible world but without infringing upon its laws. (Kant 1999, 38).

Kant's contrast between sensible nature and supersensible nature reminds us that humans as rational animals have two perspectives on the same thing. By cultivating the "higher" rational perspective, one can relate even to one's self in such a way, and in doing so, one realizes the autonomy of the Will. In order to do so, one must conform to the Moral Law to free one's self from the animality of the body enough to be able to witness the Will's Freedom. Kant tells us, "Autonomy of the will is the property of the will by which it is a law to itself." (Kant 2002, 47). Thus, conformity with the Moral Law brings Personhood and Dignity individually, and moving from the Soul to the City, it brings about the Kingdom of Ends from out of the Kingdom of Nature.

The Kingdom of Ends and the be-ing of a Morally Good Person constitute Kant's soteriology. Also, recalling Plato and Aristotle, moving from the Soul to the City in terms of *logos* to *nomos*, Kant notes,

> The concept of every rational being as one who must regard himself as giving universal law through all the maxims of his will, so as to appraise himself and his actions from this point of view, leads to a very fruitful concept dependent upon it, namely that of a *kingdom of ends*. (Kant 2002, 41).

Further, Kant tells us, "By a kingdom I understand a systematic union of various rational beings through common laws." (Kant 2002, 41). And, "since *laws determine ends in terms of their universal validity* [emphasis added]

> if we abstract from the personal differences of rational beings as well as from all the content of their private ends we shall be able to think of a whole of all ends in systematic connection (a whole both of rational beings as ends in themselves and of the ends of his own that each may set himself), that is, a kingdom of ends, which is possible in accordance with the above principles. (Ibid).

For Kant, then the Kingdom of Ends is populated by rational be-ings with the Spirit of Goodness in their Hearts. This is the City of Happiness in which each has Dignity and Autonomy. It is "the idea of a pure world of understanding as a whole of all intelligences, to which we ourselves belong as rational beings (though on the other side we are also members of the world of sense)" (Kant 2002, 66).

Hegel: The Phenomenology of Spirit & The Philosophy of Right

§12 *Return to an Optimistic-Trinitarian Reading of Spirit*

The purpose of this section is simply to provide a passage from G.W.F. Hegel for the purpose of discussion and to show one of the German Idealist ways of reading Kant's philosophy toward its completion, that is, as it pertains to ethics. Keeping in mind the idea of Self-Realization from out of the Natural Law to Autonomy of the Will in regard to the Moral Law, consider the following from Hegel's *Philosophy of Right*:

> A person must translate his freedom into an external sphere in order to exist as Idea. Personality is the first, still wholly abstract, determination of the absolute and infinite will, and therefore this sphere distinct from the person, the sphere capable of embodying his freedom, is likewise determined as what is immediately different and separable from him. (Hegel 1967, 40).

In order to comprehend Hegel's insight, think of how the movement of Self-Realization in Kant ends with an awareness of the Freedom of the Will; however, it must have been the case that the Will was constitutionally Free the whole time. In other words, it was what Plato might call the not Recollecting the appropriate *logos* that causes the Self to not realize it is Free, despite its inherent Freedom. Thus, with Hegel we can take the Freedom of the Will and the Autonomous Self to be present at the beginning (cf. Hegel 1977, §§157, 165, & 176), though present without the excellence and perfection of Self-Knowledge (i.e., it is a Self that has not completed the movement of "Know thy Self").

In this way, note the first line of the Hegel quote above. It is as if we "translate" our Freedom into "an external sphere" when we satisfy the various Desires we have, for example, for Property and various forms of Recognition. In doing so, it is not the Self so much that is revealing itself through the "translation," but rather the progress of the Self in its movement toward Self-Realization. Hence, for Hegel, the universal Spirit (2) of which we are individual expressions is always already Good (1), and its return into itself at the level of each individual (3), which brings about the Kingdom of Ends, is the Self-Realization of Spirit Itself.

Schopenhauer: The World as Will & Representation

§13 *Return to a Pessimistic-Skeptical Reading of the Stoic Craftsman-like Fire*

We ought to be able to see Hegel's reworking of Kant's Kingdom of Ends as optimistic, since the attributes of Harmony, Justice, and Goodness are associated with the movement of Self-Realization. However, Arthur

Schopenhauer provides a more pessimistic reading of Kant. Schopenhauer seems to have a strong grasp on Kant's "transcendental" relation to reality. Famously Schopenhauer began his book *The World as Will and Representation* with the following homage to Kant's Revolution:

> "The world is my representation": this is a truth valid with reference to every living and knowing being, although man alone can bring it into reflective, abstract consciousness. If he really does so, philosophical discernment has dawned on him. It then becomes clear and certain to him that he does not know a sun and an earth, but only an eye that sees a sun, a hand that feels an earth; that the world around him is there only as representation, in other words, only in reference to another thing, namely that which represents, and this is himself. If any truth can be expressed *a priori*, it is this; for it is the statement of that form of all possible and conceivable experience, a form that is more general than all others, than time, space, and causality, for all these presuppose it. (Schopenhauer 1969, 3).

Of all that could be said of Schopenhauer's comment here, we want to recognize that he is emphasizing the Will as the "condition for the possibility" of experiencing the world. In this way, Schopenhauer is emphasizing the universal Will as more primary than its individual expressions. The idea, as we will see in more detail shortly, is that the universal Will expresses itself as individual rational human beings, and at the level of each individual "the world around him is there only as representation." Now, as we have seen above, on the one hand, this representation is relative to the individual expression of the Will's self-realization. On the other hand, also consistent with Kant, it begins in Nature and perfects itself toward the Kingdom of Ends.

The pessimistic reading comes, then, from what Schopenhauer takes to be a twofold insight. First, the attributes of Harmony, Justice, and Goodness apply to the universal Will, yet the human must *live* the individual expression of the universal at the level of the multiplicity of individual selves, which are all in the process of striving for Self-Realization. Moreover, Schopenhauer sees the universal Will as blind to the suffering of its individual expressions, especially insofar as the human lived-experience of that suffering functions as a Willing sacrifice by the universal Will to return to itself. Second, and this point is illuminated by the previous points, from the perspective of the lived-experience of the human along the trajectory of Self-Realization, much of life is illusion. What is more, combining the two points, it is illusion, that is, filled with illusory representations relative to the Self-Realization of our autonomy, and, moreover, we are subjected to the viciousness of the less Self-Realized individuals.

It is in this context that Schopenhauer's comments regarding women should be understood. He is lamenting what he calls the "conjurer's trick" of Nature. That is, that the world is represented as if holding a tremendous amount of hope, promise, and beauty; however, he understands this to be a "trick" of Nature for the sake of procreation and continuation of the species. In even just one of Schopenhauer's aphorisms we find three of his infamously oft-quoted pinnacles of pessimism. From his essay titled "On the Suffering of the World" from §156 we hear the following:

(1) "We can also regard our life as a uselessly disturbing episode in the blissful repose of nothingness. At all events even the man who has fared tolerably well, becomes more clearly aware, the longer he

lives, that life on the whole is *a disappointment, nay a cheat*, in other words, bears the character of a great mystification or even a fraud."

(2) "Whoever lives *two* or *three generations*, feels like the spectator who, during the fair, sees the performances of all kinds of jugglers and, if he remains seated in the booth, sees them repeated two or three times. As the tricks were meant only for one performance, they no longer make any impression after the illusion and novelty have worn off."

(3) "Let us for a moment imagine that the act of procreation were not a necessity or accompanied by intense pleasure, but a matter of pure rational deliberation; could then the human race really continue to exist? Would not everyone rather feel so much sympathy for the coming generation that he would prefer to spare it the burden of existence, or at any rate would not like to assume in cold blood the responsibility of imposing on it such a burden?—The world is just a *hell* and in it human beings are the tortured souls on the one hand, and the devils, on the other." (Schopenhauer 2005, 35–36).

Thus Schopenhauer is in harmony with the sentiment expressed in Shakespeare's first Scene from *Much Ado about Nothing*:

"Friendship is constant in all other things,
Save in the office and affairs of love:
Therefore, all hearts in love use their own tongues;
Let every eye negotiate for itself,
And trust no agent: for beauty is a witch,
Against whose charms faith melteth into blood."

Hence, it is as if Schopenhauer's pessimistic reading of the Target Analogy would suggest that we select various targets in regard to Natural Function; however, were we at a greater stage of Self-Realization, we would know better, and in this way, Nature is illusory and punishes us even for playing along. The lived-experience in the service of the universal Will's return to itself is like a torturous Wheel of (re)incarnation.

Appendix I

§1 *Ancient Greek "Socratic" Wisdom School Charts*

There are ten primary questions and topics which we can examine in order to differentiate between the Socratic schools. Those questions and topics are: (a) How should we relate to pleasure? (b) What is a wise person (sage) like? (c) Should we follow social conventions? (d) What is the purpose of speaking (Is it/why is it good to speak)? (e) How should we relate to/think of death? (f) How should we relate to/think of chance/fate? (g) How should we relate to/think of possessions? (h) What does it mean to be in a state of /how can we find tranquility? (i) What is the proper use of rationality, or what can be known? (j) When is it/what is appropriate to doubt?

A. Pleasure	F. Chance/Fate
B. The Sage/The Wise Person	G. Possessions
C. Social Conventions	H. Tranquility
D. Purpose of Speech	I. Rationality/Knowledge
E. Death	J. Use of Doubt

Schools	Pleasure
Hedonist	Best of all.
Skeptic	Not certain.
Stoic	If present, enjoy. If not, then do not seek or avoid.
Cynic	Worst of all.

Schools	Death
Hedonist	Nothing to us.
Skeptic	Cannot know what it is.
Stoic	Can be motivational, but not to be feared.
Cynic	Might be best of all.

Schools	Social Conventions
Hedonist	Follow if pleasurable.
Skeptic	Follow as given, but question.
Stoic	Follow as given, but do not seek or avoid.
Cynic	Reject.

Schools	Purpose of Speech
Hedonist	Pleasure.
Skeptic	Therapy.
Stoic	Therapy.
Cynic	Repulsion/Frustration

APPENDIX I

Schools	Chance/Fate
Hedonist	Chance.
Skeptic	Cope with but cannot know.
Stoic	Fate.
Cynic	Chance.

Schools	Possessions
Hedonist	Good if they bring pleasure.
Skeptic	Cope with but cannot know.
Stoic	Not wanting to save or remove.
Cynic	Should not desire.

Schools	Use of Doubt
Hedonist	Useful for distinguishing/maintaining pleasures.
Skeptic	As needed/therapy.
Stoic	To avoid im/compulsion.
Cynic	Good to doubt others who would pervert us.

Schools	Rationality/Knowledge
Hedonist	Good b/c pleasurable. Use to direct toward pleasure.
Skeptic	Illusory
Stoic	Clear & Distinct. Use to guard against phantasms.
Cynic	Mind is only true possession. Use to avoid being persuaded toward social sentiment.

Schools	Tranquility
Hedonist	Pleasure.
Skeptic	*Aporetic*.
Stoic	Not seeking/avoiding.
Cynic	Away from society.

Schools	Sage
Hedonist	Maximizes pleasure.
Skeptic	Remains at *aporia*.
Stoic	Affirms fate.
Cynic	Saves mind from imprisonment.

Appendix II

19ᵗʰ-Century Existentialism: The Solitude of Existence & The Mystery of Life

> "What I really need is to get clear about what I must do…
> What matters is to find a purpose … the crucial thing is to find a truth which is truth for me,
> to find the idea for which I am willing to live and die."[31]
> ~Søren Kierkegaard

Kierkegaard: Purity of Heart is to Will One Thing

§1 *Stages Along Life's Way: Life is not a problem to be solved; it is a mystery to be lived*

In what may be understood as Søren Kierkegaard's (1813–1855 AD) Christianized reading of Plato's *scala amoris* or his existential reading of Self-Realization toward the Kingdom of Ends, the notion of "Stages Along Life's Way" refers to a key theme from his writings (Kierkegaard 1988). There are three (3) stages. They are (1) the aesthetic, (2) the ethical, and (3) the religious (cf. Kierkegaard 1983; cf. Kierkegaard 1987; cf. Kierkegaard 1988). As if attempting to synthesize Hegel and Schopenhauer, while ultimately returning to Kant, Kierkegaard understands each of these stages as coinciding with a kind of despair. Thus, the different types of despair are: (1) "in despair not to be conscious of having a self." (2) "in despair not to will to be oneself," and (3) "in despair to will to be oneself," respectively. Kierkegaard defines despair as a condition characterized by "constantly dying," despite "not being able to die" (Kierkegaard 1980; cf. Kierkegaard 2009; cf. Kierkegaard 1998). According to Kierkegaard, the individual's self is not able to die until it establishes a relation to something that does not change; otherwise, it must continue to change, that is, "constantly die." Though a number of clarifications need to be made, the one constant, according to Kierkegaard, which does not change is God. Therefore, the relation to God allows one to be lifted from despair and to accomplish the perfection of Self-Realization.

There are two hidden references to Plato. First, "constantly dying" could refer to the Wheel of (re) incarnation; however, Kierkegaard, following Augustine, does not believe in reincarnation, so this type of "constantly dying" must refer to a process taking place during one's lifetime. Second, recall the Platonic idea (we quoted Heraclitus regarding it also) that suggested our current state of *embodiment is death for the soul.* It is as if Kierkegaard has Christianized that idea and combined it with Kant's Kingdom of Ends. In other words, just as Plato was concerned with Divine Justice and the self-perfection of Self-Realization through Harmony with Divine Justice, Kant's movement of Self-Realization resulted in *autonomy in relation* to the *unchanging* Moral Law. Finally, just as Kant suggested he was critiquing reason to make room for faith, Kierkegaard's stages are such that the second still clings to reason and the third clings to faith. Hence, the idea that the individual Self "can die" may be contextualized as release from the Wheel of (re)incarnation in Plato or Self-Realization as an individual expression of universal Spirit/Will in German Idealism.

Now, before hearing Kierkegaard's technical definition of the Self, consider the Character Types he associates with each Stage along Life's Way. First, because the aesthetic stage (associated with the perennial "libertine and seducer" Don Juan, depicted for example in Mozart's 1787 opera *Don Giovanni*) may be characterized in terms of a willingness toward *self*-destruction, Kierkegaard suggests the type of despair associated with the aesthetic stage is not "despair in the strict sense." Therefore, there are really only two forms of despair in the strict sense. The first type of genuine despair coincides with the ethical stage, and an individual in this stage is known as the "Knight of Infinite Resignation" (KIR). The second type coincides with the religious stage, and such an individual is known as the "Knight of Faith" (KOF).

Kierkegaard's explication of these two forms of despair provides his understanding of the "self." According to Kierkegaard,

> A human being is spirit. But what is spirit? Spirit is the self. But what is the self? The self is a relation that relates itself to itself or is the relation's relating itself to itself in the relation; the self is not the relation but is the relation's relating itself to itself. … thus under the qualification of the psychical the relation between the psychical and the physical is a relation. If, however, the relation relates itself to itself, this relation is the positive third, and this is the self. [Lastly,] Such a relation that relates itself to itself, a self, must either have established itself or have been established by another. (Kierkegaard 1980, 13).

Notice, there are three points we want to be clear on from the above. First, Kierkegaard indicates two different answers regarding the identity of the Self. On the one hand, the Self is a relation that relates itself to itself. This will be the first strict form of despair and the Character Type involved here is the Knight of Infinite Resignation. On the other hand, the Self may be the relation that relates itself to itself while in relation to an absolute unchanging dimension. As we have seen, for Plato that is Divine Justice, for Kant it is the Moral Law, and for Kierkegaard it is God. Whereas both of the two constitutions of the Self may relate to others, only the latter enters into a relation with a being that does not change, that is, God.

Second, because Kierkegaard understands human be-ing to be a spiritual kind of be-ing, the relation between what may be termed the "soul" and the "body" is "under the qualification of the psychical." In other words, the body ultimately expresses the soul and the soul's activity; therefore, concern for the soul takes primacy over concern for the body. Though it is true that for Kierkegaard, "Death erases all distinctions…"

(1962, 74), the soul retains the quality (developed through embodied existence) of its relation to the absolute (cf. Scalambrino 2015b). This is Kierkegaard's way of providing a Christianized version of what throughout this book we have been calling the excellence of Self-Perfection in regard to Self-Realization. Put another way, in order for a Person to realize the Dignity of Self, there must be a stable Self so that through the lived-experience, that is, "when the single individual fights for himself with himself within himself" (Kierkegaard 1993, 143; cf. Kierkegaard 1983; cf. Kierkegaard 1987), the individual may acquire "self-ownership." However, by resisting God's Judgment, an individual is unable to be their true Self, rather pursuing "one of anxiety's possibilities … leads [one] away from [one's] self" (Kierkegaard 1980, 37; cf. Kierkegaard 1981), and therefore the individual cannot "own" their own existence. Thus, without the Harmony of such a Self-relation, the individual retains the "sickness unto death."

§2 *Mysterium Coniunctionis: The Hierosgamos of Piety*

In addition to characterizing each of the Stages and Character Types in terms of Death, Kierkegaard also characterizes them in terms of Love. That is, each Self along the trajectory of Self-Realization toward the Kingdom of Ends may be characterized in terms of Self-Love. According to Kant, the three types are animality, humanity, and personality. Kierkegaard provides the exact same typology, though more explicitly Christianized. That is, the aesthetic understands love in terms of animality, and thus seems to want to not be conscious of being an individual expression of universal Spirit/Will, that is, having a Self. At the same time, the Knight of Infinite Resignation still clings to a rational Self-understanding. Moreover, in a move hearkening back to our discussion of Orpheus, Kierkegaard's description of the Character Types in regard to the loss of love may be even more telling.

Following Kierkegaard's discussion of the theme, imagine you are deeply in love with someone. Now, suppose that person dies. How do you react? The question is not asking whether you become upset. The question is asking, how do you live afterward? If you eventually "move on" and find someone else to love, then Kierkegaard would locate you in the aesthetic stage. For Kierkegaard the stage a Character Type occupies, in terms of love, doubly reflects itself. That is to say, for the aesthetic stage, this means both that you believe the one you love is replaceable and that you have a kind of Self-Love that seems open to continually changing what it loves. This is why Kierkegaard suggests it is a kind of Will to Self-destruction, in that such an individual does not try to stop the "constant dying," the constantly changing as a Person in relation to what they love.

Next, keeping with the example, suppose you decide that you loved the person who is now dead, so much that you refuse to "move on." That is, with perfect rationality, you recognize that you cannot be with this person, since the person is dead, and so you stand "infinitely resigned" to accept a destiny of never loving another again. This is the approach of the Knight of Infinite Resignation. Can you notice how this Character Type lines up with a Person of Good Morals in Kant or the Incontinent Type in Aristotle? The idea is basically that the Knight of Infinite Resignation performs the right action; however, the Self-Love is one that is filled with melancholia. This kind of Self-Love is not perfect. It is not in Harmony with the universal Spirit's Self-Love.

Finally, consider how the Knight of Faith responds. Kierkegaard tells us the Knight of Faith believes that "with God all things are possible." This is beyond Reason. Whereas the aesthetic used Reason for its own gain, and the Knight of Infinite Resignation used Reason in the attempt to determine itself, the Knight of Faith is the only one who truly allows its Self to be determined through a true relation to God. Thus, both the Knight of Infinite Resignation and the Knight of Faith stand their ground; however the latter—like the Morally Good Person and the Virtuous Person—is able to die. Toward understanding this, consider the following question which comes from Kierkegaard's writings titled *Works of Love*:

"Which is more difficult:
to awaken one who sleeps;
or, to awaken one who, awake, dreams he is awake?"

Though the question may be perplexing at first, the Knight of Infinite Resignation is awake; however, it *dreams* it is awake. That is, it still asserts a human Will, with a human Self-Love, and knows its Self, not in terms of Divine Justice, but rather in terms of its own dream of what is valuable.

In terms of the Theological Virtues, the Knight of Faith has the Virtue of Piety (*hosios*). In terms of Kant's Kingdom of Ends, the Knight of Faith has perfected its Self by merging, as much as possible while still embodied, with universal Spirit, we called this Celestial Be-ing in the Plato chapter. The ancient Greek term which may be translated as Piety, Godliness, Holiness or "sanctioned by the Law of God" is *hosios*, and its verb form means "to purify." (Balz & Schneider 1993, 536). Now, notice the family resemblance between this term and a term used to describe initiation into ancient mysteries, such as the Eleusinian Mysteries associated with Persephone and discussed regarding Plato's *Meno*, that is, the term *hosiosis*, which means subsistence together—though the more common term is *henosis*. This latter term, then, was used to describe "merging" with "the god." The terminology used by "philosophical or spiritual alchemists" is *Mysterium Coniunctionis*, which refers to a "mysterious conjunction" or a "holy marriage," that is, *hierosgamos*. Hence, it is as if the Knight of Faith accomplishes the *mysterious conjunction* into the Kingdom of Ends, and as autonomous has the lived-experience of Happiness (*Eudaimonia*) as its Will surrenders itself to being the expression of universal Spirit mysteriously beyond the grasp of human reason.

Nietzsche: Will-to-Power & Original Nature

"In fact, the question is not:
is blameworthy existence responsible or not?
But is existence blameworthy ... or innocent?" [32]
~Gilles Deleuze

§3 On Schopenhauer: From Will to Will-to-Power

Friedrich Nietzsche (1844–1900 AD) studied the Classics, that is, ancient Greek Tragedies and Comedies, Mythological, and Philosophical texts. Nietzsche's life was filled with suffering. Though an account of his life is beyond the scope of our present inquiry, it is contextualizing to note that his life was filled by a series of miseries and illness. Hence, the optimism of his philosophy is all the more remarkable. Moreover, for our purposes in an introduction to ethics, we will not be addressing Nietzsche's more controversial claims, for example, the infamous "God is Dead" phrase. My reading of Nietzsche in regard to this phrase may be found in my book *Full Throttle Heart: Nietzsche Beyond Either/Or*.

To understand the dynamics of Nietzsche's conversion of Schopenhauer's pessimistic Will to the optimistic Will-to-Power, we need to recall a number of items from Plato and combine them with Schopenhauer, specifically the second of the twofold insight from which Schopenhauer read Kant's Kingdom of Ends. The idea is that from the perspective of the lived-experience of the individual existence, as an expression of universal Will, recall life "*is a disappointment, nay a cheat*," (Schopenhauer 2005, 35). What is more, insofar as individual existence must be continually lived, until the universal Will no longer expresses itself into the material dimension, then the existence of human life as suffering may even take on the quality of endless suffering. Nietzsche may be understood, then, as reading this activity of the universal Will through Plato's Myth of Er with an emphasis on Aristotle's Great-Souled Person.

The idea is that our existential situation becomes optimistic by understanding it in terms of a Heroic Contest. With the gods as our witness, we strive to overcome the challenges of human embodied existence. One of the challenges may be the subterfuge of Nature; however, that too will contribute to our character as it is forged in the existential kiln of human be-ing. Just like all those who came before us, life is a contest in which we compete with ourselves, that is, we strive to express the Will-to-Power that we are as the individual expression of universal Will Self-Realizing. In this way, we become *worthy* of Happiness, that is, we may stand tall in front of ourselves and with dignity. Recalling the wisdom of Plato and Aristotle, such a self-relation from which we may have dignity is about our existence; therefore, neither our poverty nor our loneliness should make us feel shame. That we can withstand more than the pampered, that *we can do more* with less material comfort, proves both that we are favored, not by men so much as, by the gods and that our Souls are Greater than those of the pampered (cf. Nietzsche 1989a, §225).

§4 *The State of Nature: The Homeric Contest*

A Nietzschean reading of the State of Nature follows directly from the previous section's conclusion. The idea is quite explicit from Nietzsche's posthumously published, though written in 1872 work "Homer's Contest." According to Nietzsche,

> When one speaks of humanity, the idea is fundamental that this is something which separates and distinguishes man from nature. In reality, however, there is no such separation: "natural" qualities and those called truly "human" are inseparably grown together. Man, in his highest and noblest capacities, is wholly nature and embodies its uncanny dual character. Those of his abilities which are terrifying and considered inhuman may even be the fertile soil out of which alone all humanity can grow in impulse, deed, and work. (1977, 32).

Thus, Nietzsche hopes to help us more accurately recollect the notion of Nature on which the Western Tradition is founded. Recall Aristotle noted that the Great-Souled Person is "right to despise others."

APPENDIX II

Nietzsche, invoking the name of Aristotle's most famous pupil, associates the quality of "lust to annihilate" with the dignity of the ancient Greeks.

> Thus the Greeks, the most humane men of ancient times, have a strain [Zug] of cruelty, a tigerish lust to annihilate —a trait that is also very distinct in that grotesquely enlarged mirror image of the Hellenes, in Alexander the Great, but also in their whole history just as much so in their mythology, which must put into anxiety any who come up against it with the soft concept of modern humanity.[33] (Nietzsche 1977, 32–33).

Hence, Nietzsche is calling into question Hobbes' suggestion that it is Natural—in the State of Nature—to "seek peace," since as such, War would be against our Natural inclinations to *humanity* (cf. Nietzsche 1979, 81).

Nietzsche goes further with two suggestions that may seem shocking to contemporary ears. First, for the ancient Greeks the discharge of hatred and violence, even violence and cruelty against the weak, was a celebration.

> When Alexander has the feet of Batis, the brave defender of Gaza, pierced, and ties him, alive, to his carriage, to drag him about while his soldiers mock, that is a revolting caricature of Achilles, who maltreats Hector's corpse in a similar fashion at night; and even this trait is offensive to us and makes us shudder. Here we look into the abyss of hatred. (Nietzsche 1977, 33).

Second, hearkening back to the theme of Natural Law running consistently through the Western Tradition and again reminiscent of Aristotle's description of the Great-Souled Person, the discharge of hatred and violence was seen as Natural, in accordance with Natural Justice (if not also Divine Justice), and a kind of birthright.

> With the same feeling we may also observe the mutual laceration, bloody and insatiable, of two Greek parties, for example, in the Corcyrean revolution. When the victor in a fight among the cities executes the entire male citizenry in accordance with the laws of war, and sells all the women and children into slavery, we see in the sanction of such a law that the Greeks considered it an earnest necessity to let their hatred flow forth fully … Why must the Greek sculptor give form again and again to war and combat in innumerable repetitions: distended human bodies, their sinews tense with hatred or with the arrogance of triumph: writhing bodies, wounded; dying bodies, expiring? Why did the whole Greek world exult over the combat scenes of the *Iliad*? (Nietzsche 1977).

Hence, for Nietzsche it seems as if the more Natural response to the State of Nature as a State of War would be to delight in the existential throws[34] of such a contest as if it were a carnival, that is, a celebration of the gods tilling the soil of generation with the victors as their plow.

§5 *On the Genealogy of Morals: Autonomy and the Great-Souled Person*

An entire course in ethics could be taught from Nietzsche's *On the Genealogy of Morals*. For our introductory purposes, we will only note the following. First, there are three sections to Nietzsche's *On the Genealogy*

APPENDIX II

of Morals, each section contains one key idea which we will examine. However, there is also a specific relation across the three sections, which we need to recognize. The three ideas across the sections are (1) resentment, (2) bad conscience, and (3) life-denying ascetic ideals, respectively. The sections culminate into what Nietzsche calls "Slave Morality." Slave Morality is contrasted with Master Morality, and the latter is the morality of the Great-Souled Person.

The first section of *On the Genealogy of Morals* is title "'Good and Evil,' 'Good and Bad,'" and in this section Nietzsche contrasts the two different ways of understanding the opposite of Good. He claims that the word Good referred to knightly-aristocratic value judgments determined by Masters and conquerors. Thus, the value judgment that something is good was Self-centered and not "unegotistical." In contrast, Nietzsche refers to altruism as (turning a phrase from Aristotle) a "herd instinct." Nietzsche sees the sense in which Slaves must band together as the evolution of a herd instinct, though to be sure he believes the weak, ignorant, and sickly Naturally have a herd instinct for the sake of surviving. Further, he claims that a "spiritual vengeance" permeates the Slave herd because they want to wield the power of a Master.

However, because they are not Naturally endowed to be Masters, they must use cunning. Nietzsche characterizes the motivational force of such vengeful deceptiveness as "resentment" (i.e. *ressentiment*—note Nietzsche tends to use French words to denote a concept born out of decadence and nihilism). Nietzsche notes, "*Ressentiment* itself, if it should appear in the noble man, consummates and exhausts itself in an immediate reaction, and therefore does not poison: on the other hand, it fails to appear at all on countless occasions on which it inevitably appears in the weak and impotent." (Nietzsche 1989b, 39).

In this way, Nietzsche draws his conclusion that "the noble man … conceives the basic concept 'good' in advance and spontaneously out of himself and only then creates for himself an idea of 'bad,'" and thus, "This 'bad' [is] of noble origin and that 'evil' [comes] out of the cauldron of unsatisfied hatred." (Nietzsche 1989b, 39–40). Moreover, the Slave comes to see the Great-Souled Person and their concept of "good" as "evil," that is, "interpreted in another fashion … by the *venomous eye of ressentiment*." (Nietzsche 1989b, 40).

Nietzsche calls Slave resentment "the most abysmal hatred." It is not the hatred of the Great-Souled Person. Nietzsche calls the Great-Souled Person "Noble" because they are able to acknowledge a slight as "bad," yet forget about it, and not "lower" themselves to seek vengeance. However, the Slaves consider slights against them to indicate the presence of "evil," and lust for revenge. Further, according to Nietzsche, whereas the Great-Souled Person associates Happiness with activity, Slaves associate Happiness with passivity, that is, with being able to stop working or to not have to work. When this is combined with the second section of *On the Genealogy of Morals*, which is titled "'Guilt,' 'Bad Conscience,' and the Like,'" Nietzsche believes he has isolated the mechanism by which such Slave mentality spread, and through which the "slave revolt in morality" was accomplished.

According to Nietzsche, "Guilt" originally only meant "Debt." Thus, if you did not repay your debt you were considered guilty, and the creditor could exact the amount from you which was owed.

> Throughout the greater part of human history punishment was *not* imposed *because* one held the wrong-doer responsible for his deed, thus not on the presupposition that only the guilty one should be punished: rather, as parents still punish their children, from anger at some harm or injury, vented

on the one who caused it—but this anger is held in check and modified by the idea that every injury has its *equivalent* and can actually be paid back, even if only through the *pain* of the culprit. And whence did this primeval, deeply rooted, perhaps by now ineradicable idea draw its power—this idea of an equivalence between injury and pain? … in the contractual relationship between creditor and debtor, which is as old as the idea of "legal subjects" and in turn points back to the fundamental forms of buying, selling, barter, trade, and traffic. (Nietzsche 1989b, 63).

Nietzsche further explains the "logic of this form of compensation" noting,

An equivalence is provided by the creditor's receiving, in place of a literal compensation for an injury … a recompense in the form of a kind of pleasure … the enjoyment of violation. This enjoyment will be the greater the lower the creditor stands in the social order, and can easily appear to him as a most delicious morsel, indeed as a foretaste of higher rank. In "punishing" the debtor, the creditor participates in a *right of the masters*: at last he, too, may experience for once the exalted sensation of being allowed to despise and mistreat someone as "beneath him." … The compensation, then, consists in a warrant for and title to cruelty. (Nietzsche 1989b, 64–65).

Thus, Nietzsche draws a twofold conclusion here. First, notice it is by way of making someone indebted to them—by extending them credit—that Slaves set up a situation in which to discharge their resentment on those in their debt. Second, this idea of an "equivalence," which Nietzsche suggests was only associated with the "guilt" of not repaying one's debt ultimately becomes "internalized." Hence, "It was in this sphere then, the sphere of legal obligations, that the moral conceptual world of 'guilt,' 'conscience,' 'duty,' 'sacredness of duty" had its origin". (Nietzsche 1989, 65).

The effect of the internalization of the "equivalence" for "guilt" is "bad conscience." Whereas initially the punishment was for the action of breaking the promise or contractual agreement, for example, with one's creditor, the idea of an equivalence for guilt enabled one to enter into a self-relation from which one could keep a running tally of their guilt. When this internalization was coupled with the Slave notion of "evil," then it became possible to suggest to people that they were being punished for their own "good," as if their actions had incurred a debt for which they owe its equivalence in punishment. Further, because the Slaves had identified the strengths of the Great-Souled Person as "evil," the stage was set for what Nietzsche called their "spiritual revenge and the revaluation of all values." In fact, Nietzsche believes that this kind of thinking is now so pervasive that he repeatedly and explicitly says the Slaves have successfully revolted, and the world we now occupy is permeated with Slave mentality. According to Nietzsche, "Man has all too long had an 'evil eye' for his natural inclinations, so they have finally become inseparable from his 'bad conscience'" (Nietzsche 1989b, 95).

Finally, the third section of *On the Genealogy of Morals*, which is titled "'What is the Meaning of Ascetic Ideals?'" discusses the manner in which interpretations of Christianity which perpetuate such Slave mentality constitute what he calls "Slave Morality." Thus, ascetic priests have made an ideal out of the notions of evil

APPENDIX II

and guilt and renounce any inclinations toward Greatness of Soul. In particular, Nietzsche is upset regarding what he sees as a shifting of the Kingdom of Ends to "another world." Whereas Self-Realization for the ancient Greeks meant achievement in this life, and along the lines discussed above regarding the Homeric Contest, Nietzsche sees Slave Morality as having posited another world after this life to complete the internalization of guilt, that is, there had to be some threat of force. However, because the Great-Souled Person's integrity and dignity are not to be shaken, Slave Morality suggests that somewhere else and by someone else the Great-Souled Person will be punished. Hence, Nietzsche may be seen criticizing Hobbes' "English," (rather than ancient Greek), way of understanding the State of Nature. For it would be the herd instinct of Slave mentality that seeks contracts as a means to escape a State of War, only to wage a different type of war. Moreover, Nietzsche would seem to agree with Hume over Hobbes that there could be art and beauty, and so on, in a State of Nature insofar as the Great-Souled respected each other's Self-Realization and lived in Harmony in accordance with *that* Natural Divine Justice.

Now that we have seen Nietzsche's account of the opposition between Master and Slave Morality, we can ask the question of how all this would appear were one to return to the point of view of the Great-Souled Person, that is, in terms of Master Morality. In his excellent book, *Nietzsche & Philosophy*, Gilles Deleuze (1925–1995 AD) discussed the relation between the Great-Souled Person and ascetic ideals in terms of "the intensity of forces." Thus, as if from a metaphysical perspective, ascetic ideals are accounted for, not in terms of heritable traits or tribal practices but, in terms of forces. According to Deleuze, "Nietzsche devotes a whole book to the analysis of the figures of reactive triumph in the human world—*ressentiment*, bad conscience and the ascetic ideal" (Deleuze 2006, 57). And, "In each case [Nietzsche] shows that reactive forces do not triumph by forming a superior force but by 'separating' active forces" (Ibid). That is to say, the Slave revolt is accomplished when "Active force is separated from what it can do" (Ibid). Hence, "the words 'vile', 'ignoble', and 'slave' ... designate the state of reactive forces that place themselves on high and entice active force into a trap, replacing masters with slaves" (Deleuze 2006, 57–58).

Deleuze's articulation provides some insight into how one might think about the Freedom of the Great-Souled Person in the wake of the success of the Slave revolt. On the one hand, insofar as the Norms of Social interaction are coded in terms of Slave Morality's having permeated the City, one may need to look "within" to recognize the metaphysical presence of such coding; that is, so that one can—thinking of the Analogy of the City and the Soul and Plato's types of lovers—replace the oligarchic tyranny of money-lovers with a philosopher-king. On the other hand, by returning to a metaphysical characterization, we may see Nietzsche's existential post-German Idealist way of returning to the ancient Greeks.

Recall from Nietzsche's *Beyond Good & Evil* his famous saying, "Whoever fights monsters should see to it that in the process he does not become a monster" (Nietzsche 1989a, 89), since in becoming a monster you have allowed the "monsters" to separate you from what you can do. Further, recalling how Nietzsche referred to the hatred of the Slaves as an "abysmal hatred," recall the conclusion of the "monsters" quote: "And when you look long into an abyss, the abyss also looks into you." (Ibid). When you hear the Slave *logos*, does it ring true to you? Has your internalization of the *logos* separated you from what you can do, i.e. from the Self-Realization of becoming who you are?

151

APPENDIX II

Amor Fati: Nietzsche's Return to the Myth of Er

"You tremble carcass?
You would tremble a lot more
if you knew where I am taking you."[35]
~Turenne

§6 *On Truth & Lies in a Non-moral Sense: From the Ubiquity of Interpretation to Daimonic Self-Love*

In regard to an early essay (written in 1873) from Nietzsche titled "On Truth and Lies in a Non-moral Sense," we may recognize that Nietzsche speaks of the Will, the Heart, and the Spirit as masculine, and he speaks of the intellect as feminine. In fact, in this particular essay, it is as if he has shifted Schopenhauer's description of "woman" to the intellect. Thinking of the intellect as feminine immediately explicates the meaning of the essay's title. That is to say, Nietzsche dislikes liars. That is clear. However, Nietzsche identifies different dimensions to which the intellect may relate. Employed in its instrumental mathematical use in terms of abstracting from and calculating in regard to reality, especially social reality, there is a clear distinction to be made between truth telling and lying. If you claim to understand existentialism, but you do not, then you are a liar. In this regard, Nietzsche chastises the intellect for falling so far into dissimulation that one has lost touch with reality (cf. Nietzsche 1979, 81). Yet, Nietzsche emphasizes a different aspect of the intellect's femininity in regard to the metaphysics of its relation beyond its instrumentality of abstracting and calculating.

Nietzsche's non-calculative intellect, then, is feminine insofar as it receives metaphysical input, as if from "beyond" the dimension of the physically calculable. Thus Nietzsche presents an overview of his philosophy of attitude, which we will read as culminating with his notion of *Amor Fati*. For now, notice Nietzsche's illumination of this dimension when in §17 of *Beyond Good and Evil* regarding the "superstitions of logicians," he notes, "I shall never tire of emphasizing a small terse fact, which these superstitious minds hate to concede —namely, that a thought comes when 'it' wishes, and not when 'I' wish" (Nietzsche 1989a, 24). Going further, Nietzsche suggests that the tendency to clever calculative fabrications, or the Will-to-dissimulation, may lie even here, then, when one attempts to deny the presence of a dimension beyond the physically calculable. Thus, according to Nietzsche, "it is a falsification of the facts of the case to say that the subject 'I' is the condition of the predicate 'think.' *It* thinks" (Nietzsche 1989a, 24). In order to understand the depth of Nietzsche's thought here, recognize that there are two parts to his thought.

The first part is that this dimension beyond the physically calculable, *precisely because* it is beyond the physically calculable, necessarily involves *interpretation*, that is, this is Nietzsche's notion of the "ubiquity of interpretation" (cf. *Beyond Good & Evil* §22). In other words, one cannot rely on instrumental rationality to calculate the beyond. Rather, the intellect must interpret whatever it encounters in relation to such a dimension. The second part, then, is that interpretations of this dimension may be divided into Master and Slave interpretations. Nietzsche sees "life affirming" interpretations as those of Masters and "life denying" interpretations as those of Slaves. Hence, he concludes §17 of *Beyond Good and Evil* noting but that this 'it' is precisely the famous old 'ego' is, to put it mildly, only a supposition, an assertion, and assuredly not an 'immediate certainty.' After all, one has even gone too far with this 'it thinks'—even the 'it' contains *interpretation* of the process, and does not belong to the process itself (Nietzsche 1989a, 24).

Notice, the ability to remain open to the process entering the intellect, reminiscent of *ataraxia*, is a more honest relation to reality than attempts to calculate its components, as if humans were capable of manipulating the dimension of Fate. Most importantly, then, Nietzsche highlights the manner in which the construction of interpretations regarding the dimension beyond the physically calculable involves "far more delicate conceptual material which [a human] first has to manufacture *from himself* [emphasis added]." (Nietzsche 1979, 85). Thus, again, when you look into the abyss, the abyss looks into you. Your interpretations of life reflect who, what, and how you are.

What is needed in regard to the dimension beyond the physically calculable is an "artist." One should be artistic when they interpret the meaning of life, and they should be healthy enough to provide a life affirming interpretation; for a more in-depth rendering of this topic see my *Full Throttle Heart* (Scalambrino 2015a). Notice, Nietzsche's return to the ancient Greek way of thinking in the following passage.

Pascal is right in maintaining that if the same dream came to us every night we would be just as occupied with it as we are with the things that we see every day. "If a workman were sure to dream for twelve straight hours every night that he was king," said Pascal, "I believe that he would be just as happy as a king who dreamt for twelve hours every night that he was a workman." In fact, because of the way that myth takes it for granted that miracles are always happening, the waking life of a mythically inspired people—the ancient Greeks, for instance—more closely resembles a dream than it does the waking world of a scientifically disenchanted thinker. (Nietzsche 1979, 89).

Thus, when with a life affirming attitude one artistically interprets the dimension beyond the physically calculable, it is as if one expresses oneself "as a member of a higher community." For Nietzsche the ancient Greek component which many may miss in considering the Great-Souled Person *from Plato and Aristotle* is the innocence and artistry constituting its life affirming attitude. Nietzsche concludes,

When every tree can suddenly speak as a nymph, when a god in the shape of a bull can drag away maidens, when even the goddess Athena herself is suddenly seen in the company of Peisastratus driving through the market place of Athens with a beautiful team of horses—and this is what the honest Athenian believed—then, as in a dream, anything is possible at each moment [(cf. Kierkegaard's Knight of Faith)], and all of nature swarms around man as if it were nothing but a masquerade of these gods, who were merely amusing themselves by deceiving men in all these shapes. (Ibid).

In regard to earlier themes in this book, we can see the above as Nietzsche's strategy for recollecting a Master relation to reality and perfecting the process of Self-Realization by restoring an appropriate relation to the Divine.

Finally, as if showing us how to overcome Schopenhauer's pessimism while also avoiding the liar's life of Slave Mentality and Slave Morality, Nietzsche distinguishes between "rational" and "intuitive" Character Types. These could just as well be called Slave and Master or Scientist and Artist, respectively, in regard to their attitudes toward life.

> There are ages in which the rational man and the intuitive man stand side by side, the one in fear of intuition, the other with scorn for abstraction. The latter is just as irrational as the former is inartistic. They both desire to rule over life: the former, by knowing how to meet his principle needs by means of foresight, prudence, and regularity; the latter, by disregarding these needs and, as an "overjoyed hero," counting as real only that life which has been disguised as illusion and beauty. Whenever, as was perhaps the case in ancient Greece, the intuitive man handles his weapons more authoritatively and victoriously than his opponent, then, under favorable circumstances, a culture can take shape and art's mastery over life can be established. (Nietzsche 1979, 90).

Nietzsche's indictment of the calculative Type and attitude does not deny that such types often survive longer; rather, he points to the idea of survival for its own sake as antithetical to true Happiness.

> The man who is guided by concepts and abstractions only succeeds by such means in warding off misfortune, without ever gaining any happiness for himself from these abstractions. And while he aims for the greatest possible freedom from pain, the intuitive man, standing in the midst of a culture, already reaps from his intuition a harvest of continually inflowing illumination, cheer, and redemption—in addition to obtaining a defense against misfortune. To be sure, he suffers more intensely, *when* he suffers; he even suffers more frequently, since he does not understand how to learn from experience and keeps falling over and over again into the same ditch. He is then just as irrational in sorrow as he is in happiness: he cries aloud and will not be consoled. (Nietzsche 1979, 91).

§7 *Amor Fati: "Then I will be one who makes things beautiful…"*

There are four (4) ideas we want to learn from this section. For our purposes, they are Nietzsche's views on "pity," "adventure," "destiny," and "fate." We will discuss these ideas by looking at three (3) passages from Nietzsche. The first is an epigram from *Beyond Good & Evil* (§225)[36] in which he explicitly criticizes Hedonism, Pessimism, and Utilitarianism. The second is his discussion of the Eternal Return from *The Cheerful Science* (not *Thus Spoke Zarathustra*). Finally, the third passage, also from *The Cheerful Science*, is titled *Amor Fati*, that is, the Love of Fate.

Nietzsche's views on "pity" need not be overly complicated. The basic idea is that we first need to keep in mind his above discussion regarding the internalization of Slave Mentality. As we will see, he thinks pity comes from an imbalance in the soul. The following passage from *Beyond Good & Evil* (§225) is lengthy, so we will discuss it piecemeal. He begins by noting,

APPENDIX II

> Whether it is hedonism or pessimism, utilitarianism or eudaemonism[37] —all these ways of thinking that measure the value of things in accordance with *pleasure* and *pain*, which are mere epiphenomena and wholly secondary, are ways of thinking that stay in the foreground and naïvetés on which everyone conscious of *creative* powers and an artistic conscience will look down not without derision, nor without pity. (Nietzsche 1989a, 153).

Notice the word "value." Nietzsche is contrasting the way the Great-Souled Person determines value with a "lower" bodily style of evaluation, that is, in terms of Pleasure and pain. Further, Nietzsche shows us here that he does not reject the notion of "conscience" wholesale; rather, there is a kind of conscience which urges us on. It is the creative conscience of the artist, and let us not forget that "conscience" is the modern term for "*daimon*."

The above quote ends with the word "pity." However, as we will see, Nietzsche begins, here, to articulate two different kinds of pity: pity which stems from Slave Mentality and pity which stems from Master Mentality. Hence, as we continue to read §225, we need to keep in mind that Nietzsche is speaking from the Master position, that is, the "our" and "we" refer to we Masters, and the "you" and "your" accusations are made toward the Slaves as those with Slave Mentality.

> Our pity toward *you*—that, of course, is not pity in your sense: it is not pity with social "distress," with "society" and its sick and unfortunate members, with those addicted to vice and maimed from the start, though the ground around us is littered with them; it is even less pity with grumbling, sorely pressed, rebellious slave strata who long for dominion, calling it "freedom." (Nietzsche 1989a, 153).

Before taking up Nietzsche's clarification between the way Slaves pity and how Masters pity, notice how he not only gestures toward linking Slave Mentality with Vice (and ultimately decadence elsewhere) but also how he associates slave rebellion with Dominion, thereby also pointing to a Slave Mentality understanding of Freedom. He continues,

> *Our* pity is a higher and more farsighted pity: we see how man makes himself smaller, how *you* make him smaller—and there are moments when we behold *your* very pity with indescribable anxiety, when we resist this pity—when we find your seriousness more dangerous than any frivolity. You want, if possible—and there is no more insane "if possible"—*to abolish suffering*. And we? It really seems that *we* would rather have it higher and worse than ever. Well-being as you understand it—that is no goal, it seems to us only an *end*, a state that soon makes man ridiculous and contemptible—that makes his overcoming *desirable*. (Nietzsche 1989a, 153-4).

After clarifying the difference between the Slave and Master understanding of pity, in a move reminiscent of the movement from "bad conscience" to the "ascetic ideals," Nietzsche suggests the desire to "abolish all suffering" is "insane" and makes humans "ridiculous and contemptible." Therefore, "overcoming" such an attitude is desirable and may be understood as the call of (Master) conscience to overcome the presence of ascetic ideals in the soul, such as pity.[38]

APPENDIX II

Nietzsche goes on to make this last point explicit. Recalling the manner in which the Personhood of the Great-Souled Person positions them in relation to the Divine in terms of Self-Knowledge and Self-Realization, Nietzsche speaks of suffering as if it were a Divine gift. Affirming life as an adventure, both internally and externally, it is through the fire that we accomplish an awareness of Divinity, and the presence of the Divine Will in our actions.

> The discipline of suffering, of *great* suffering—do you not know that only *this* discipline has created all enhancements of man so far? That tension of the soul in unhappiness which cultivates its strength, its shudders face to face with great ruin, its inventiveness and courage in enduring, persevering, interpreting, and exploiting suffering, and whatever has been granted to it of profundity, secret, mask, spirit, cunning, greatness – was it not granted to it through suffering, through the discipline of great suffering? (Nietzsche 1989a, 154).

In regard to the higher and lower parts of the soul, mapping onto what we called Congruence and Incongruence as divisions of Aristotle's Character Types in relation to Self-Realization, Nietzsche explains the following.

> In man *creature* and *creator* are united: in man there is material, fragment, excess, clay, dirt, nonsense, chaos; but in man there is also creator, form-giver, hammer hardness, spectator divinity, and seventh day: do you understand this contrast? ... And *your* pity is for the "creature in man," for what must be formed, broken, forged, torn, burnt, made incandescent, and purified—that which *necessarily* must and *should* suffer? And *our* pity—do you not comprehend for whom our *converse* pity is when it resists your pity as the worst of all pamperings and weaknesses?
> Thus it is pity *versus* pity.
> But to say it once more: there are higher problems than all problems of pleasure, pain, and pity; and every philosophy that stops with them is a naïveté. (Nietzsche 1989a, 154).

Notice, three points. First, when Nietzsche asks if we "understand this contrast" he is directly referring to the contrast which we also saw in §5 above in which he associated a desire to avoid doing work with Slave Mentality. Second, the distinction between creature and creator may be seen as referring to the Person's relation to the *daimon* and the *hierosgamos*, that is, the holy marriage of the soul with the Divine, received into the intellect. Third, Nietzsche reminds us that the Dignity of the Great-Souled Person is not preoccupied with Pleasure and pain; moreover, Slave pity comes from a softened spirit's attempt to treat abstract instrumental rationality as if it were absolute truth (cf. Nietzsche 1989a, §225). That is, the calculative animal connives to increase Pleasure and decrease pain, and, thereby, the intellect's highest concerns are with the comfort of its body.

Finally, it is as if, from Nietzsche's perspective, we can fix the relation between Kant's discussion of the Kingdom of Ends and Nietzsche's in terms of the relation between Plato's Myth of the Metals and his Myth of Er. Notice the following from Kant,

> the idea of a pure world of understanding as a whole of all intelligences, to which we ourselves belong as rational beings (though on the other side we are also members of the world of sense),

APPENDIX II

remains always a useful and permitted idea for the sake of a rational belief, even if all knowledge stops at its boundary—useful and permitted for producing in us a lively interest in the moral law by means of the noble ideal of a universal kingdom of ends in themselves to which we can belong as members only when we carefully conduct ourselves in accordance with maxims of freedom as if they were laws of nature. (Kant 2002, 66).

On the one hand, when Nietzsche, after Kant, asks "What is Noble?" we can see him as orienting those "who have the ears for it" to a Master understanding of Kant's Kingdom of Ends—notice the language of "the noble *ideal* of the kingdom of ends." Recall, the Myth of the Metals was the Myth told to the non-philosophers. Thus, through an artistic twofold reading of the Kingdom of Ends, first, Nietzsche re-articulates the "Noble" by suggesting the lower "metals" have successfully rebelled against the higher. Second, moving from the City to the Soul he recommends we test our metal, as it were, to see the extent to which the rebellion has separated us from being who we are.

On the other hand, we can see Nietzsche providing the Myth of Er to emphasize the metaphysical "side" of human be-ing and, thereby providing a reading of the "laws of nature." Notice the language of "a pure world of understanding." This pushes us into a metaphysical discussion, for example, in regard to the "noetic cosmos" oft-discussed regarding "theurgy," and, explicitly so in regard to autonomy and Fate. We will complete this discussion in the next section; however, for now, having discussed the ideas of "pity" and "adventure" above, we will begin the discussion regarding "destiny" and "fate" by invoking Nietzsche's famous "Eternal Return," or abbreviated: ER.

We will examine the following passage from Nietzsche's "The Cheerful Science" titled "The greatest weight." The passage naturally divides into two parts. So, we will look at the first part, which will provide us with a version of the Eternal Return, then we will look at the second part in order to understand the epigram's title and work it into a kind of Fate-filled Maxim, as if Nietzsche were articulating a kind of Conduct Ethics. Though ultimately we, of course, understand Nietzsche's ethics as emphasizing Character.

> *The greatest weight.* —What if, some day or night, a demon[or daimon] were to steal after you into your loneliest loneliness and say to you: 'This life as you now live it and have lived it, you will have to live once more and innumerable times more; and there will be nothing new in it, but every pain and every joy and every thought and every sigh and everything unutterably small or great in your life will have to return to you, all in the same succession and sequence—even this spider and this moonlight between the trees, and even this moment and I myself. The eternal hourglass of existence is turned upside down again and again, and you with it… (Nietzsche 1974, 273).

This, then, is what we refer to as the "Eternal Return." The idea, simply put, is that all of your life's experiences will return to you to experience again, without end. Nietzsche follows this up with the question: "Would you not throw yourself down and gnash your teeth and curse the demon [or daimon] who spoke thus?" (Nietzsche 1974). On the one hand, it may seem like this question is meaningless. For if everything in your life is already determined, then wouldn't your reaction be determined too? However, it seems, reminiscent of Stoicism, that Nietzsche at least holds open the possibility of our affirming or denying the determined content of life. So, we cannot circumvent the question with sophisticated logic. On the other hand, Nietzsche's use of the term, which may be translated as either demon or daimon depending upon one's response to the message, immediately suggests for us a link to Plato's Myth of Er and the question of how to relate to Fate.

It is in regard, then, to the second part of the passage that we can employ the epigram's title as a Maxim. Nietzsche concludes "The Greatest Weight" noting,

> Would you not throw yourself down and gnash your teeth and curse the demon [or daimon] who spoke thus? Or have you once experienced a tremendous moment when you would have answered him 'You are a god and never have I heard anything more divine.' If this thought gained possession of you, it would change you as you are or perhaps crush you. The question in each and everything, 'Do you desire this once more and innumerable times more?' would lie upon your actions as the greatest weight. Or how well disposed would you have to become to yourself and to life to crave nothing more fervently than this ultimate eternal confirmation and seal? (Nietzsche 1974, 273-4).

Notice the language of a thought "gaining possession of you." This is the idea that when one recognizes one's position in regard to Divine Justice that one achieves Self-Realization, that is, Personhood. In this way, by affirming the Divinity of the *daimon*, one affirms one's relation to Divinity. Thus, the weight has the potential to "crush you" because it is "above" you. Further, to "crave nothing more fervently" sounds much like accepting one's Divine Judgment. Moreover, if we cannot change our Fate, *Eudaimonia* becomes establishing the appropriate attitude to it; to be a virtuoso at living the Eternal Return, we must become the Great-Souled Person. We will discuss this attitude in concluding this section.

Lastly, notice how we can make the Eternal Return into a kind of Categorical Imperative in relation to the Myth of Er, rather than the Myth of the Metals. In this way, "the greatest weight" may be treated as a kind of Maxim in determining how we should conduct ourselves by performing the action regarding which we are deliberating. That is to say, if you are about to perform some action, you should ask yourself "Would I want to have this experience return to me endlessly?" If so, then it would seem to pass the Categorical Imperative of the Eternal Return, if not, then we should ask ourselves, "So, then, why are we doing this?"

Now, the final part to consider in this section is Nietzsche's epigram titled: *Amor Fati*. Clearly it is a statement of his prescribed attitude toward Fate. However, there are a number of other aspects we want to notice, as they link with previous ideas mentioned in this section. First, notice Nietzsche's "creative conscience" of the "artistic" Type is reaffirmed. Second, Nietzsche's refusal to "accuse the accusers" speaks to his belief that resentment is indicative of Slave Mentality. Third, there is an emphasis on the inevitable presence of the intellect, which some twentieth century existentialists have taken up as commenting on suicide. That is, that if one is not going to commit suicide, then one will continue to live and continue to think. Thus, since (recall from above) thoughts come to us, we do not come to thoughts, we should orient our attitude to what is coming, that is, to what is Fated.

> *To the new year*—Still I live, still I think: I must still live, then I must still think… Today everyone allows the speaking out of wishful and heartfelt thinking: so now I also want to say, what I wish for myself today and which thought first ran across my heart this year, —which thought shall be my

foundation, certainty, and sweetness for the rest of my life! I want to learn more and more, to see the necessary in things as beautiful: —then I will be one who makes things beautiful. *Amor fati*: shall be my love from now on! I do not want to wage war on what is ugly. I do not want to accuse, I do not even want to accuse the accusers. Looking away will be my only negation. And, all in all and on the whole: I wish to be only a Yes-sayer! (Nietzsche 1974, 223).

Given the contemporary context, we should perhaps clarify that being a "Yes-sayer" is not being a spineless "Yes-Man." Nietzsche is not advocating for social flattery, and so on. Rather, Nietzsche advocates for a kind of attitude, here, toward what is the dimension beyond the physically calculable. The "intuitive" artistic type finds a way to relate to the particular-fated configuration of this life, not to merely "endure it," but rather to make it beautiful.

Nietzsche's Cheerful Science: The Secret to Happiness is Overcoming Yourself Again and Again and …

§8 *Freedom, Destiny, & Self-Realization: Becoming Who You Are*

To begin, we must get clear on the distinction between "destiny" and "fate." For our purposes, Fate cannot be changed. If an event is Fated, then there is no way to escape it. Now, destiny is different. Notice the word "destiny" looks like the word "destination." Thus, we may say that just as you may or may not reach your destination, you may or may not fulfill your destiny. However, you cannot escape your Fate. Hence, when we put these two ideas together, we should express a twofold conclusion.

On the one hand, it is as if were we to constellate the events that have been Fated to you in a way that coincides with your accomplishment of Self-Realization, Self-Knowledge, and Self-Perfection (though it is still open to philosophical debate, and not immediately clear, how to interpret each of those terms across the history of the Western Tradition), then the result of that constellation may refer to the events and activities that you may be able to make into reality. If you are able to make those events and activities into reality, then you have manifested your destiny. Notice, in a way Fate limits your destiny, though it is up to you whether it will manifest. On the other hand, we may reaffirm the value of developing the most appropriate attitude, which means "relation" including an account (*logos*), for example, *Amor Fati* is a *logos* with which to face the future. Hence, a chain appears which we have sufficient power and autonomy to determine, and that chain conditions how we will navigate our Fate. The chain is our progress in regard to Self-Realization, and that, of course, involves Self-Knowledge. Further, recall from the Myth of Er discussion, this Self-Realization was deemed soteriological and teleological. In other words, it involved developing one's Natural be-ing in relation to the Divine, and the relation to the Divine constituted a kind of salvation.

Consider the following three (3) thoughts from Nietzsche:

1. "What does your conscience say? —'You shall become who you are.'" (Nietzsche 1974, 219).
2. "What is the seal of liberation? —No longer being ashamed in front of oneself." (Nietzsche 1974, 220).
3. "That which does not kill me, makes me stronger." (Nietzsche 1990, §8).

We can read these as suggesting, first, that the voice of conscience (i.e., the daimon) calls you to Self-Realization; second, that Freedom means being able to accept the constellation of Fate that essentially makes you who you are (if we were talking about Plato we would add: "This time around."), and essentially establishes your destiny. When you stop resisting this—notice you can't change it anyway—then you are *Free* to intentionally pursue the manifestation of your destiny (this is existential "authenticity" or "self-ownership"). Otherwise, the destiny just sits there (because it supervenes on your Fate constellation), and you do not reach it because you are too busy resisting becoming who you are. Finally, the idea that if the experience does not kill you, then it makes you stronger links not only to Self-Realization but also to the idea that life is an adventure, a contest at which Divinity is, at least, a spectator, and in which we are the playthings of the gods.

§9 *Full Throttle Heart: The Craftsman-like Spirit-Fire Dances through Me*

If we look for Nietzsche's aesthetic ideal to counter the ascetic ideal, then we may characterize the search as for the metaphysical dimension in which our Fate is given to us in the Now. Without going too deeply into this here, the idea is that, given Fate, the future is already determined to at least some extent. Thus, it is as if the content of the present moment were pouring-in from the future. When the appropriate attitude is accomplished, then one is able to recognize not only that the content of the environment is pouring-in from the future but also we ourselves are pouring-in from the future. To be sure, this is hardcore metaphysics! However, Nietzsche talks about this beautifully in a number of places, and it should be no surprise that he discusses this primarily through the ancient Greeks. Hence, we will look at some of his comments regarding the very same Mystery initiations which were mentioned in Plato.

Now, though it would seem antithetical to Nietzsche's position to suggest he is hoping to "escape" a Wheel of (re)incarnation, in a kind of "inversion" of such an interpretation of the Myth of Er, Nietzsche repeatedly affirms the idea of *hierosgamos*, that is, the *henosis* of a *mysterium coniunctionis*. This idea has been found throughout the history of the Western Tradition. In fact, it is the very same idea as Self-Realization and Self-Perfection via Self-Knowledge if we read Nietzsche's *Amor Fati* as the culmination of Self-Perfection regarding attitude. Read in this way, the idea of Full Throttle Heart refers to the witnessing of the metaphysical, the dimension beyond the physically calculable, as it pours-into the Now from the future. The universal Will or Spirit or Craftsman-like Fire flows through the heart. Hence, the existential reality of the *Amor Fati* attitude may be characterized by the idea of Full Throttle Heart. Notice the relation to the Kingdom of Ends, Nietzsche tells us, "The 'Kingdom of Heaven' is a condition of the heart" (Nietzsche 1990, 159); and, "The 'kingdom of God' is not something one waits for; it has no yesterday or tomorrow, it does not come 'in a thousand years'—it is an experience within a heart; it is everywhere, it is nowhere…" (Nietzsche 1990, 159).

Nietzsche asks, "Can it perhaps have been yet another merit of the ancients that the deepest pathos was with them merely aesthetic play" (Nietzsche 1967, 132; cf. Ruck 1986, 2006)? What he means here by "aesthetic play" is reality pouring-into the Now from the future. He pushes this to the point of true *henosis* with the Divine. This is a metaphysical description of the human experience of the Divine, and as such it is a description of the phenomenology of Happiness, that is, *Eudaimonia*.

an overflowing wealth of the most multifarious forces and the most dexterous power of 'free willing' and lordly command dwell amicably together in one man; *the spirit is then as much at home in the senses as the senses are at home in the spirit*; and whatever takes place in the *spirit* must enkindle a subtle extraordinary happiness and *play* in the senses (Nietzsche 1968, §1051; emphasis added; cf. Nietzsche 1967, 37–38).

Further,

we may assume that we are merely images and artistic projections for the true author, and that we have our highest dignity in our significance as works of art — for it is only as an *aesthetic phenomenon* that existence and the world are eternally *justified* ... as the sole author and spectator of this comedy of art (Nietzsche 1967, 52).

And, connecting these ideas explicitly with the initiation into the Mysteries noted in Plato's *Meno*,

In song and in dance man expresses himself as a member of a higher community; he has forgotten how to walk and speak and is on the way toward flying into the air, dancing. His very gestures express enchantment. ... *He is no longer an artist, he has become a work of art* [emphasis added]: in these paroxysms of intoxication the artistic power of all nature reveals itself to the highest gratification of the primordial unity. The noblest clay, the most costly marble, man, is here kneaded and cut, and to the sound of the chisel strokes of the Dionysian world-artist rings out the cry of the Eleusinian mysteries ... 'Do you sense your Maker, world?' (Nietzsche 1967, 37–38).

Thus, Nietzsche directs these thoughts toward Self-Realization,

I learned to walk, since then I let myself run. I learned to fly, since then I do not wait to be pushed to move from the spot. Now I am light, now I fly, now I see myself beneath me, now a god dances through me (Nietzsche 2006, 28).

Hence, it seems *Eudaimonia* for Nietzsche could not include ascetic ideals such as survival or Pleasure of the body; for he seems to have return to a strong—albeit however "inverted" — reading of Plato's Myth of Er, such that Self-Knowledge and Self-Realization condition a Self-Perfection which changes us right here, right Now, that is, not in another world, and this Self-Perfection is tantamount to the *Eudaimonia* of *henosis* through *hierosgamos* with the *daimon*. Nietzsche tells us how to become one (with the one) who makes things beautiful (i.e., pours-in the Divine from the future), and how to understand *henosis* as our human destiny:

I love him who reserveth no share of spirit for himself, but wanteth to be wholly the spirit of his virtue: thus walketh he as spirit... I love him who maketh his virtue his inclination and destiny: thus, for the sake of his virtue, he is willing to live on, or live no more (Nietzsche 1909, 9; cf. Clissord 1829).

Notes

1. Aristotle (2009).
2. I am indebted to Dr. Nicholas Rescher's discussion "The Canons of Distributive Justice" for assistance in constructing this list.
3. I am indebted to Dr. Philip Pettit's excellent book *A Theory of Freedom: From the Psychology to the Politics of Agency* for the specific terms used here; however, the characterization of the positions is my own.
4. Whitehead (1985, 39).
5. Scalambrino (2016, 90).
6. "Dimension" may be simply understood as the "measurement of."
7. Kennedy musical structure of the dialogs.
8. It may be helpful for later discussions in the book to consider the ancient Greek term *polis* or "City," here, as synonymous with the term used later in the Western Tradition, "Kingdom."
9. The movie *Compliance* (2012) was based on true events dealing with this issue at the level of employment
10. The ancient Greek *hosios* links with *hosiosis* and *henosis* as a *hierosgamos* and *mysterium coniunctionis*. For a more in-depth discussion, see my *Meditations on Orpheus* (2016).
11. Aristotle (2009).
12. This is like leaving your signature on the situation.
13. I do not claim originality regarding this chart. I have developed it throughout the years of teaching Aristotle and acquired and developed it piecemeal from others and my reading of Aristotle. I do not know the exact trajectory of its origination. I am aware of multiple authors who use similar looking charts; however, I have not excerpted these charts wholesale from any other author.
14. Plato (1997a, 38a).
15. This saying comes from Nietzsche, and though he was not a Hedonist, it is tempting to characterize his philosophy in terms of "attitudinal Hedonism."
16. *English Standard Version.*
17. Notice the Platonic logic which clarifies the Christian notion of Grace. If we think of the *logoi* as laws, that is, divine commands, we can combine the idea of Personhood with the idea of the care of souls, and, of course, the "Good order-ing" myth from Plato's *Timaeus* is the context here. What we see is that it is as if the divine revelation of commands for ordering material nature functions as an act of love insofar as it liberates us, especially tyrants, enabling us to be truly Happy. At the same time it allows us awareness of ourselves as Person's in the Kingdom of such ends, that is, the Divine City, and it reveals that the act of love's divine origin is also a "Person" in relation to this Divine Kingdom.
18. Gramsci (2013, 164).; quoted in Gramsci (1971, 447–48).
19. I would like to thank Zachary Willcutt for his helpful comments regarding Augustine after reading an earlier draft of this chapter.
20. Aquinas. (1947, ST I-II, 34, a4).

NOTES

21 Hobbes (1994, 75; Ch. 13, §3).
22 It may be fruitful for discussion to examine the relationship between the dilemma in Plato's *Euthyphro* and this dilemma regarding Natural Law. Further, the link to Leibniz's discussion of the "best of all possible worlds" would also be fruitful to discuss here.
23 It is interesting to wonder regarding the relationship between "contemplation" as it appears in the writings of Plato and Aristotle and our "original state." For example, were we so deep in contemplation (of God) that we did not notice our nakedness?
24 The question to what extent Freemasonry, the founding principles of America, the ideas of Equality, and Tolerance toward Freedom of Religion stem from Hobbes' type of thinking, here, is outside the scope of our present investigation.
25 This term was, at least, inspired by Deleuze. If Deleuze uses this term, I apologize that I have lost the reference.
26 This distinction comes from the following work: Byron (2015). I would like to thank Dr. Byron for our conversations regarding ethics in general and Hobbes in particular.
27 Shakespeare. *Hamlet*, Act 2, Scene 2.
28 From Hume's: *Treatise of Human Nature*, Bk III.
29 Kant (2012).
30 Beck (1950, 1).
31 Søren Kierkegaard, *Journal I*.
32 Deleuze (2006, 22).
33 Translation slightly modified.
34 I would like to point out to "Grouchy Grammarians" that this word is not a typo. It is not a misspelling of the word "throes," which connotes *pathos* and the pangs of sorrow; rather, this term comes from Martin Heidegger' *Being & Time*, and refers to the idea that the movement of (universal) Being "throws" itself as individual beings, and the individual being-in-the-throw has the lived-experience of its life.
35 Epigraph for "Book Five: We Fearless Ones" of Nietzsche's *Cheerful Science*.
36 I have made minor corrections to Kaufmann's translation of this section throughout.
37 Nietzsche's reference to Eudaimonism here is not a reference to the Platonic and Aristotelian models.
38 Nietzsche's position here can also be read as extreme here: it is a call to public policy. Rather than allow the sick, weak, and feeble to survive, while a "priestly" class profits from diminishing their suffering, Nietzsche may be read (whether he intended this or not is controversial) as advocating for euthanasia and eugenics.

Bibliography

Allen, Michael J. B. 1984. *The Platonism of Marsilio Ficino: A Study of his Phaedrus Commentary, Its Sources and Genesis*. Berkeley: University of California Press.

Aquinas, St. Thomas. 1928. *On Buying and Selling on Credit*. Translated by A. O'Rahilly. *Irish Ecclesiastical Record* 31.

———. 1947. *The Summa Theologica of St. Thomas Aquinas*. Translated by Fathers of the English Dominican Province. New York: Benzinger Brothers.

Aristophanes. 1908. *The Birds of Aristophanes: Acted at Athens at the Great Dionysia B.C. 414*. Translated by B. B. Rogers. London: George Bell & Sons.

———. 2002. *Frogs. Assemblywomen. Wealth*. Translated by J. Henderson. Cambridge, MA: Harvard University Press.

Aristotle. 1924. *Metaphysics*. Translated by W. D. Ross. In *The Complete Works of Aristotle: The Revised Oxford Translation*, Vol. II, edited by J. Barnes, 1552–728. Princeton, NJ: Princeton University Press.

———. 1950. *Physics*. Translated by W. D. Ross. R. P. Hardie and Revised by R. K. Gaye. In *The Complete Works of Aristotle*, Vol. II, edited by J. Barnes, 315–446. Princeton, NJ: Princeton University Press.

———. 1984. *On the Soul*. Translated by J. A. Smith. In *The Complete Works of Aristotle: The Revised Oxford Translation*, Vol. II, edited by J. Barnes, 641–92. Princeton, NJ: Princeton University Press.

———. 1995a. *Poetics*. Translated by I. Bywater. In *The Complete Works of Aristotle*, Vol. II, edited by J. Barnes, 2316–40. Princeton, NJ: Princeton University Press.

———. 1995b. *Politics*. Translated by B. Jowett. In *The Complete Works of Aristotle*, Vol. II, edited by J. Barnes, 1986–2129. Princeton, NJ: Princeton University Press.

———. 2009. *Nicomachean Ethics*. Translated by R. Crisp. Cambridge: Cambridge University Press.

Athanasius. (2016). *On the Incarnation*. A. Robertson (Trans.). New York: Witaker House.

Augustine. 1958. *The City of God*. Translated by V. J. Bourke. Garden City, NY: Image.

———. 1986. *Confessions of St. Augustine*. Brewster, MA: Paraclete Press

———. 1993. *On Free Choice of the Will*. Translated by T. Williams. New York: Hackett.

———. 2002. *On the Trinity: Books 8–15*. Translated by S. McKenna. Cambridge: Cambridge University Press.

Balz, Horst R., and Gerhard Schneider. 1993. *Exegetical Dictionary of the New Testament*. Grand Rapids, MI: Eerdmans.

Barker, Ernest. 1906. *The Political Thought of Plato and Aristotle*. New York: G. P. Putnam's Sons

Beck, Lewis White. 1950. Introduction: Kant and his Predecessors. *Critique of Practical Reason and Other Writings in Moral Philosophy*. Chicago, IL: University of Chicago Press.

Beckman, James. 1979. *The Religious Dimension of Socrates' Thought*. Ontario: Wilfrid Laurier University Press.

Bellamy, Richard. 2010. Dirty Hands and Clean Gloves: Liberal Ideals and Real Politics. *European Journal of Political Theory* 9(4): 412–30.

Benner, Erica. 2009. *Machiavelli's Ethics*. Princeton, NJ: Princeton University Press.

Berlin, Isaiah. 1958. The Originality of Machiavelli. In *Against the Current: Essays in the History of Ideas*, edited by H. Hardy, 25–79. Oxford: Oxford University Press.

BIBLIOGRAPHY

Byron, Michael. 2015. *Submission and Subjection in Leviathan: Good Subjects in the Hobbesian Commonwealth*. London: Palgrave Macmillan.

Cicero. 1976. *De Inventione*. Translated by H. Hubbell. *Works*, Vol. II. London: Heinemann.

Clissord, Henry. 1829. *The last hours of eminent Christians*. London: C. J. G. & F. Rivington.

Deleuze, Gilles. 1994. *Difference & Repetition*. Translated by P. Patton. New York: Columbia University.

_____. 2005. *Expressionism in Philosophy: Spinoza*. Translated by M. Joughin. New York: Zone Books.

_____. 2006. *Nietzsche & Philosophy*. Translated by M. Hardt. New York: Columbia University Press.

Duns Scotus, John. 1968. *Duns Scotus on the Will and Morality*. Translated by A. B. Wolter. Washington, DC: Catholic University Press.

Epictetus. 1998. *Encheiridion*. Translated by W. I. Matson. In *Classics of Philosophy*, Vol I, edited by L. P. Pojman. Oxford: Oxford University Press.

Feingold, Lawrence. 2010. *The Natural Desire to See God According to St. Thomas Aquinas and His Interpreters*. Ave Maria, FL: Sapientia Press.

Ficino, Marsilio. 1559. *Theologia Platonica de immortalitate animorum*. Paris: Apud Aegidium Gorbinum.

_____. 1981. *Marsilio Ficino and the Phaedran Charioteer*. Translated and introduction by M. J. B. Allen. Berkeley: University of California Press.

Finnis, John. 1980. *Natural Law and Natural Rights*. Oxford: Oxford University Press.

Girard, René. 1979. *Violence and the Sacred*. Translated by P. Gregory. Baltimore, MD: Johns Hopkins University Press.

Gramsci, Antonio. 1971. *Selections from the Prison Notebooks*. Translated and edited by Q. Horare and G. N. Smith. London: Lawrence & Wishart.

_____. 2013. *Quaderni dal carcere*. Vol. IV: *Passato e presente*. Torino: Giulio Einaudi.

Gurney, Joseph J. 1880. *On the Distinguishing Views and Practices of the Society of Friends*. New York: William Wood & Company.

Guthrie, W. K. C. 1979. *A History of Greek Philosophy, vol. II: The Presocratic Tradition from Parmenides to Democritus*. Cambridge: Cambridge University Press.

Hampshire, Stuart. 1978. *Public and Private Morality*. In *Public and Private Morality*, edited by S. Hampshire, 23–54. Cambridge: Cambridge University Press.

_____. 2001. *Justice is Conflict*. Princeton, NJ: Princeton University Press.

Hansen, William. 2005. *Classical Mythology: A Guide to the Mythical World of the Greeks and Romans*. Oxford: Oxford University Press.

Hegel, G. W. F. 1967. *Philosophy of Right*. Translated by T. M. Knox. Oxford: Oxford University Press.

_____. 1977. *Phenomenology of Spirit*. Translated by A. V. Miller. Oxford: Oxford University Press.

Heidegger, Martin. 1984. *Early Greek Thinking*. Translated by D. F. Krell and F. A. Capuzzi. New York: Harper & Row.

_____. 2001. "What Are Poets for?" In *Poetry, Language, Thought*. Translated by A. Hofstadter, 87–140. . New York: Harper & Row.

Heidegger, Martin, and Eugen Fink. 1979. *Heraclitus Seminar*. Translated by C. H. Seibert. Tuscaloosa: The University of Alabama Press.

Heraclitus. 1981. *The Art and Thought of Heraclitus: An Edition of the Fragments with Translation and Commentary*. Translated by C. H. Kahn. New York: Cambridge University.

_____. 2003. *Fragments*. Translated by J. Hillman and B. Haxton. New York: Penguin Books.

Hobbes, Thomas. 1994. *Leviathan*. Indianapolis, IN: Hackett Publishing.

Hoffmann, Tobias. 2010. Intellectualism and Voluntarism. In *The Cambridge History of Medieval Philosophy*, edited by R. Pasnau, 414–27. Cambridge: Cambridge University Press.

Hume, David. 1751. *An Enquiry Concerning the Principles of Morals*. London: A. Millar.

_____. 1874. *A Treatise on Human Nature*, Vol. I. London: Longmans, Gree, and Co.

BIBLIOGRAPHY

———. 1985. *Essays, Moral, Political, and Literary*. New York: Cosimo.

———. 1999. *An Enquiry Concerning Human Understanding*. Indianapolis, IN: Hackett Publishing.

Jaeger, Werner. 1945. *Paideia: The Ideals of Greek Culture, Vol. I: Archaic Greece, The Mind of Athens*. Translated by Gilbert Highet. New York: Oxford.

Kant, Immanuel. 1960. *Religion Within the Limits of Reason Alone*. Translated by T. M. Greene and H. H. Hudson. New York: Harper & Row.

———. 1996. "On the Miscarriage of All Philosophical Trials in Theodicy." In *Religion and Rational Theology*. Translated by P. Guyer and E. Matthews, 19–38. Cambridge: Cambridge University Press.

———. 1997. *Lectures on Ethics*. Translated by P. Heath. Cambridge: Cambridge University Press.

———. 1998. *Critique of Pure Reason*. Translated by P. Guyer and A. W. Wood. Cambridge: Cambridge University Press.

———. 1999. *Critique of Practical Reason*. Translated by M. Gregor. Cambridge: Cambridge University Press.

———. 2001. *Lectures on Metaphysics*. Translated by K. Ameriks and S. Naragon. New York: Cambridge University Press.

———. 2002. *Groundwork of the Metaphysics of Morals*. Translated by M. J. Gregor and J. Timmermann. Cambridge: Cambridge University Press.Press.

———. 2012. *The Metaphysics of Morals*. Translated by M. J. Gregor. Cambridge: Cambridge University Press.

Kantorowicz, E. 1957. *The King's Two Bodies: A Study in Medieval Political Theology*. Princeton, NJ: Princeton University Press.

Kavka, Gregory S. 1986. *Hobbesian Moral and Political Theory*. Princeton, NJ: Princeton University Press.

Kennedy, J. B. 2011. *The Musical Structure of Plato's Dialogues*. New York: Acumen.

Kierkegaard, Søren. 1962. *Works of Love*. Translated by H. V. Hong and E. H. Hong. New York: Harper & Brothers.

———. 1980. *The Sickness Unto Death*. Translated by H. V. Hong and E. H. Hong. Princeton, NJ: Princeton University Press.

———. 1981. *The Concept of Anxiety*. Translated by H. V. Hong and E. H. Hong. Princeton, NJ: Princeton University Press.

———. 1983. *Fear & Trembling and Repetition*. Translated by H. V. Hong and E. H. Hong. Princeton, NJ: Princeton University Press.

———. 1987. *Either/Or, Vol. I*. Translated by H. V. Hong and E. H. Hong. Princeton, NJ: Princeton University Press.

———. 1988. *Stages on Life's Way*. Translated by H. V. Hong and E. H. Hong. Princeton, NJ: Princeton University Press.

———. 1992. *Eighteen Upbuilding Discourses*. Translated by H. V. Hong and E. H. Hong. Princeton, NJ: Princeton University Press.

———. 1993. *Upbuilding Discourses in Various Spirits*. Translated by H. V. Hong and E. H. Hong. Princeton, NJ: Princeton University Press.

———. 1998. *The Point of View*. Translated by H. V. Hong and E. H. Hong. Princeton, NJ: Princeton University Press.

———. 2009. *"The Moment" and Late Writings*. Translated by H. V. Hong and E. H. Hong. Princeton, NJ: Princeton University Press.

Kohlberg, L. 1976. *Moral stages and moralization*. In T. Lickona (Ed.). *Handbook of Socialization Theory*. (pp. 31–53). New York: Holt, Rinehart & Winston.

Kohn, Hans. 1967. *The Idea of Nationalism*. New York: Collier Books.

Korsgaard, Christine M. 2006. Introduction. In *Immanuel Kant's Groundwork of the Metaphysics of Morals*. Translated by M. Gregor, vii–xxx. Cambridge: Cambridge University Press.

Laertius, Diogenes. 1925/1979. *Lives of Eminent Philosophers*, Vol. I–II. Translated by R. D. Hicks. Cambridge: Cambridge University Press.

Lewis, David K. 1986. *The Plurality of Worlds*. Oxford: Oxford University Press.

Liddell, Henry George, and Robert Scott. 1883. *A Greek-English Lexicon*. New York: Harper & Brothers.

Machiavelli, Niccolò. 1995. *The Prince*. Translated by D. Wootton. Indianapolis, IN: Hackett Publishing.

Manchester, Peter. (1986). *The Religious Experience of Time and Eternity*. In A.H. Armstrong (Ed.). *Classical Mediterranean Spirituality: Egyptian, Greek, Roman*. London: Routledge & Kegan Paul.

BIBLIOGRAPHY

Mead, G.R.S. (1896). *Orpheus*. London: Theosophical Publishing Society,

Merriam-Webster.com 2016. Accessed June 2, 2016. http://www.merriam-webster.com

Mill, D. V. 2001. *Liberty, Rationality, and Agency in Hobbes' Leviathan*. Albany: SUNY Press.

Mill, J. S. 1874. On Nature. In *Nature: The Utility of Religion and Theism*. London: Longmans, Green, Reader, and Dyer.

_____. 1960. *Autobiography*. New York: Columbia University Press.

_____. 2002. *Utilitarianism*. Indianapolis, IN: Hackett Publishing.

Nietzsche, Friedrich. 1967. *The Birth of Tragedy Out of the Spirit of Music*. Translated by W. Kaufmann. New York: Vintage Books.

_____. 1968. *The Will to Power*. Edited and translated by W. Kaufmann and R. J. Hollingdale. New York: Vintage Books.

_____. 1974. *The Gay Science*. Translated by W. Kaufmann. New York: Vintage Books.

_____. 1977. *Homer's Contest*. Edited and translated by W. Kaufmann and The Portable Nietzsche. London: Penguin.

_____. 1979. "On Truth and Lies in a Nonmoral Sense." In *Philosophy and Truth: Selections from Nietzsche's Notebooks of the Early 1870's*, edited and translated by D. Breazeale, 79–97. Atlantic Highlands, NJ: Humanities Press.

_____. 1989a. *Beyond Good & Evil: Prelude to a Philosophy of the Future*. Translated by W. Kaufmann. New York: Vintage Books.

_____. 1989b. *On the Genealogy of Morals/Ecce Homo*. Translated by W. Kaufmann. New York: Vintage Books.

_____. 1990. *Twilight of the Idols/The Anti-Christian*. Translated by R. J. Hollingdale. London: Penguin Books.

_____. 2006. *Thus Spoke Zarathustra*. Translated by A. Del Caro. Cambridge: Cambridge University Press.

O'Connor, D.J. (1967). *Aquinas and Natural Law*. New York, NY: Palgrave.

Pettit, Philip. 2001. *A Theory of Freedom: From the Psychology to the Politics of Agency*. Oxford: Oxford University Press.

Plato. 1997a. *Apology*. Translated by G. M. A. Grube. *Plato Complete Works*. Edited by John M. Cooper. Indianapolis, IN: Hackett Publishing.

_____. 1997b. *Cratylus*. Translated by G. M. A. Grube. In *Plato Complete Works*, edited by John M. Cooper. Indianapolis, IN: Hackett Publishing.

_____. 1997c. *Gorgias*. Translated by G. M. A. Grube. In *Plato Complete Works*, edited by John M. Cooper. Indianapolis, IN: Hackett Publishing.

_____. 1997d. *Ion*. Translated by G. M. A. Grube. In *Plato Complete Works*, edited by John M. Cooper. Indianapolis, IN: Hackett Publishing.

_____. 1997e. *Laws*. Translated by G. M. A. Grube. In *Plato Complete Works*, edited by John M. Cooper. Indianapolis, IN: Hackett Publishing.

_____. 1997f. *Meno*. Translated by G. M. A. Grube. In *Plato Complete Works*, edited by John M. Cooper. Indianapolis, IN: Hackett Publishing.

_____. 1997g. *Phaedo*. Translated by G. M. A. Grube. In *Plato Complete Works*, edited by John M. Cooper. Indianapolis, IN: Hackett Publishing.

_____. 1997h. *Phaedrus*. Translated by A. Nehamas and P. Woodruff. In *Plato Complete Works*, edited by John M. Cooper. Indianapolis, IN: Hackett Publishing.

_____. 1997i. *Philebus*. Translated by A. Nehamas and P. Woodruff. In *Plato Complete Works*, edited by John M. Cooper. Indianapolis, IN: Hackett Publishing.

_____. 1997j. *Protagoras*. Translated by G. M. A. Grube. In *Plato Complete Works*, edited by John M. Cooper. Indianapolis, IN: Hackett Publishing.

_____. 1997k. *Republic*. Translated by G. M. A. Grube and Revised by C. D. C. Reeve. In *Plato Complete Works*, edited by John M. Cooper. Indianapolis, IN: Hackett Publishing.

_____. 1997l. *Sophist*. Translated by N. P. White. In *Plato Complete Works*, edited by John M. Cooper. Cambridge: Hackett Publishing.

_____. 1997m. *Symposium*. Translated by A. Nehamas and P. Woodruff. In *Plato Complete Works*, edited by John M. Cooper. Indianapolis, IN: Hackett Publishing.

BIBLIOGRAPHY

_____. 1997n. *Theaetetus*. Translated by M. J. Levett and Revised by M. Burnyeat. In *Plato Complete Works*, edited by John M. Cooper. Indianapolis, IN: Hackett Publishing.

_____. 1997o. *Timaeus*. Translated by D. J. Zeyl. In *Plato Complete Works*, edited by John M. Cooper. Indianapolis, IN: Hackett Publishing.

Rachels, James. 2003. *The Elements of Moral Philosophy*. Boston, MA: McGraw Hill.

Rogers, Carl R. 1957. "The Necessary and Sufficient Conditions of Therapeutic Personality Change." *Journal of Consulting Psychology* 21(2): 95–103.

de Romilly, J. (1968). *Time in Greek Tragedy*. Ithaca, NY: Cornell University Press.

Rommen, Heinrich A. 1998. *The Natural Law: A Study in Legal and Social History and Philosophy*. Translated by T. R. Hanley. Indianapolis, IN: Liberty Fund.

Ruck, Carl A. P. 1981. "Mushrooms and Philosophers." *Journal of Ethnopharmacology* 4(2): 179–205.

_____. 2006. *Sacred Mushrooms of the Goddess and the Secrets of Eleusis*. Berkeley, CA: Ronin Publishing.

Ruck, Carl A. P., and Danny Staples. 1994. *The World of Classical Myth: Gods and Goddesses, Heroines and Heroes*. Durham, NC: Carolina Academic Press.

Scalambrino, Frank. 2011. *Non-Being & Memory*. (Doctoral Dissertation). Retrieved from ProQuest. (UMI: 3466382).

_____. 2015a. *Full Throttle Heart: Nietzsche, Beyond Either/Or*. New Philadelphia, OH: The Eleusinian Press.

_____. 2015b. The Temporality of Damnation. In *The Concept of Hell*, edited by R. Arp and B. McCraw, 66–82. New York: Palgrave.

_____. 2015c. "The Vanishing Subject: Becoming Who You Cybernetically Are." In *Social Epistemology & Technology*, edited by F. Scalambrino, 197–206. London: Roman & Littlefield International.

_____. 2016. *Meditations on Orpheus: Love, Death, and Transformation*. Pittsburgh, PA: Black Water Phoenix Press.

Schneewind, J. B. 1998. *The Invention of Autonomy*. Cambridge: Cambridge University Press.

Schopenhauer, Arthur. 1926. *Selected Essays of Schopenhauer*. Edited and translated by E. B. Bax. London: G. Bell and Sons.

_____. 1969. *The World as Will and Representation*, Vol. 1. Translated by E. F. J. Payne. New York: Dover Publications.

_____. 2005. *Philosophical Writings*. Translated by W. Schirmacher. New York: Continuum, 2005.

Warden, John. 1982. *Orpheus, the Metamorphoses of a Myth*. Toronto: University of Toronto Press.

Watkins, J. W. N. 1973. *Hobbes's System of Ideas*. London: Hutchinson University Library.

Whitehead, Alfred North. 1985. *Process and Reality*. New York: Free Press.

Zuntz, Günther. 1971. *Persephone: Three Essays on Religion and Thought in Magna Graecia*. Oxford: Clarendon Press.

Index

A
Absolute monarchy, 46
Absolutism, 7, 8
   divine command theory, 8
   functionalism, 8
Abstractions, 154
Academic skepticism, 70
Action
   involuntary, 51, 52
   judgment in, 12–13
   prescriptive ethics, 3. *See also* Behavior, prescriptive ethics
   virtuous, 49–50
   voluntary, 50
Actuality
   defined, 44
   potentiality and, 44–45
Act Utilitarianism, 117
Adam and Eve, 80
Aesthetic stage, 144
After life, 80
Agent, 11. *See also* Action
   virtuous, necessary conditions for, 49
Alexander the Great, 43, 67
Altruism, 6
   Nietzsche on, 149
Amor Fati, 152, 154–159, 160
Analytical division of ethics, 2–3
Anamnesis, 18, 21, 38–40
Anaximander, 36
Ancient period (600 BC–400 AD), 1, 2
Angelic beings, 88
Anger, 56
Animality, 125
Animi intentio, 90

Anxiety, 56
Apatheia, 76–78
Aporia, 72
Appetites, intellect and, 53
Applied ethics, 3
Aquinas, Thomas, 83, 87, 88, 89, 91–94
Arbitrary rule, 46
Archimedes, 60
Aristippus, 68
Aristotle, 1, 17, 43–63
   on characters, 52–53
   on choice, 50–52
   on city, 45–46
   Doctrine of the Mean, 54–55
   Four Causes, 43–44, 85
   on friendship, 60–61
   on ignorance of particulars, 51
   on inclinations, 48–49
   on justice, 46–47
   on moral and intellectual virtues, 53–55
   Natural Law and, 45, 46–47
   on partnerships, 45
   on pleasure, 57–58
   on potentiality and actuality, 44–45
   on self-love, 58–60
   on self-realization, 55–57
   on soul, 48
   on virtue, 49
   on virtuous action, 49–50
Artificial virtues, 114, 115
Ascetic ideals, 150–51
Askesis, 67, 76–78
Ataraxia, 68–69, 71–72, 88
Augustine, 88–91
Aurelius, Marcus, 74

INDEX

Autarkeia, 67
Autobiography (Mill), 118

B
Bad conscience, 150
Beatitude, 87–88
   Theodicy and, 95–96
Beethoven, Ludwig van, 124
Behavior, prescriptive ethics, 3. *See also* Action, prescriptive ethics
Being & Time (Heidegger), 164n34
Bentham, Jeremy, 111, 116, 117–118
Beyond Good & Evil (Nietzsche), 151, 154
Bioethics, 3
Blameworthiness, 51
Body and soul, 144–145
Bonaventure, 94–96
Business ethics, 3

C
Calvin, John, 93
Campbell, Joseph, 36
Cardinal virtues, 22–23
Casuistical, 120
Categorical imperative, 131–133
Catholic Church. *See* Church
Catholic Ethics, 79
Catholicism, 79
Catholic Revolution, 79–109
Cave Allegory, 17–19
Celestial Be-ing, 23–24, 31, 58, 81, 129, 146
Characterological disorder, 7. *See also* Egoism; Narcissism
Characters, 3
   Aritotle on, 52–53
   phenomenological reading of, 53
   types of, 52–53
Charioteer Allegory, 19–20. *See also* Tripartite soul
Charmides (Plato), 22
The Cheerful Science (Nietzsche), 154
Choice, Aristotle on, 50–52
Christ, 79–80
Christianity, 79
Chrysippus of Soli, 73, 77–78

Church, 79–80
   political influence, 99
   state and, 108–109
Churchil, Winston, 121
Cicero, 3, 75
   on cardinal virtues, 22
City, 106. *See also* Kingdom
   Aristotle on, 45–46, 88
   just, 22
   Kant on, 131–133, 136–137
   and soul, analogy, 22–23, 30, 39, 76, 98, 100, 131–133
   unjust, 22
The City of God (Augustine), 88, 136
City of Man, 88. *See also* City
Cleanthes, 73
Cognition, 9
Cognitive behavioral therapy, 78
Commutative justice, 4, 47. *See also* Justice
Comparative ethics, 3. *See also* Normative ethics
Compliance, 163n9
Conative control. *See* Volitional control
Conception, 14
Concepts, 154
Congruence, 56
   trust and, 61. *See also* Friendship
Conscience, 56
   bad, 150
   heart and, 87
   Nietzsche on, 155
Consequentialism, 97–99
Constitutional democracy, 115
Contemplation, 58, 164n23
Contemporary period (1901 AD – present), 1, 2
Continent character, 52, 53
Contract, 115
Convention, 115
Conventionalism, 9, 115–116
Conventional Justice, 47
Copper Rule, 107
Corporeal world, 74
Cosmopolitanism, 66–67, 108
Courage, 22. *See also* Fortitude
Cratylus (Plato), 37, 38
Critique of Practical Reason (Kant), 123, 136
Critique of Pure Reason (Kant), 124

INDEX

Cultural relativism, 9
Cynic Crates of Thebes, 73
Cynicism, 66–67
Cynosarges, 66
Cyrenaic hedonism, 68
Cyrenaic School, 68

D
Daimon, 35
Daimonic self-love, 152–154
Dante, 44
De Anima (Aristotle), 48
Debt, 149–150
Decalogue, 86
Decision-making, 44
Deleuze, Gilles, 105–106, 151
Deliberation, 50
Delphos, 21
Descriptive ethics, 3. See also Normative ethics
Descriptive psychological egoism, 6
Desires, 13, 69–70
    natural and necessary, 69
    natural but non-necessary, 69
    vain and empty, 69
Despair, aesthetic stage and, 144
Destiny *vs.* fate, 159–160
Determinism, freedom and, 12
Dignity, 77–78, 134
Dike, 13
Dimensions of Becoming and Being, 18, 21
Diogenes of Sinope, 66, 67
Diotima, 21
Dirty Hands, 103
Discursive control, 13
Dissimulation, 103
Distributive justice, 4, 47. See also Justice
Divine Command Theory, 8, 11–12. See also Absolutism
    criticisms of, 11–12
    defined, 11
Divine Justice, 47
Divine justice, 5. See also Justice
Doctrine of the Mean, 54–55
Dominican intellectualism, 91–94
Don Giovanni (Mozart), 144

Duns Scotus, 94–96
Duties, 108
Duty, 15

E
Efficient Cause, 44
Egoism, 6–7
    altruism *vs.*, 6
    characterological disorder, 7
    descriptive psychological, 6
    ethical, 7
    pathology, 7
    prescriptive psychological, 6
The Elements of Moral Philosophy (Rachels), 11
Eleusinian Mysteries, 31, 35–41
Eleutheria, 67
Empiricism, Hume on, 116
Empiricus, Sextus, 3
Epictetus, 74, 75, 76, 77–78
Epicurean hedonism, 68
Epicurus, 68, 69, 115
Epithumia, 20
Epoche, 71
Erôs, 20
Erotic desire, 20. See also Love
Eternal Return, 157–158
Ethical egoism, 7
Ethics
    analytical division, 2–3
    applied, 3
    defined, 4
    etymology, 3
    historical division, 2
    meta-ethics, 2
    morality *vs.*, 3–4
    normative, 2–3
Ethike, 52
Ethikos, 3
Ethos, 3
Eudaimonia, 54, 58. See also Happiness
    ataraxia and, 68–69
    Catholic Revolution and, 87–88. See also Beatitude
    Nietzsche and, 160–161
    Plato on, 31–34
    teleological, 62–63

INDEX

Eudaimonism, 31–34
Euripides, 41
Evil, 85–86. *See also* Sin
    Kant on, 126–127
Excellence of soul, 29

F
Families, 45–46
Fatalism, 12, 78
Fatalism, freedom and, 12
Fate
    destiny *vs.*, 159–160
    Machiavelli on, 101
Fichte, Johann Gottlieb, 124
Ficino, Marsilio, 19, 21, 81
Final Cause, 44
Finnis, John, 47, 86, 107
Five senses, 18
Formal Cause, 44
Forms, 18–19
    being immutable, 18
    soul as, 19
    spiritual dimension toward, 21
Fortitude, 22
Fortuna, 102
Fortuna (Machiavelli), 101
Four Causes, 43–44, 85
Fourfold division of historical periods, 1, 2
Franciscan voluntarism, 94–97
Frankness, 61
Freedom, 12–14, 160
    dignity and, 134
    fatalism, 12
    future and, 13–14
    hard determinism, 12
    indeterminism, 12
    necessity and, 134–135
    soft determinism, 12
Freedom of speech, 67
"Freedom of the Will," 12
Freemasonry, 164n24
Free self, 13
Free Will, 108
    intention and, 89–91
Friendship, 60–61

Full Throttle Heart (Scalambrino), 153
Functionalism, 8. *See also* Absolutism
Future, and freedom, 13–14

G
"The Garden of Eden," 5
German Idealism, 124
God
    and Hell, 93–94
    will of, 94–95
Golden Rule, 107
Good
    Kant on, 125
    Nietzsche on, 149
Good Will, 133–135
Grace, 84–85
Graphein, 3
The Greatest Weight (Nietzsche), 157, 158
Great-Souled Person, 58–60, 101
    Nietzsche on, 149
Greek, 3
Grotius, Hugo, 86
Grouchy Grammarians, 164n34
Guilt, 149–150

H
Happiness. *See also* Eudaimonia
    Aristotle on, 58–63, 98
    Epicureans and, 68–69
    excellence of soul and, 29, 30
    as feeling, 14
    as human destiny, 62–63
    Kant on, 133–137
    Nietzsche on, 159–161
    Plato on, 31–41
    psychological aspect, 14
    soteriological aspect, 14
    super-natural, 83, 87–88
    supervenience, 15
    teleological aspect, 14
    utilitarianism, 116–121
Hard determinism, freedom and, 12
Harm, 119–120
Harmonic manifestation. *See* Supervenience
Harmonic visualization, 77

INDEX

Harmony, 12, 13, 14, 15, 29, 31, 132. *See also* Happiness; Virtues
  Four Causes and, 85
  friendships and, 61
  perfecting powers of soul by, 55–56, 89
  providence and predetermination in, 89–91
Heart
  conscience and, 87
  goodness, 127, 133–137
  law written in, 87
  purity of, 143–146
  will with moral law and, 127
Hedonic Calculus, 117, 118, 119
Hedonism, 117
Hedonism, 68–70
Hegel, Georg Wilhelm Friedrich, 124, 137
Heidegger, Martin, 36, 164n34
Hell and God, 93–94
Henosis, 146, 160
Herd instinct, 149
Hesiod, 36
Hierosgamos, 146, 160
Hippies, 66
Historical division, of ethics, 2
Historical periods, 1
  four, 1, 2
  nine, 1, 2
Hitler, Adolf, 121
Hobbes, Thomas, 5, 103–109
Hölderlin, Friedrich, 34, 124
Holy Spirit, 81
Holy Trinity, 81
Honor, 59–60
  praise *vs.,* 59–60
Hosios, 146, 163n10
Hosiosis, 146
Human freedom. *See* Freedom
Humanity, 125
Human sacrifice, utilitarianism and, 120–121
Hume, David, 12, 111–116

I
Ignorance of particulars, 51
Imperatives, 127–129
Impetuosity, 56
Inclinations, 48–49
Incommensurability, 9–10. *See also* Relativism
Incontinence, 56
Incontinent character, 52, 53
Indeterminism, freedom and, 12
Individual, 11
  justice and, 22
Instrumental rationality, 152
Instrumental/relativist orientation, 6
Integrity, 102
Intellect, 21
  appetites and, 53
  as feminine, 152
  Nietzsche on, 152
  on-calculative, 152
Intellectualism, 91–93
Intellectual virtues, 53–55
Intention
  free will and, 89–91
Intentionalism, 88–91
Intentions, 50–52
Interest, 48
An Introduction to Catholic Ethics, 79
Intuitive man, 154
Involuntary actions, 51, 52
Is and Ought, 113–114

J
Jaeger, Werner, 36
Jesus, 81
Judgment, 9
  in action, 12–13
Juridical person, 11
Just city, 22
Justice, 22
  Aristotle's vision of, 46–47
  commutative, 4
  distributive, 4
  divine, 5
  individual and, 22
  interpretations of, 5
  legal, 5
  pleasant life and, 22
  social, 5
  spheres of, 4–5

INDEX

Justice (*continued*)
  suspension of, 72–73
  as utility, 116–117
  violence and, 99–100

K

Kant, Immanuel, 23, 24, 123–137
  on categorical imperative, 131–133
  on evil in human nature, 126–127
  on Good Will, 133–135
  on imperatives, 127–129
  Kingdom of Ends, 136–137
  propensities *vs.* predispositions, 126–127
  on self-gold, 125–126
  on virtue, 129–130
Kantian Copernican Revolution, 124
Katalepsis, 74–76
Kharakteristikos, 3
Kharassein, 3
Kierkegaard, Søren, 143–146
Kingdom, 106, 108–109, 136–137. *See also* City
Kingdom of Ends, 124, 136–137
Kingdom of Nature, 136
KIR. *See* Knight of Infinite Resignation (KIR)
Knight of Faith (KOF), 144, 146
Knight of Infinite Resignation (KIR), 144, 146
Kohlberg, Lawrence, 5

L

Ladder of love. *See Scala amoris*
Laertius, Diogenes, 32
Latin, 3
Law of Attraction, 81
Laws, 22–23
Laws (Plato), 22, 24
Learning, Plato and, 18
Lectures on Ethics (Kant), 136
Lectures on Metaphysics (Kant), 23, 126
Legal justice, 5. *See also* Justice
Leviathan, 108–109
Liberty, 119, 120
Life, Aristotle on, 45
Locus of control, 77
Logoi, 21, 22–23

Logos
  Aristotle, 50, 51, 56–57
  Plato on, 24–27
  as virtue ethics, 21
Longtin, Lucien F., 79
Lord of the Rings (Tolkien), 22
Love
  Aristotle on, 58–60
  Charioteer Allegory, 19–20
  embodied soul and, 21
  Kierkegaard on, 145–146
  Platonic, 20–21
  scala amoris, 21
Lying, Nietzsche on, 152

M

Machiavelli, Niccolò, 97–103
Man, as political animal, 45
Masters. *See also* Slaves
  morality, 149, 151
  pity, 155
  and slaves partnership, 45
Material Cause, 44
Meditations on Orpheus (Scalambrino), 35
Melancholia, 145
Men and women partnership, 45
Meno (Plato), 37, 160
Meta-ethics, 2
The Metaphysics of Morals (Kant), 129
Middle ages (401–1600 AD), 1, 2
Mill, John Stuart, 111, 116, 118–120
Miracles, 94–95
Moderation, 54
Modern period (1601–1900 AD), 1, 2
Moral conventionalism, 9, 10. *See also* Relativism
Moralis, 3
Morality
  defined, 4
  ethics *vs.*, 3–4
Moral Justice, 47
Moral Law, 124
Morally bankrupt, 121
Morally good person *vs.* person of good morals, 135
Moral self-esteem, 126
Moral virtues, 53–55

INDEX

Mother Teresa, 84–85
Mozart, 144
Much Ado about Nothingi (Shakespeare), 139
Multi-culturalism, 9
Mysterium coniunctionis, 145–146, 160
Mythico/religious interpretation of justice, 5
Myth of Er, 32, 156–157
    Noble Lie *vs.*, 34–35
Myth of Narcissus, 58

N
Narcissism, 7
    self-love *vs.*, 58–59
National Catholic Educational Association, 79
Natural and necessary desires, 69
Natural but non-necessary desires, 69
Natural functions, 49
Natural harmony, 89
Natural justice, 46
Natural Law
    Aristotle and, 45, 46–47
    intellectualism and, 91
    Kant and, 123, 127–129, 132
    Plato and, 27–31
    Rommen on, 86
    Stoics and, 74–76, 82
    Ten Commandments and, 86–87
    voluntarism and, 103–105
The Natural Law (Rommen), 76
Natural Law and Natural Rights (Finnis), 47, 86
Natural law of Antiquity, 105
Natural person, 11
Natural right, 46
Nature, 23–31
    rational order-ing of, 27–31
Nazi Blitzkrieg, 121
Negative visualization, 78
Nicomachean Ethics (Aristotle), 43, 46, 49, 50, 57, 58, 60–61, 115, 130
Nietzsche, Friedrich, 146–160
    Amor Fati, 152, 154–159, 160
    Eudaimonia and, 160–161
    On the Genealogy of Morals, 148–151
    The Greatest Weight, 157, 158
    Homer's Contest, 147–148
    on Noble, 157
    on pity, 155
    on Schopenhauer, 146–147
    on State of Nature, 147–148
    on ubiquity of interpretation, 152–154
Nietzsche & Philosophy (Deleuze), 151
Nihilism, 8, 9
    Hume on, 115–116
Ninefold division of historical periods, 1, 2
Noble Lie *vs.* Myth of Er, 34–35
Nomos, 22
Noncognitivism, 9. *See also* Nihilism
Normative ethics, 2–3, 15
Normative relativism. *See* Moral conventionalism
Norms, 3
Novalis, 124

O
Obedience orientation. *See* Punishment and obedience orientation
Objectivism, 7. *See also* Ethical egoism
Old Testament, 126
On the Genealogy of Morals (Nietzsche), 148–151
On the Trinity (Augustine), 90
"On Truth and Lies in a Non-moral Sense" (Nietzsche), 152
Optimistic nature, 5
Order, interpretation of justice, 5
Original Sin, 80
Orpheus, 31, 32, 36–37, 38, 81, 145
Ought and Is, 113–114
Ownership, 10–11

P
Panoramic wisdom, 55–57. *See also* Self-realization
Pantheists, 74
Paradise, 88
Parmenides of Elea, 19
Parrhesia, 67
Particularistic Normative Theory, 116
Partnerships, Aristotle on, 45
Passions, 112–113
Pathos, 7, 56
Perception, 14
Persephone, 31, 32, 35–41

INDEX

Person
    good morals *vs.* morally good, 135
    Great-Souled, 58–60
    juridical, 11
    legal concept, 11
    natural, 11
Personal egoism, 7. *See also* Ethical egoism
Personalty, 125
    defined, 10
    rights, 10–11
Pessimistic nature, 5
Pettit, Philip, 163*n*3
Phaedo (Plato), 40–41
Phaedrus (Plato), 19
Phantasia, 71
Philadelphia, 21
Philia, 20–21, 58. *See also* Platonic love
Philosophy of Right (Hegel), 137
Physics (Aristotle), 44
Piety *(hosios)*, 22
Pindar, 38
Pity, 155
Plato, 17–41, 43
    cardinal virtues, 22–23
    Cave Allegory, 17–19
    Charioteer Allegory, 19–20
    creation myth, 23
    on *Eudaimonia*, 31–34
    learning and, 18
    on love, 19–21
    on Natural Law, 27–31
    on Noble Lie, 34–35
    on Persephone Myth, 35–41
    on pleasant life, 22
Platonic love, 20–21
Pleasure, 56, 57–58, 61
    dynamics of, 69–70
Plutarch, 60
Pneuma, 74
Political justice, 46, 47
Politics (Aristotle), 45
Positivism, Hume's position on, 115–116
Potentiality, and actuality, 44–45
Practical wisdom. *See* Prudence

Praise, 59–60
Predestination, 84–85
Predispositions
    to animality, 125
    to humanity, 125
    human nature, 125
    to personality, 125
    propensities *vs.*, 126–127
Prescriptive ethics, 3. *See also* Normative ethics
Prescriptive psychological egoism, 6
The Prince (Machiavelli), 75
Prisoner's Dilemma, 107
Privacy, rights to, 10
"The Problem of Evil." *See* Theodicy
Propensities *vs.* predispositions, 126–127
Property
    Hobbes on, 106–108
    rights to, 10–11
    types, 10
Providence, 84–85, 93–94, 101–102
    Theodicy and, 93–94
Proximate cause, 93
Prudence, 22, 53–54, 55. *See also* Intellectual virtues
Psyche, 48
Psychology
    motivation theories, 6–7
    Stages of Moral Development, 5, 6
Psychopaths, 7. *See also* Sociopaths
Psychopathy, 7
    sociopathy *vs.*, 7
Public interest, 115
Punishment and obedience orientation, 6
Pyrrhonian skepticism, 70–71
Pyrrho of Elis, 70, 72
Pythagoras, 32

R
Rachels, James, 11
Rackman, H., 51
Rape, 107
Rational animal, human as, 58
Rational control, 13
Rational emotive therapy, 78
Rational man, 154

INDEX

Rational order-ing of nature, 27–31
Realism, 97–99
Reality
  defined, 10
  rights to, 10
Realpolitik, 97, 98–99
Reason, 112–113
Reciprocal justice, 47
Recollecting, 18
Reincarnation, 19
Relativism, 8–9
  moral conventionalism, 9
  subjective naturalism, 8–9
  subjectivism, 9
Religion, Theodicy, 13–14
Remembering, 18
Republic (Plato), 17, 18
Resentment, 149
Ressentiment, 151
Retributive justice. *See* Commutative justice
Rhetoric (Aristotle), 47
Rights
  Hobbes on, 107–108
  to privacy, 10
  to property, 10–11
Rodin, Auguste, 44
Rogers, Carl, 56–57
Romans, 3
Rommen, Heinrich, 76
Ross, W. D., 57
Rule of Law, 46, 107
Rule Utilitarianism, 117
Ruthlessness, 100

S

Sacrifices, 80
Scala amoris, 21
Schelling, Friedrich Wilhelm Joseph, 124
Schopenhauer, Arthur, 124, 137–139
Scriptures, 11
Second Punic War, 60
Self, 11
  free, 13
  Kierkegaard on, 144–145
Self concept, 56–57

Self-destruction, 144
Self-esteem, 126
Self-knowledge, 159
Self-love, 58–60
  daimonic, 152–154
  Kant on, 125–126
  narcissism *vs.*, 58–59
Self-mastery, 55–56
Self-ownership, 41, 145
Self-possession, 60
Self-realization, 53, 55–57
  Nietzsche and, 159, 160, 161
Self-willingness, 13
Seneca, Annaeus, 74, 75, 78
Sensation, 14
Sex, 69–70
Sin, 85–86. *See also* Evil
Skepticism, 70–73
Slave Morality, 141, 150–51
Slave resentment, 149
Slaves. *See also* Masters
  Great-Souled Person and, 150
  happiness and, 149
  mentality, 150
  morality, 149, 151
  pity, 155
Social contract, 6, 115
Social groups, 6
Social justice, 5. *See also* Justice
Sociopaths, 7. *See also* Psychopaths
Sociopathy, 7
  psychopathy *vs.*, 7
Socrates, 25, 27, 28, 29, 30, 32–33, 34, 37–40, 43, 47, 61, 65
Socrates (Plato's character), 18, 21
Socratic wisdom school charts, 141–142
Soft determinism, freedom and, 12
Soul
  Aristotle on, 48
  being immortal, 19
  body and, 144–145
  and city, analogy, 22–23
  embodied, 21
  excellence of, 29
  as form, 19
  intellect and, 21

Soul (*continued*)
   Kierkegaard on, 144–145
   time and, 19
   tripartite, 19–20
   types of, 48
Sovereignty, 98
Species-specific organic conditions, 14
Spirit, 35, 161
   Kierkegaard on, 144
   optimistic-trinitarian reading, 137
   phenomenology of, 137
Spiritual be-ing, 24
Spiritual subsistence, 88
Spiritual vengeance, 149
Stages Along Life's Way (Kierkegaard), 143–145
Stages of Moral Development, 5, 6
State, 106, 108–109
State of Nature
   Aristotle and, 45–46
   Catholic ethics and, 85–86
   concept of, 5
   divine justice and, 29
   Garden of Eden and, 80
   Hobbes and, 105–106, 107–108, 115
   laws in, 34
   Nietzschean reading of, 147–148
   Plato and, 23–24
Stoa poikile, 73
Stoicism, 73–78
The Stoic Manual (Epictetus), 75
Structural Model, 4
Subjective naturalism, 8–9. *See also* Relativism
Subjectivism, 9. *See also* Relativism
Superhuman Prudence, 99
Supervenience, 15
Syllogisms, 44, 51
Symposium (Plato), 21
Synchronicity, 81
Synderesis, 91–93
Syracuse, 60

T
Target Analogy, 24–25, 48, 77
   pessimistic reading of, 139

Temperance, 22
Ten Commandments, 86–87
Tension state, 56
Theaetetus (Plato), 26
Theodicy, 13–14
   Beatitude and, 95–96
   Kant on, 126
   providence and, 93–94
Theological virtues, 22, 83
A Theory of Freedom: From the Psychology to the Politics of Agency (Pettit), 163n3
Theos, 13
Thinking, 14
Thrasymachus, 22
Throes, 164n34
Timaeus (Plato), 23
Time
   forms and, 18, 19
   soul and, 19
Traditionalism, 9–10
Tranquility, 71–73
Transcendentals, 83–84
Tripartite soul, 19–20
Trismegistus, Hermes, 32
Trust, 61. *See also* Friendship

U
Ubiquity of interpretation, 152–154
Underworld, 36–37
Universal-ethical-principle orientation, 6
Universal spirit, 137
Universal will, 138
Unjust city, 22
Utilitarianism, 111–121
   Bentham on, 117–118
   criticisms, 120–121
   happiness and, 116–117
   human sacrifice and, 120–121
   Hume on, 111–116
   Mill on, 118–120
Utility, 15
   defined, 116
   justice as, 116–117
Utility, interpretation of justice, 5

INDEX

V

Vain and empty desires, 69
Value judgments, 6, 9
Vice, 59
Vicious characters, 52, 53
Violence, 99–100
Virtù, 102
Virtues, 15, 20
    Aristotle on, 49
    artificial, 114, 115
    cardinal, 22–23
    defined, 22
    intellectual, 53–55
    Kant on, 129–130
    Machiavelli on, 101–102
    moral, 53–55
    naturalistic account, 114–115
    theological, 22
Virtuous action, 49–50
Virtuous character, 52, 53
Virtuous kindness, 54
Volitional control, 13
Voluntarism, 94–95, 103–105
Voluntary action, 50

W

"The Way of Truth" (Parmenides of Elea), 19
Weakness, 56
Wheel of (re)incarnation, 41, 88, 101
Wheel of Ixion, 101
Whitehead, Alfred North, 17
Will, 12
    of God, 94–95
    good, 133–135
    goodness and, 134
    necessity and, 134–135
    pessimistic reading of, 137–139
    universal, 138
Will-to-Power, 147
Wisdom, 22
Women and men. *See* Men and women partnership
Works of Love (Kierkegaard), 146
The World as Will and Representation (Schopenhauer), 138
World War II, 120–121

Z

Zeno of Citium, 73, 75
Zoroaster, 32

About the Author

Professor Frank Scalambrino has received recognition for teaching excellence in Ohio, Pennsylvania, Illinois, and Texas, and has presented his work internationally. He holds degrees in psychology and philosophy (including an MA with a concentration in ethics), and graduated with his Ph.D. from Duquesne University in August of 2011. He is the first person in the history of Western philosophy to explicitly solve the problem of "non-being."

Before age 27 he founded a Community Mental Health Suicide Prevention Respite Unit and Clinical Intervention Center, and has worked in various direct service provision capacities in psychiatric emergency rooms and trauma settings, such as Mercy Medical Center (Canton, OH), the University of Pittsburgh Medical Center (UPMC Braddock), and the Tuscarawas County Health Department. He was inducted into Chi Sigma Iota, the National Counseling Honor Society in 2003, and is an alumnus member of Beta Theta Pi (Kenyon College).

He has been teaching university level courses since January, 2004, and he has taught both philosophy and psychology graduate coursework.

He regularly teaches courses on the history of philosophy (especially Leibniz to Heidegger), metaphysics, ethics, and critical thinking. His recent publications include: *Full Throttle Heart* (2015), *Social Epistemology and Technology* (2015), *Meditations on Orpheus* (2016), and *Introduction to Ethics: A Primer for the Western Tradition* (2016). His work has appeared in *The Review of Metaphysics, Philosophical Psychology, Phenomenology and Mind, Topos, Reason Papers, Philosophy in Review, Social Epistemology Review and Reply Collective*, and the *Internet Encyclopedia of Philosophy*.

CPSIA information can be obtained
at www.ICGtesting.com
Printed in the USA
LVOW02s0630221216
518035LV00006B/17/P